A History of U.S.
Military Forces in Germany

About the Book and Author

Since the diplomatic relationship between the U.S. and the FRG is the heartbeat of the Atlantic Alliance, West Germany is the most strategically vital European member of the alliance. U.S. forces have been stationed in the country since the end of World War II, constituting the largest U.S. overseas contingent. Discussing why the U.S. will remain in the FRG for the foreseeable future, Dr. Nelson examines the U.S. military presence in broad historical perspective. He shows how that presence has affected the development of the political and diplomatic relationship between the two countries and has contributed to a dense network of military/civilian relationships, including kinships through marriage and individual friendships. Exploring the military side of this close and abiding partnership, the book analyzes U.S. successes and failures, pointing to changes necessary for maintaining the cohesiveness and viability of the U.S. presence on an ally's soil.

Daniel J. Nelson is associate professor of political science at Auburn University.

To Myles Nelson
and to the memory of
David Nelson

A History of U.S.
Military Forces in Germany

Daniel J. Nelson

Westview Press / Boulder and London

Westview Special Studies in Military Affairs

Copyright © 1987 by Westview Press, Inc.

Published in 1987 in the United States of America by Westview Press, Inc.; Frederick A. Praeger, Publisher; 5500 Central Avenue, Boulder, Colorado 80301

Library of Congress Cataloging-in-Publication Data
A history of U.S. military forces in Germany.
   (Westview special studies in military affairs)
   Bibliography: p.
   Includes index.
   1. United States—Armed Forces—Germany (West)
2. United States—Military relations—Germany (West)
3. Germany (West)—Military relations—United States.
I. Title. II. Title: History of U.S. military forces in
Germany. III. Series.
UA26.G3N45 1987   355'.033043   86-22471
ISBN 0-8133-7333-6

Printed and bound in the United States of America

The paper used in this publication meets the requirements of the American National Standard for Permanence of Paper for Printed Library Materials Z39.48-1984.

6   5   4   3   2   1

CONTENTS

TABLES

PREFACE

Military history was one of the casualties of the Vietnam War. Long out of fashion among social scientists and historians because of the unhappy outcome of that conflagration, military history has been rediscovered again in recent years. Indeed it has achieved a new kind of vitality through the addition of sociological and socio-political dimensions to the more usual concern with strategy and tactics. This book is military history of a peculiar sort, since it concerns itself as much with politics and diplomacy as with armies, equipment, and strategies. It attempts to focus upon the military dimension of a diplomatic relationship which is central to U.S.-European relations. For the vitality of the NATO alliance there is no single bilateral relationship which is more critical than the relationship between the Federal Republic of Germany and the United States. And central to the relationship between the U.S. and West Germany is the fact of the massive American military presence physically on West German soil. As a student of West German-American relations for many years, I find it intriguing that no one has attempted up to this time to construct a history of the American military presence in Germany, for it is that very presence which imparts many of the basic definitional characteristics to the relationship. This book is an attempt to fill that gap.

The earlier portions of this study (Chapters One through Three) were constructed largely from existing secondary sources. The major historical scholarship in reference to German-American relations from the end of World War Two until the late 1960s has already been produced. My task in these chapters was to gather together all the strands of that historical scholarship which focus upon the U.S. military presence in West Germany and to weave them together within the framework of a coherent and historically defensible interpretation. From the early 1970s onward much of the historical scholarship is still lacking. Hence, it was necessary to plow some new ground in Chapters Four and Five with the use of those historical materials now available.

Though many kinds of sources were at times helpful, I have tended to rely heavily upon accounts given in the German press in these chapters. Though there may be lacunae which are plainly evident to the trained historical eye, I shall justify my heavy use of the German press primarily in terms of the focus I have attempted to develop for this study. One of the primary goals has been to portray the American military presence in West Germany as it is experienced by the German civilian population. We know much more about American preoccupations, goals, and views, either explicitly or implicitly, in the first place. What we too often tend to neglect is the German dimension - how the massive American presence looks and feels from the German point of view. If Stoessinger is right in his emphasis upon empathy as a key to historical understanding, and this author believes that he is, then it behooves us to make a special effort to put ourselves in the shoes of the Germans and to experience the American presence, and its implications for policy in reference to German-American relations, as they do.

Two items related to the author's responsibility require specific mention. All translations from German sources into English, including translations of government documents and articles in the press, are the author's own. The author accepts full responsibility for the accuracy of the translation as well as the sense or contextual meaning of the original source. Footnotes which cite articles from the German press give the name of the newspaper and the date of publication, but not the page of the material quoted. This is because the filing system for newspaper clippings at the Federal Press and Information Office in Bonn is organized topically according to date and name of newspaper, but without exact page numbers.

I have been aided immensely in this endeavor by many research institutions and individuals in both West Germany and the United States. To name even some of them is to risk omitting others who may have been equally helpful. Unfortunately, it is possible to list here only the individuals and organizations without whose help the manuscript could not have been completed.

First and foremost I am indebted to the Hoover Institution on War, Revolution and Peace, Stanford University, which supported the project with funding for a full year of unencumbered research and writing. Much of the manuscript was written during the period of my appointment as Edward Teller National Fellow at the Hoover Institution. The Institution's excellent facilities and genial ambience provided an atmosphere most conducive to the scholar's craft. I extend many thanks to my colleagues and Senior Fellows at Hoover, Lewis Gann, Peter Duignan, and Dennis Bark for advice, aid, and encouragement during many months of labor. I am also indebted to Auburn University, which provided a faculty research grant-in-aid for several months of field research in Germany. An enormous debt of gratitude is due to my talented research assistant at Stanford, Conrad Rubin, for his help throughout an entire academic year. Mr. Rubin provided excellent background material for the construction of the historical accounts in the first three chapters. My research assistant at Auburn University, Michael Rasmussen, also helped to advance the project with incredible skill and talent. Mr. Rasmussen assembled the bibliography in final form, constructed the tables, and did much useful editorial work. William C. Flick, computer systems support specialist at Auburn University, contributed his special genius to the management and use of complex data sets on a mainframe computer.

Scholars and research institutions in the Federal Republic were unfailingly cooperative and helpful during the period of field research in Germany. Frau Klimmer at the Federal Press and Information Office in Bonn provided abundant help with the newspaper clippings files of the German Federal Government. Frau Ilsemarie Querner, Senior Librarian, provided extensive help with the use of materials at the Library of the German *Bundestag* in Bonn. My friend and colleague Herr Klaus Schuler, Senior Analyst, Legislative Reference Service, The German *Bundestag,* rendered indispensable help with many phases of the research. In addition, his abundant expertise in German politics and diplomacy was a constant source of valuable information. Herr Helmut Schuler and Frau Herta Schuler have provided a wonderful second home for me in Germany since my student days at the University of Bonn.

Despite help from these and many others, the author assumes full responsibility for the accuracy of the factual information and the quality of the historical analysis. The views expressed in this book do not represent the views of the Hoover Institution or any other research institution which rendered assistance.

Daniel J. Nelson

A History of U.S.
Military Forces in Germany

INTRODUCTION: THE PROTRACTED AMERICAN MILITARY PRESENCE IN GERMANY

History not only explains the past and illuminates the present. It also provides basic understanding for interpreting the signposts of the future. Military history has its own peculiar *raison d'etre* through its ability to illuminate salient dimensions of a nation's security policy. The security policy of the United States since World War II has rested, as most analysts understand it, on two fundamental pillars: containment and deterrence. Rightly or wrongly America's primary preoccupation in the security sphere has been the containment of communist expansion. With containment as the primary goal, deterrence, either through conventional military forces or through the threat of nuclear weapons, has been the primary means of achieving the goal.

The United States, as a continental-sized power with an ocean on either side, defines its security in global terms. It maintains a network of alliance relationships with strategically important nations all over the world. In terms of the primary goal of containment, however, one geographic region assumes a strategic importance not equalled by any other. That region is of course Western Europe. By virtue of culture, history, and community of values, Western Europe is linked more closely to the United States' past, present, and future than any other region of the world. Hence, the security of the United States tends to be linked to, or defined in terms of, European security first and the security of other regions in a secondary fashion. Though this perception of security is sometimes more implicit than explicit, it is nevertheless very real. It is reflected in the term "forward defense," which is widely used to describe the basic nature of the security relationship between the United States and Western Europe. Though the United States has vital security interests in many parts of the world, only in Europe does the U.S. maintain what is described as forward defense, which translates into a

1

large contingent of troops, large supplies of war materials, and the stationing of tactical and medium-range nuclear weapons. Though the U.S. also maintains a form of forward defense in South Korea, in the Pacific with the navy, and at other geographical locations, only in reference to Europe is the term "forward defense" used constantly with a well understood meaning. Such usage merely underscores the basic fact that of all the security and alliance relationships the United States maintains around the world, the NATO alliance is by far the most strategic for the basic defense needs of the United States.

If NATO is the lynchpin of the U.S. security system, there is one country within NATO which in turn is the lynchpin of the western alliance. That is the Federal Republic of Germany. No other country matters quite so much to the United States. U.S. policy makers may fret and worry about political and economic developments in other Western European countries, but they tend to panic whenever events appear to be destabilizing in West Germany. For many years after World War II analyses of U.S. security policy made reference to a "special relationship" between the United States and Britain. The term was heard less frequently in the 1970s and today is heard only seldom. What may have not been noticed but in fact happened is that West Germany over the years largely supplanted Britain as the European power with which the United States has a special relationship. It is a special relationship with a very peculiar dimension not present in the relationship with other European countries, namely, the massive American military presence. The U.S. of course maintains various levels of military presence in several West European countries, but nothing approaches the huge dimensions of the military presence in West Germany. What is even more noteworthy about the U.S.-West German relationship is that this formidable military presence has existed ever since World War II, a period of over forty years.

This brings us to the reasons for constructing a history of the U.S. military presence in West Germany. The German-American political and diplomatic relationship evolved over the years against the backdrop of the American military presence, which has imparted to the relationship a peculiar cast. What distinguishes this relationship is the heavy element of security woven into it. The postwar era of German-American relations began with several million American troops on German soil in the role of an occupation army. Today over a quarter of a million American troops remain on German soil as the crucial linkage mechanism between American and European security policies. Without the American military presence, the history of German-American relations might have been vastly different. Hence, the military dimension assumes an importance in the history of

German-American relations much more prominently than it does in the history of American relations with most other countries. If the scholarly community has "discovered" military history as valid in its own right in recent years, then the case can be made that the military history of U.S.-West German relations since World War II is a particularly important case study of the genre. And though there is a plethora of excellent scholarship available on West German diplomacy and German-American relations, there is at the same time a paucity of scholarship on the history of the military relationship between West Germany and the United States. This book attempts to fill that gap at least partially.

The focus of the book centers on a central theme and a central question. The theme is the progressive development of a relationship of security dependency between West Germany and the United States, with Germany as the dependent partner and the United States as the dominant partner. The related central question can then be stated as follows: how has the American military presence in Germany affected the development of the political relationship between the Federal Republic and the United States from the end of World War II to the present time? I suggest the question can be answered in two ways. First, the American military presence served as a formidable influence upon the West German government in its formative years when the security orientation of the new regime was emerging. The West German government opted for an alliance with the United States within the framework of the NATO alliance. More importantly, the alliance relationship was cemented over time with an ever deepening web of political and security commitments between the U.S. and the Federal Republic. Second, in a somewhat parallel fashion, the huge American military presence in West Germany contributed to an ever deepening web of social relationships between American military personnel and the German population, which had the effect of reinforcing the political and alliance relationship.

There was, in fact, a kind of "americanization" which took place in West Germany in the years after World War II. In the social and political vacuum which followed the collapse of the Nazi regime, the Germans tended to adopt American manners and conventions in many aspects of their collective life. The entire political culture of the country was rewoven, more or less from whole cloth, with American ideas and orientations serving as a powerful influence. Standards of scholarship, musical tastes, dance styles, eating habits, advertising modes, school and university curricula, lifestyle forms - all of these and many more aspects of German life were altered, sometimes transformed, in the direction of American forms. Most important, however, was the recasting of political life in a western democratic mode and the articulation of security and defense policies oriented toward the United States. All of this might have happened despite the presence or absence of American forces. There are, after all, larger geopolitical forces at work in the political history of postwar Germany. Nevertheless, there is something absolutely compelling in the fact that West German politics and policy developed in the postwar period in the shadow of the physical presence of American forces.

The chapters which follow attempt to establish a historical thesis which, though hardly revolutionary, is somewhat different from many which have appeared in print to date. It is a thesis which, I am convinced, is historically valid and which has much to contribute to a mature understanding of West German-American relations. The core concept of the thesis is a phenomenon which I have labelled *security dependency*. Viewed in its larger dimensions, the forty year period since World War II has been characterized by the development of a relationship of security dependency between West Germany and the United States. Security dependency means that the Germans have no way to guarantee or safeguard the country's security from external threat without a firm military relationship with the United States. The Federal Republic began its postwar existence with its security almost totally dependent upon the United States. Despite Germany's emergence as a major global power in recent years, the basic condition of security dependency has not been altered. Indeed, West Germany's dependence upon the United States for its basic security guarantee is perhaps greater now than it has ever been. There are, of course, other states which also rely upon an American guarantee, such as Japan, South Korea, and other states in Europe. West Germany is, however, a special case, owing to the division of the country into two states and the presence of large contingents of foreign military forces in both parts of the country. If a conventional attack were to occur in Western Europe it would most likely occur through the accessible land corridors in West Germany, i.e. the Hof Corridor, the Fulda Gap, or the North German Plain. Hence, the Soviet military threat possesses an immediacy in West Germany much greater than in any other country. In addition, West Germany has a special and peculiar psychological relationship with the United States which stems from the period of the military occupation. The American mantle of military protection was placed around West Germany in the early years after World War II and remained in place during the period of economic and political reconstruction. The West German economy was rebuilt with the massive Marshall Plan aid extended by the United States. The West German government recovered its sovereignty and acquired its authority under the tutelage of the United States. The German armed forces were eventually rebuilt with the blessing of the allied powers under the watchful eye of the United States. For at least the first twenty-five years of its existence the Federal Republic existed in a kind of younger brother relationship with a stronger sibling. When the country finally emerged as a major world power in the 1970s, it assumed responsibility for its own welfare with the exception of its security, which still remained heavily dependent upon the presence of American forces. The circumstance of security dependency had a permanency which no wishful thinking could alter.

Security dependency has an unpleasant psychological dimension which can manifest itself in malevolent ways. No person individually or no people collectively enjoys being dependent upon someone else for protection or security. Dependency means not being fully in control of one's fate, an inability to be wholly self-sufficient. It leads sometimes to outbursts borne of frustration. Relationships of dependency are difficult to manage in any case, and those involving a security factor are probably even more difficult than others. Inevitably, West German security dependency upon the United States was bound to lead to stresses and strains. Such stresses became noticeable in the decade of the 1970s, and they have become stronger in the decade of the 1980s.

The stresses affect both parties to the relationship. Many West Germans would like to free themselves from dependence upon the United States in the security sphere. It seems somehow unnatural to have the military forces of six foreign nations stationed in one's country. With vital decisions on security sometimes made in a foreign capital thousands of miles away, it is not difficult for the Germans to become resentful that they must acquiesce to U.S. demands more often than they would like. It seems to many Germans that the United States is most of the time overly critical of their defense efforts, when from the German point of view the country is making a greater sacrifice than is required and one that is very often misunderstood in Washington. From the American side also there are visible strains. Many members of Congress are convinced that the West Germans do not bear their fair share of the burden of western defense. Recent American presidents and secretaries of defense have criticized the Germans for spending less on defense than they ought to. Most Americans believe that the United States shoulders an immense burden by continuing to station over a quarter of a million American troops in West Germany. Why should we continue to shoulder such a burden when the West Germans contribute less than their share to the common defense? It is now commonplace for members of Congress to threaten massive withdrawals of of American troops from Germany if the Germans do not acquiesce in demands for greater burden sharing.

In general, the history of German-American relations throughout the postwar period has been a record of productive and mutually beneficial contact. The very record of success has, however, created its own backlash. The Germans wonder whether or not the country has become too americanized for its own good. The close relationship with the United States for so many years has, it would seem, left the Germans bereft of the special national identity and character essential to a country's national well being. There is a natural tendency for many Germans to wish for greater independence from the United States in all aspects of the country's existence including the sphere of security. It is perhaps an inherently attractive idea for Germans to think of their country without foreign troops stationed on its soil. A different national self consciousness could develop in a country fully responsible for its own security.

The backlash phenemon in German-American relations can properly be understood as a natural occurrence. It should have been expected all along. Even in the best of human relationships stresses and strains appear. Backlash is not an unusual reaction to a longterm condition which is somewhat unnatural or uncomfortable for one of the parties. What is necessary is to understand the real causes of the phenomenon and to devise a strategy which can mitigate the effects.

Despite the wish for greater security independence, which is probably widely shared in the West German population, one of the assumptions upon which this book is based is that the situation of security dependency is likely to continue for a long time in the relationship between the Federal Republic and the United States. Given the geopolitical realities in Western Europe, there is simply no choice for either the Germans or the Americans. The relationship of security dependency will, however, be much more difficult to manage for both sides in the future than it has been in the past. For West Germany, the younger sibling relationship is no longer appropriate for a country which has produced one of the strongest economies in the world. If the relationship is likely to be more sensitive and difficult in the future, then perhaps a better understanding of its development and management in the past will provide needed insight.

Military history, like any other kind of history, illuminates understanding only to the extent that it can be meshed with, indeed embedded within the larger socio-political considerations of a historical period. The history of the American military presence in West Germany is only one strand in the larger history of German-American relations. While I have attempted to keep the focus clearly upon the American military presence, I have attempted also to embed this particular segment of history within the larger historical forces of the postwar period. The readers must be the judge as to whether the attempt has been successful.

The history of the American military presence in Germany can be divided into five fairly coherent periods, as reflected in the chapter titles. The first is the period of the military occupation, which lasted from 1945 to 1949. The approach taken in this chapter is to discuss events in terms of the major substantive areas of policy articulated by the United States as the sovereign power in its zone of occupation. From a historical standpoint what is most interesting to consider is the ways in which the American occupation policies were revised and softened throughout the occupation period in preparation for the reestablishment of a sovereign government in the western two-thirds of Germany. The larger historical forces which shape the postwar period, most especially the western perception of the Soviet threat and the need to reestablish a healthy, prosperous West Germany as a bulwark against Soviet expansion, are much in evidence here. The importance of the period is perhaps best understood in terms of the legacy it left to German-American relations for the duration of the postwar period. The essential building blocks of the western alliance system, with West Germany as a potential European pillar of the alliance, were laid during this period.

Chapter Two looks at the period of semi-sovereignty from 1949 to 1955. This was a period in which the German-American relationship was rather profoundly transformed from one of occupation to one of partnership. Momentous decisions were made which in effect represented a point of no-return in German-American relations. The NATO alliance was created, and the decision made by the Truman administration to bring back a large contingent of American troops to German soil. The decision to rearm West Germany within the framework of NATO, and the rise and demise of the plan for a European Defense Community are important themes in this crucial period. The chapter concludes with a discussion of the web of relationships which were developing between Germans and American military personnel by the mid-1950s which would profoundly affect the course of the future relationship between the two countries.

Chapter Three covers the period from 1955 to 1967, which is perhaps the calmest and most stable period of German-American relations in the postwar period. The alliance relationship was fully consolidated and elaborated, and the two countries learned to cope with highly troublesome issues in a professional diplomatic manner without threats or use of force. Differences over nuclear weapons issues appeared for the first time, as relected in the debates over the plan to create a multilateral force. Sresses were also created by the Mansfield initiative to withdraw American troops from Germany and the disputes over offset payments. Toward the end of the period one begins to see clearly the spillover effects of the Vietnam War in the American forces stationed in Germany, effects which would eventually create of plethora of nearly insoluable problems.

In Chapter Four the discussion delves into the darkest period of the American military presence which extends from 1967 until approximately 1973. The period was delineated by major shifts in U.S. military policy which caused political uncertainty on both sides of the Atlantic. The spillover effects of the Vietnam War served as a contributory factor to the overall decline in both the quality and quantity of American forces. Race relations in the forces became exceedingly acrimonious, while problems with drugs, criminal behavior, and violence appeared to reel out of control. As signs of poverty appeared due to the precipitous decline in the value of the dollar, a kind of psychological estrangement between Germans and American military personnel appeared which left a lasting imprint upon German-American relations.

The final chapter in the book analyzes the American military presence in the most recent period, from 1973 until the mid-1980s. The year 1973 was selected as a dividing line, since the shift from conscription forces to the all-volunteer force was completed that year. The period can be characterized largely as a period of struggle to rebuild and reregenerate American forces in Germany and to reconstruct the politico-military relationship between the United States and West Germany on a transformed, more healthy basis of partnership. The earlier part of the period saw the final struggles over the offset payments issue and the Mansfield troop withdrawal initiative as well as some fundamental changes in force structure and force locations. In the mid to late 1970s a major change occurred by virtue of the decision to establish a major military presence for the first time in North Germany. The early 1980s saw the beginning of major debates on issues such as force readiness, nuclear weapons and weapons security, and changing strategic concepts which continued on into the later years of the decade. In addition there was the so-called "Stoessel Demarche," which led eventually to a new treaty between the United States and West Germany in 1982. The Wartime Host Nation Support Treaty, as it is known, supplements existing military arrangements in an entirely new way by making possible rapid and massive U.S. reinforcements in crisis or war by utilizing new contingents of German army reservists. The period concludes with a discussion of as yet unsettled issues relating to major revisions in NATO strategy for the 1990s and beyond.

Military history is fascinating to military personnel and analysts of international politics alike. There is inherent drama in the kind of history which deals directly with the possibility of and preparations for violent conflict. There is also, however, a deeply human and personal side to military history which is perhaps too often neglected. This is the aspect which treats the phenomena of command and control of some human beings by others, of male bonding (and more recently male-female bonding) in military communities, and the relationships of military personnel to their civilian surroundings and communities. In the case of military history which reviews the military presence of one country on the soil of another, the drama is heightened because one is dealing with vagaries and complexities of intercultural relations. West Germany and the United States are strongly allied to each other in the common purpose of providing for the defense of the western world. Much more than that, however, the citizens of both countries have for a long time considered themselves good friends. To this day Americans receive a kind of red carpet treatment in Germany unmatched by any other country in the world. This means that the socio-political dimension of the American military presence in Germany is crucial because of its sheer sensitivity. I have attempted to highlight this dimension as much as possible in the chapters to follow. Managing the relationships between siblings or close friends is sometimes more complex than managing the relationships among adversaries. If the assumption is true that it will be necessary to station a fairly large contingent of American forces on German soil for the indefinite future, pending some larger settlement of the East-West confrontation, then it behooves us to study the history of the American military presence in Germany to learn as much as possible from our past mistakes and to divine the signposts of the future as accurately as possible.

MILITARY OCCUPATION
1945-1949

The allied military occupation of Germany after World War II had a profound impact upon the country's political future and the psyche of its people. Though there were five zones of occupation, one for each of the major allies and a fifth zone of joint responsibility for Berlin, this historical analysis concentrates only upon the American occupation regime. We cannot, of course, investigate comprehensively all aspects of the U.S. military presence. The central focus here is on those aspects which were most significant in the development of a dense network of socio-political relationships between the U.S. military and the German population and which, consequently, had an impact upon the texture of political relations over time. Though we refer frequently to political decisions made in both the United States and Germany, neither decision-making nor the nature of the policy process in either country is the primary subject of interest. Broadly speaking, our analysis centers on the social and political impacts of U.S. forces in West Germany in the years following World War II. The socio-political effects, in turn, form the basis for an assessment of how the military presence affected the political and diplomatic relationship between West Germany and the United States over the years.

The Chain of Command and Early Occupation Policy

At the time of Germany's final collapse in May, 1945, the United States had sixty-nine ground force divisions in Germany with over two million men. The redeployment of allied forces into the zones of occupation defined by the European Advisory Commission and approved at the Yalta Conference took place in early July, 1945.[1] From this time on U.S. forces were located in the American zone of occupation in southern and southwestern Germany, except for a contingent of forces in Berlin and a small garrison at the northern port of Bremerhaven. French forces occupied a small southwestern corner of Germany, British forces occupied the northwestern portion of the country, and Soviet forces were in the East. Berlin was a fifth zone of occupation subject to a special four-power regime under the auspices of the Allied Kommandatura. Each allied power possessed supreme political jurisdiction in its zone of occupation, though the Potsdam Agreements envisaged a joint economic administration of the country with relatively free movement of goods, services, and people between the occupation zones. The Allied Control Council in Berlin was established as a mechanism for overall cooperation, consultation, and where possible, joint administration by the military occupation authorities. Despite the fact that the allied agreements provided for a unified effort in the postwar governance of Germany, the four zones of occupation rapidly became four separate regimes with little cooperation between them and almost no cooperation between the three western powers and the Soviet Union.

In anticipation of the occupation the Americans established in the spring of 1944 a zonal command center within Supreme Headquarters, Allied Expeditionary Forces (SHAEF) in London under the command of General Eisenhower. The organization moved from London to Paris after the liberation of Paris by allied forces in the fall of 1944. SHAEF was dissolved after Germany's surrender in July, 1945, and replaced by United States Forces, European Theater (USFET), located in Frankfurt, and the U.S. Group in the Allied Control Council (ACC) in Berlin. Friction over jurisdictional responsibilities rapidly developed between the two groups, leading finally to the creation of a new organization in the fall of 1945, the Office of Military Government of the United States for Germany (OMGUS). OMGUS was situated in Berlin, but exercised its responsibilities for the governance of the American zone initially through the old USFET structure in Frankfurt with branches throughout the American zone. OMGUS functioned through a lengthy and complex chain of command, which underwent several changes in the first two years. By 1946 there were three major units of military government which reported directly to OMGUS, one for each of three Laender (German states) in the American zone - Bavaria, Hesse, and Wuerttemberg-Baden. From the Land (state) organization command trickled down to the local military governments (MG's), which varied in size according to the size of the German community. After the local German elections of January, 1946, local MG's were ordered not to interfere directly in the affairs within the jurisdiction of the local German administrations, limiting them to the role of indirect overseers of local German affairs. This role, of course, varied from community to community.

There were four military governors of the American zone in Germany during the occupation period: General Dwight Eisenhower, General Joseph McNarney, General Lucius Clay, and John J. McCloy. The one who served for virtually the entire four year period, however, and with whose name the occupation is generally associated was General Clay. The way in which Clay exercised his authority set the tone for the entire occupation period. Without the modifications he was able to bring to the policies of hardnosed bureaucrats in the State and War Departments, the American occupation might have left a very different imprint upon postwar German history.

In its original inception American occupation policy was designed to punish rather than reconstruct defeated Germany, for understandable reasons. The brutal nature of the Nazi regime, the heavy American casualties required for Germany's defeat, and the influence of Treasury Secretary Morgenthau all combined to give American policy an edge of revenge and punishment. As far as military government was concerned, an unofficial policy was first articulated by the German Country Unit of SHAEF, which in the summer of 1944 published a *Handbook for Military Government in Germany* in loose leaf edition. The *Handbook* was designed simply as a set of *ad-hoc* and temporary guidelines for military commanders should the German government collapse, requiring military occupation to go into immediate effect upon short notice. Though the *Handbook* never became official policy through presidential endorsement, it was published and distributed widely among local MG's at the outset of the occupation in the summer of 1945. John Gimbel notes that, "it did provide a convenient list of duties for military government officers when they entered a city."[2] Official policy was expressed in a directive issued by the Joint Chiefs of Staff known as JCS 1067. JCS 1067 originated in late 1944 also as a precautionary order for U.S. commanders faced with an unexpected German surrender. Though it had gone through many drafts before receiving President Roosevelt's approval, it bore the unmistakeable imprint of the ill-fated Morgenthau Plan for the reduction of Germany to a pastoral society. Its wording was purely negative. Demilitarization, denazification, strict rationing, deindustrialization, strict obedience - these were the policy guidelines for American commanders during the occupation.

Revisions of Occupation Policy, 1945-1947

From the outset JCS 1067 caused conflict among U.S. policymakers and generated confusion at the highest levels of OMGUS. General Clay found both its tone and its specific injunctions deeply disturbing. As early as April, 1945, as deputy to Eisenhower, he stated that, "Washington must revise its thinking relative to destruction of Germany's war potential.....₃ The progress of the war has accomplished that end."[3] Fortunately, the Potsdam Agreements, signed by the three major allies in August, 1945, provided a means of escape for Clay from the most onerous provisions of JCS 1067. By invoking international treaty commitments upon existing U.S. policy Clay was able to pay lip service to official U.S. policy while actually blazing a policy trail of his own. The Potsdam Agreements called for the treatment of Germany as an economic unit by all four allied powers, a provision which at least implied certain changes in JCS 1067. In actuality, Potsdam set in motion a process of reversing American policy in Germany. The softening was implicit at first, but the escalating difficulties with the Russians caused increasing concern in Washington that communism might engulf all of Germany if the harsher provisions of JCS 1067 were not modified. On December 12, 1945, the State Department issued a statement saying that, "the United States intends....to permit the German people....to develop their own resources and to work toward a higher standard of living subject only to such restrictions designed to prevent production of armaments as may be laid down in the peace settlement."[4] This gave Clay a fairly free hand in interpreting JCS 1067 as he saw fit.

As the Soviet Union became increasingly intransigent in negotiations with the western powers and proceeded to sovietize its zone of occupation as rapidly as possible, the United States became more lenient in its occupation administration, gradually replacing its earlier punishment of Germany with policies of rebuilding. In Washington the confusion engendered by the competing fears of latent Naziism and expansionist communism resulted in highly ambiguous policy directives to OMGUS, leaving the interpretation to General Clay. Armed with overlapping directives, Clay "could do more or less as he pleased in Germany, as long as he observed the formalities and accepted JCS 1067 as the general guideline."[5] Meanwhile, Clay and Secretary of State James F. Byrnes jointly campaigned for an official set of replacement policies from President Truman.

In September, 1946, Byrnes gave an address to an assembly of German political leaders in Stuttgart which presaged a more restrained policy and also indicated the American intention to begin rebuilding a German political structure. While reiterating many of the points of the Potsdam Agreement and mentioning JCS 1067 he made clear American intentions with the statement that, "It is the view of the American government that the German people throughout Germany, under proper safeguards, should now be given the primary responsibility for the running of their own affairs."[6]

The difference between official policy and the actual functioning of OMGUS created a certain amount of confusion during the first two years of the occupation. The official policy directives emanating from Washington seemed strangely removed from the realities of life in occupied Germany. General Clay had already been forging a new softened policy for nearly two years before there was an official retreat from the hard line by Washington. Finally, however, in the summer of 1947, an official new policy was transmitted to Clay from the War Department in the form of JCS 1779. The new document represented in essence the policies Clay had advocated and had been pursuing for some time. Hence, JCS 1779 did not change the direction of OMGUS; it merely confirmed the *status quo*.

We turn now to the actual policies pursued by the American Military Government in Germany and to the impact they had upon the German population. OMGUS began its work in the summer of 1945 with a great burst of energy, attempting to implement all aspects of JCS 1067 and to govern and reform Germany all at once. The implementation of the various policies often had unintended effects, which required modifications of the policies on an *ad hoc* basis, sometimes frequently. Some policies seemed to be internally contradictory, and some policies conflicted rather directly with others. This led to a confusing array of directives from OMGUS to the local military governments, with no apparent connection sometimes between one set of directives and another. In addition, the local military commanders were often successful in enlarging their own area of discretion, with the result that military government varied widely in texture and quality from one area to another.

The Policy of Nonfraternization

Perhaps the first policy implemented and the earliest one abandoned was the policy of nonfraternization between American military personnel and Germans. Initially, Eisenhower had adopted the rule to prevent leakage of secret information during the war and to hold down the level of promiscuity, thus keeping the troops' minds focused on the main goal of winning the war. Before the surrender most soldiers understood the requirement well enough not to argue with it, but after V-E Day it became progressively more difficult to enforce. In 1946 Allied Radio carried admonitions such as, "If in a German town you bow to a pretty girl or pat a blond child....you bow to Hitler and his reign of blood....You caress the ideology that means death and persecution. Don't fraternize."[7]

In the early months of the occupation harsh penalties, even courts-martial, acted as an effective deterrent to breaking the rule. As the Americans gradually lost their fear of the German people, however, the rule seemed to make less and less sense. Homeless and hungry, most of the Germans came to be viewed as victims rather than enemies. When the backlog of cases awaiting court-martial grew to over a thousand, OMGUS urged Washington to repeal the nonfraternization rule. It was modified several times, until by the end of 1946 only the clauses forbidding marriage and prohibiting the quartering of Americans and Germans in the same house remained. By mid 1947 OMGUS ceased enforcing the rule at all.

To most Germans the nonfraternization rule was patently offensive. Especially to the many German opponents of Naziism, who came to the occupation authorities after the war to offer their support and cooperation, the rule seemed unsavory. In many cases the local commanders were forbidden even to shake their hands. The nonfraternization policy might have left a bitter legacy for decades to come except for the fact that it proved highly adaptable in the hands of most local commanders. Fortunately, the policy did not do much, if any, permanent damage for the simple reason that it was not enforced vigorously after the first few months of the occupation. It was a case where the difference between the official policy and the actual behavior of the American authorities proved to have salutary effects over the longterm.

The Policy of Denazification

There was firm agreement among the Allies that Germany would have to undergo a thorough process of denazification after the war. The policy was articulated in the Potsdam Agreements as well as JCS 1067. Soon after the German surrender SHAEF Headquarters issued an order that all Nazi party members who joined the party before 1933 must be removed from positions of authority. All materials with Nazi emblems and all books extolling Nazi ideology were to be confiscated. It soon became obvious that every segment of society required thorough examination if the roots of Nazi ideology were to be removed. In September, 1945, OMGUS promulgated Military Government Law #8, which extended the process of denazification to all public and private sectors of society, with the exception of agriculture.

By the fall of 1945 most of the highest ranking Nazi leaders had been interned by the occupation authorities, fled the country, or committed suicide. The Nuremburg trials, beginning in November, 1945, and ending in October, 1946, processed the top echelon of the Nazi leadership. The more complex problem, of course, was how to deal with the rest of the society. In the American zone each of the Laender military governments under the supervision of OMGUS established special tribunals to try Germans associated with the Nazi regime. According to Military Government Law #8 membership in a large number of National Socialist organizations required internment until trial by the special tribunals. Because the number of cases far exceeded the capacity of the courts, a huge backlog rapidly developed. By the end of 1945 the number of Germans awaiting trial in American prison camps surpassed 100,000. In December, 1945, OMGUS took steps to curtail the number of arrests. In an effort to expedite the trial process OMGUS organized local review boards comprised of Germans with clean anti-Nazi records to test the merits of each arrest. When, however, many of the military governments found the German review boards too lenient, military government review boards were established to review the work of the German review boards, enveloping the entire process in a sea of bureaucratic red tape.

As the size of the American occupation forces continued to shrink, the task of trying legions of Germans in the special courts became physically impossible. Consequently, General Clay decided to institute a German tribunal system which would, in effect, turn the entire process over to the Germans, albeit under close American supervision. The new system was established on June 1, 1946, when Clay promulgated the Law for Liberation from National Socialism and Militarism. The new system required that each county (Kreis) have a tribunal consisting of a chairman, two assessors and a prosecutor, all appointed by the Land Minister for Political Liberation who, in turn, reported directly to the local military governor. The law required all Germans over age eighteen to register and to supply specific data to the tribunal on a questionnaire (Meldebogen). On the basis of the information provided every German would be classified in one of five categories: Major Offenders (Class I), Offenders (Class II), Minor Offenders (Class III), Followers or Nominal Nazis (Class IV), and Persons Exonerated (Class V). The class into which a person was placed depended upon Nazi party membership tenure, offices held, economic gains under the Nazi regime, and other information on the questionnaire.[8] The law required punishment for the Major Offender and Offender classes, rehabilitation for Lesser Offenders, and mild sanctions for the Followers.

It is difficult to render a judgment on whether the German tribunal system was better or worse than the American military tribunals. The German tribunals were certainly much more expedient, but they were also more lenient. In November, 1946, General Clay expressed great disappointment over the leniency of the German tribunals to the Laenderrat, which at that time was the highest German administrative organ. Nevertheless, OMGUS needed to get on with the process as rapidly as possible. In an effort to ease the enormous backlog of cases, OMGUS ordered a youth amnesty on July 8, 1946, automatically clearing all persons born after January 1, 1919. In December OMGUS ordered a Christmas amnesty, freeing all persons whose incomes amounted to less than RM3,600 annually or, in effect, all persons of modest means. The amnesties reduced the number of cases pending from 1,800,000 to approximately 1,000,000, still far too great a number to process with any kind of efficiency. Since, however, OMGUS was far too short of personnel to reinvolve itself in the denazification process, and reinvolvement would only serve to undermine the integrity of the German tribunals in any case, the Germans were left on their own to continue the process. Clay's earlier warning concerning leniency had little effect. As time progressed, the German tribunals tended to dispose of greater numbers of cases with greater dispatch and with ever increasing leniency. By late 1948 most of the tribunals had ceased to function, and the denazification program was quietly laid to rest.

There were, of course, obvious problems with such a grandiose program from the outset. Though the goals of the program were laudable, the sheer scale of a process which set out to purge an entire society of people compromised by a miserable ideology set a goal which could not possibly be accomplished by mortal human beings. One problem was the different types of sanctions imposed by the two systems of tribunals, German and American. The Americans hastened to deal with the small cases first, leaving the more serious cases to later, so as to decrease the internment period of lesser offenders and clear out the prison camps. The German tribunals tended to do it the other way around. When OMGUS turned the major portion of the program over to the Germans, the German tribunals had little choice but to indulge a higher level of leniency if the process were ever to be terminated. The German tribunals tended to sentence most of those convicted to the term they had already served in detention. The sentences handed down by the earlier American tribunals were, by contrast, considerably harsher.

The real results of the denazification program will probably always remain controversial. On the one hand, some kind of denazification process had to be attempted if the influence of

Naziism on German society was to be weakened. The value of the program in educating Germans to the depravity of the Nazi leadership and value system was probably profound. In addition, it was essential that the occupation regime destroy as much as possible of the Nazi influence structure. On the other hand, political and social value systems change only slowly, and they change perhaps because of the quality of justice and the quality of leadership more than as a result of sanction. A program of vast proportions which attempts to discipline and reform an entire society in a short period of time is bound to have disappointing results. So it was with the denazification program in the American occupation zone. Nevertheless, the program succeeded in achieving some of its goals. Nazi influence has never figured largely in West Germany since the occupation. Germans have by and large turned away from all varieties of extremism. The only political parties in postwar Germany which have achieved anything near a mass voting appeal have been strictly democratic, liberal, and moderate. Perhaps the fruits of the denazification program can be seen in these intangible ways.

The Policy of Deindustrialization

One feature of the Morgenthau Plan which figured prominently in JCS 1067 was the proposal to deindustrialize Germany after the war. Morgenthau had proposed that the Allies protect themselves against any resurgence of German militarism by reducing the country to a pastoral economy. Heavy industry should be eliminated and the coal and iron mines should be shut down. In a less extreme form the basic tenets of the Morgenthau Plan became part of JCS 1067. In addition, the Potsdam Agreements sanctioned deindustrialization by providing that the Germans must pay war reparations to the Allies and other European nations in the form of German capital equipment. The Russian sum was to consist of all the industrial equipment in the Soviet zone, plus one-quarter of the much larger pool of industrial equipment in the western zones. There were, however two restrictions on the reparation payments. First, Germany was to be left enough of her nonmilitary industries to maintain a standard of living at the same level as the rest of Europe. Second, no reparations were to be paid out of current production until Germany could earn enough money by exports to pay for necessary imports. In short, Germany must support herself economically.

The deindustrialization policy was carried through in the American zone only in a limited manner and only in the initial stages of the occupation. In the first place, the American zone in southern Germany contained less heavy industry than any of the other zones of occupation. Secondly, much of the German industrial infrastructure was severely damaged by the war. In addition, there were three major pressures which worked against deindustrialization from the outset: Russian intransigence on the reparations question, pressures from the American business establishment, and the fear of communist expansion.

Soviet policy in the Soviet zone of occupation very quickly undermined the determination to deindustrialize Germany in the American occupation zone. The Soviets not only rapidly dismantled most German industry in their occupation zone with a vengence, shipping huge quantities of industrial materials to the Soviet Union, but they also remained adamant on the question of receiving reparations from the western zones. The French also proceeded to dismantle industry rapidly in their zone of occupation. It became obvious to OMGUS early on that Germany would be driven to total economic collapse if all the reparations provided for in the Potsdam Agreements were actually extracted. In Clay's view both the Russians and the French were violating the provisions of the Potsdam Agreements by dismantling industry beyond what was necessary for peaceful survival and by refusing to treat Germany as an economic unit. Economic collapse in Germany would necessitate a gigantic supply operation from the United States to keep the population fed, clothed, and housed. Faced with the refusal of the Russians and the French to cooperate even minimally with the Americans and the British in fashioning a joint economic program, Clay ordered a halt to any further dismantling of German industry in the American zone in May, 1946. Reparation payments to the Soviet Union were also suspended. In the Allied Control Council Clay made urgent requests to the other Allied Powers to avoid the creation of four separate economic entities in Germany and to carry out the provisions of Potsdam by treating Germany as an economic unit.

Pressure from the American business community also worked against deindustrialization. Business, together with labor and other powerful interest groups, lobbied strongly in Congress and government agencies against any actions which would cause Germany to become economically dependent on American taxpayers. American businessmen also wished to preserve the possibility that Germany might one day again serve as a haven for productive investment and a large market for American industrial output. If a healthy capitalist economy with a peaceful orientation could be created in postwar Germany, American business would be in a position to derive large profits from new productive investments.

Fear of communism was a third factor which worked against the policy of deindustrialization. If Germany were driven to economic collapse or if the Germans were forced to live in conditions of deprivation for a long period of time, communist ideology might take root in the country with results even more catastrophic than the fascist experiment. A weak, impoverished country in the western zones might tempt the Soviets to pressure the Western Powers for concessions closely tied to Soviet designs for the postwar European order. Deindustrialization seemed ever more unwise with the passage of time. Indeed, the idea which came to dominate American policy in the late 1940s was that West Germany must be rebuilt as an economic and political entity with strong ties to the West in order to serve as a bulwark against Soviet or communist expansion.

The Marshall Plan, announced in 1947, represented the embodiment of revised American policy for postwar Germany. The Plan envisaged the economic revival of the ruined and faltering economies of Europe with the help of substantial aid funds from the United States. Though the original invitation was extended to all European countries, the Soviet Union's quick rejection insured that the Plan would be used only for the economic revival of Western Europe, and much of the aid would be used for the reconstruction of West Germany. The Plan also set in motion the processes of European economic integration by requiring the Europeans to submit a plan for common needs and a common program for recovery.

The announcement of the Marshall Plan in the summer of 1947 coincided with the issuance of JCS 1779 as the replacement for JCS 1067 as official policy for OMGUS. Even prior to this time, however, the United States had made an offer to Britain and France to merge the American zone with the others in order to facilitate German economic recovery. The French rejected the offer, with the result that an economic regime known as Bizonia was created in January, 1947. (The French eventually joined in 1949, creating Trizonia, an embronic predecessor of the Federal Republic). The creation of Bizonia enabled the U.S. to make progress in revitalizing German industry, thereby ensuring that Germany would able to support itself economically without U.S. supplies.

In the reconstruction of German industry the Americans were wary of concentrating too much power in large industrial conglomerates. Consequently, the policy of decartelization appeared as an important corollary to deindustrialization in the early phases of the occupation. There were two major reasons for prohibiting cartels. First, such a prohibition would eliminate the power of the large industrial conglomerates which had willingly served the Nazi regime. Secondly, decartelization would create a healthy capitalist competitive environment in Germany, the kind of environment essential to democracy and European economic integration. Initially OMGUS proposed that only industries employing fewer than 3,000 workers and earning less than RM25,000,000 annually be allowed. The proposal was, however, not accepted by the Allied Control Council. Hence, OMGUS later adopted a softer policy which simply prohibited "cartels, trusts, syndicates, combines, ...all industrial enterprises...employing more than 10,000 persons, ...participation in international cartels, and so forth."[9] I.G. Farben, the industry which helped Hitler build his war machine, was split up. Many of the banks which had supported the Nazi regime were divided into smaller organizations. Like the deindustrialization policy, however, the decartelization program was not enforced after 1947.

The end of deindustrialization and the impetus provided by Marshall Plan aid saw the beginning of an industrial renaissance in Germany in 1948. The currency reform undertaken in June, 1948, also served as a major spur to economic revival. The major reasons for the currency reform were the rampant inflation occurring at the time and the Russian policy of flooding the western zones with newly printed Reichmarks from the East, making it difficult for the Western Allies to bring the inflation under control. The currency reform created a new currency for Bizonia, different from that of the Soviet zone. Although the reform came as a shock to business firms and Germans with savings accounts, it supplied new vitality to resume productivity and generated confidence in the future prospects for the economy. "Numerous business transactions which had been delayed were now consumated... German industry, which had moved ahead slowly and with great hesitation and at times seemed to stagnate, now started the striking advance which brought it by 1950 to a point level with the prewar period."[10]

Policies on Food and Housing

At the end of the war life was a struggle for mere survival for most Germans. Professor Spanier has aptly described conditions in Germany in 1945:

> In Germany, postwar conditions were truly horrible... Few German cities or towns had escaped Allied bombing, street fighting, or willful destruction by the Nazis themselves. Old cities like Cologne, Essen, Mannheim, and Nuremberg lay in ruins; others like Berlin, Frankfurt, Hamburg, and Munich were almost as badly damaged. Much of Germany was just a mass of broken stones, and

people found shelter among this rubble as best they could... There was only one word to describe Germany in 1945 - chaos. Millions upon millions of people were faced with the basic necessity of finding food, shelter, and work.[11]

At the beginning of the occupation OMGUS followed a policy of Americans first in reference to food and housing, regardless of the cost to Germans. This was to be expected after several years of ferocious fighting and heavy war casualties. The essential needs of the occupation troops had to be taken care of before the needs of the vanquished Germans could even be considered. The shortage of suitable housing amounted to a major crisis. Under the nonfraternization rule Americans initially could not be quartered in the same houses as Germans. Often the occupation authorities would requisition a great number of the largest suitable houses without using all available space. At the outset of the occupation only houses belonging to known Nazis were requisitioned, but as the needs of the occupation authorities increased the requisitions were expanded to include all suitable housing. Houses, once requisitioned, were often not returned to the Germans when they were vacated by troops which were relocated. By late 1947 troop relocations and the large influx of refugees from the East led to a zonal average of 1.9 people per room. Some communities, like Marburg, averaged an incredible 2.5 people per room.[12] The arrival of refugees and displaced persons aggravated an already desperate situation. In an effort to cope with the the influx the Americans often requisitioned houses long in advance, causing houses to remain empty for weeks at a time awaiting the arrival of displaced persons.

Housing was in short supply for many years after the war in West Germany. Only in the early stages of the occupation, however, were the American occupiers a source of the crisis, since massive troop withdrawals began soon after the German surrender. There were over two million American troops in Germany in the early summer of 1945. By July, 1946, the number had been reduced to 342,000, and a year later, in the summer of 1947, troop size had been reduced to 135,000.[13]

The food shortage also created near crisis conditions in Germany in the early stages of the occupation. The situation in the American zone seemed more severe than in the others because the American zone contained a smaller portion of arable land compared to the size of the zonal population. Germany's traditional breadbasket, the eastern zone, was in Soviet hands. The Russians, by exporting large quantities of foodstuffs to the Soviet Union and refusing to share what was left with the other occupation powers, aggravated the shortage in the western zones.

OMGUS was reluctant to import large supplies from the United States for fear of creating a permanent dependency and sabotaging efforts to implement the Potsdam provisions for treating Germany as an economic unit.

Though the army's medical advisors recommended a ration of 2,000 calories per day as a minimum to perform a day's work sufficiently, OMGUS established a goal of 1550 calories daily for each German in November, 1945. Even that meager goal could not be met in the early months of the occupation. In some communities the calories per day averaged as few as 700.[14] Malnutrition was widespread, and there were pockets of near starvation in some places. Even in June, 1947, the assistant secretary of war reported that OMGUS was not meeting the 1550 daily calorie ration and recommended that food shipments to Germany would have to be given priority by all government departments if there were to be any improvement in the situation.[15] Relief did come in some measure in 1948, partially because of a milder winter in 1947-48 and weather conditions which produced a bountiful harvest in the fall of 1948. As the currency reform of 1948 took effect and agricultural productivity continued to increase, food ceased to be a major problem by 1949, despite continued shortages of a few staple items.[16]

Reeducation and School Reforms

Reform of the German educational system proved to be a formidable problem for OMGUS. Nazi penetration had been thorough and profound. Nearly every German textbook had a Nazi or heavily nationalist orientation, and approximately eighty percent of the teachers had belonged to the National Socialist Teachers League. OMGUS initially intervened in the educational system with broad and sweeping changes. As in other sectors of German life, however, the intervention proved to be shortlived and less extensive than intended. Classes in all public schools were allowed in the fall of 1945, but with drastically reduced teaching staffs and few textbooks.

The task of differentiating between teachers who had joined the Nazi Teachers League by choice and those who joined out of necessity was difficult at best and impossible in reality. With the aid of advisory groups composed of known anti-Nazi Germans and teachers dismissed by the Nazi authorities, the local military governments dismissed about half of the German teaching staff.[17] Books by Nazi authors or with heavy National Socialist overtones were removed wholesale, though replacements did not become available for a long time. Even by the end of 1947 there were only 150 textbooks available for every thousand students in the American zone.[18] Consequently, large classes and few textbooks remained the order of the day in German schools for several years.

OMGUS initially attempted to revise the basic structure of the German educational system to conform more closely to the model of the American public schools. Such a reform was strongly recommended by George Zook, who headed an advisory commission to assess German education in September, 1946. The reforms were, however, strongly resisted by the new German educational leaders, as well as by other American advisors. In 1948 Alonzo Grace, another educational advisor to OMGUS, produced a report highly critical of the proposed educational reforms. The report stated that "the redirection of the goals, programs, and policies of social institutions must grow from the people," and that the existing structure of German education was entirely satisfactory as long as "what is taught, how it is taught, and by whom it is taught" remained closely controlled by OMGUS.[19] The vigorous debate over structural reform precluded the implementation of any major reforms. As the staff of OMGUS decreased in size and other more pressing problems demanded attention, OMGUS progressively shifted the responsibility for education to local German administrative organs as soon as they were established. Consequently, though the intervention in education was swift and massive, it was shortlived and less profound than originally intended. By mid-1948 OMGUS tended to pay little attention to educational matters.

Reestablishment of the Media

Control of the media was obviously a matter of high priority for the occupation authorities. What is perhaps surprising is the speed with which the military government put into operation the various media organs. In the first few months of the occupation OMGUS and the Laender Military Governments themselves printed several newspapers and periodicals with the aid of German staffs. In the summer of 1945 the MG's published ten newspapers with a combined circulation of 3,785,000. By the end of the year, however, nine of the ten American sponsored papers had been replaced by nineteen licensed German newspapers. The Americans also issued newspaper licenses to trusted anti-Nazi editors early on. The first license was issued as early as July 31, 1945, to the *Frankfurter Rundschau* which rapidly picked up a large readership. The occupation authorities were naturally careful to license "only those German newspapers and publishers whom they determined to be in sympathy with American objectives and principles."[20] As time went on, however, the military governors approved most requests to establish newspapers as long as no known Nazis were involved in the organization seeking the license. Editorial content also progressively escaped any censorship as long as Nazi ideas were not being espoused. By 1948 an Augsburg newspaper, *Die Schwaebische Landeszeitung*, was allowed to be openly critical of the military government.[21] No fewer than 113 newspapers were being published in the American zone by the end of the occupation in 1949.

Radio was a less important medium of communication in the early phases of the occupation by virtue of the fact that the Allies confiscated radio receivers en masse after the German surrender. The first radio station established by the Americans was established in the American sector of Berlin in February, 1946, as a counterweight to stations in the Russian sector which had begun broadcasting patently anti-American propaganda. It could be received only via telephone until September, 1946, when a conventional system went on the air for radio receivers under the name Radio Im Amerikanischen Sektor (RIAS). After increasing its power to overcome Soviet interference, RIAS was capable of transmitting to a large area of the Soviet zone of occupation where it was widely listened to. (Now under German ownership and management, RIAS remains one of the most prestigious stations in Germany). In the American zone of occupation proper all stations in operation during the war were taken over directly by the occupation authorities. Some ceased operation altogether, while others were put into operation in 1946 with American military personnel overseeing carefully selected German staffs. In addition, the Americans established stations broadcasting in English for military personnel in Munich, Frankfurt, Stuttgart, and Bremen. These later became part of the American Forces Network (AFN), which still exists today and is listened to avidly by millions of West Germans. As with other media, the control function of the military government was relaxed over the years, so that by the end of the occupation most German radio stations were operating under only minimal controls.

Establishment of a German Government

The process by which a new government in postwar Germany was established transcends the boundaries of this study, though it is useful to review here a few of the more important facets of the process which set the stage for later developments concerning the American military presence. What is important to note is the speed with which the decisions were taken to recreate a semblance of German political authority in the western zones of occupation. Indeed the speed with which German political authority emerged had a profound influence on the tone and texture of the occupation in the later phases. If Soviet intransigence had been less blatant or if the East-West cleavage had been less severe, it is possible that German self-government would have taken much longer to emerge. As it happened, the development of the cold war accelerated the establishment of German self-government to an extent hardly anticipated in 1945. For the Germans this meant that the occupation turned out to be much shorter than anticipated and, especially in the later phases, much more lenient. These circumstances had a powerful influence on the texture of German-American relations as they developed after 1949.

The Potsdam Agreements stipulated that local self-government was to be restored as rapidly as possible, though only for purposes of administration. Also, it would have to be consistent with military security and with the purposes of the occupation of Germany.[22] From the outset General Clay endeavored to integrate Germans into the administrative apparatus of the military government. Governing Germany would be a gigantic task, and, as American troops were likely to be withdrawn in large numbers relatively rapidly, Clay knew that the task would be impossible without the aid of trustworthy Germans. Identifying Germans who had not been compromised by Nazi ideology was a risky and hazardous process, but OMGUS did in fact accomplish the task with relatively few mistakes and with considerable dispatch. The early development of German administration is aptly described by Professor Plishke:

> At the outset, efforts were devoted to the appointment of an Oberbuergermeister (lord mayor) in each city, a Landrat (county head) in a rural community, and a Buergermeister (mayor) as well as other leaders in the Gemeinden (towns and villages). They, in turn, participated in selecting key administrative officials to assist them, who recruited staffs for lesser units of administration. Initially these were rudimentary and skeletal arrangements, but, in the course of time, they became effective elements of the new German government. Much the same process was followed in reviving political institutions at the next levels, the Regierungsbezirk (district), where such units previously existed, and the Land (state).[23]

In the fall of 1945 OMGUS selected a minister-president for each of the three Laender in the American zone. In November, Clay set up a body known as the Laenderrat (Council of States), which was simply the three ministers-president meeting together as a consultative organ for OMGUS. The Laenderrat's primary purpose was to serve as a medium through which OMGUS could relay information to the German public and to which it could refer when requiring a German consensus on administrative questions. The Laenderrat met on a monthly basis to discuss administrative coordination among the Laender bureaucracies, which were slowly being established, and to do whatever OMGUS did not wish to burden itself with. Its first project was to help with the resettlement of refugees. Later it was given responsibility for the local administration of the railroads and the postal services. With the establishment of the Bizonia economic administration in 1947 the Laenderrat ceased to have much of a function. It was reconstituted, however, in 1948 and expanded to include delegates representing state executive agencies.

Local elections for government positions in towns and villages of fewer than 20,000 inhabitants were held in January, 1946, followed by elections in larger towns and cities during the next few months. In the summer constitutional assemblies were elected to draft constitutions for the three Laender, subject to approval by OMGUS and by majority votes of the adult residents of the respective Laender. In the spring of 1947 elections were held for representatives to a Landtag (state legislature) in each Land.

With the economic fusion of the American and British zones in 1947 a number of new German political organs were established on a bizonal basis, though their jurisdiction was restricted to economic matters. Plischke summarizes these as follows:

> In essence, the German bizonal machinery was approaching the following pattern: a bicameral legislature, with a lower house popularly responsible, and an upper chamber comprised of Land executives representing their respective state legislatures, serving in a bizonal joint legislative-executive capacity; an executive branch of the cabinet type, responsible to the legislative body; a separate judiciary with its own prescribed powers; and a division of authority between the states and the German bizonal government. It is interesting to note in retrospect how these basic principles subsequently served as a precedent in the

establishment of the government of the Federal Republic of Germany. During this period more and more authority, and eventually maximum responsibility, was turned over to German officials.[24]

As the split between the Soviet Union and the western powers intensified, the United States and Britain decided the time was ripe to proceed with plans for stronger German self-government in the western zones. In February, 1948, representatives of Britain, France, the United States and the Benelux countries convened at the Western Foreign Ministers' Meeting in London. While the meeting was underway, the Soviets walked out of the Allied Control Council in Berlin, bringing all semblance of four-power administration in Germany to an abrupt end. The western allies then proceeded to design a basic outline for future political development in West Germany. In June, 1948, the Soviets instituted the Berlin Blockade with the intention of driving the western allies out of the former German capital. The effect was to accelerate the process of German self-government. The Western Military Governors met with the ministers-president of the Laender on July 1, 1948, in Frankfurt and presented them with three documents. Document I empowered the ministers-president to convene a constituent assembly not later than September 1; the assembly could proceed to draft a constitution which must be democratic and federal in character. Document II authorized the ministers-president to make recommendations concerning the boundaries of the German states. Document III reserved certain powers to the Allies until such time as the occupation should be terminated.[25]

The ministers-president were highly gratified that progress in the construction of a West German government could proceed. At the same time, however, they were unwilling to take any action which might later prejudice the reunification of Germany. In a series of negotiations between the military governors and the ministers-president it was decided that the assembly would be called a parliamentary council rather than a constituent assembly and that the document produced would be called a basic law rather than a constitution, terms which would emphasize the provisional status of the new German governmental structure which would emerge. In July, 1948, representatives to the Parliamentary Council were elected by the Land legislatures. The Council convened in Bonn on September 1.

The process of drafting the Basic Law took several months, and there were at times intense negotiations between the Germans and the military governors concerning various aspects of the new governmental structure, most especially the provisions concerning federalism. Meanwhile, however, the French government decided to join the bizonal arrangements, leading to the creation of Trizonia in January, 1949, and bringing representatives from the French zone into the proceedings of the Parliamentary Council. In plenary sessions on May 6 and 8, 1949, the Parliamentary Council gave its approval to the Basic Law. The Military Governors gave their provisional approval on May 12 with the stipulation that a new Occupation Statute, defining the residual authority of the occupying powers, would go into effect simultaneously with the Basic Law. In the ensuing months the Germans worked to prepare the machinery of the new government, while the Military Governors worked out the precise terms of the Occupation Statute.

The new constitution was then ratified by the legislatures of the Laender between May 18 and May 21. The first general postwar West Germans elections, the first general elections since 1933, were held in August, 1949, and the new Parliament convened in Bonn for its inaugural session on September 7. An official ceremony was held on September 21, 1949, to mark the official transfer of partial sovereignty from allied military government to the new German government. On that day also the Allied High Commission replaced OMGUS and the Allied Control Council as the residual organ of allied control in West Germany. The Basic Law and the Occupation Statute went into effect simultaneously, thus marking September 21, 1949, as the official birthday of the Federal Republic of Germany.

The Legacy of the Occupation Period

It remains for us to take stock of the occupation period in terms of its human dimensions and the legacy it left to the development of German-American socio-political relations in later periods. The expectations of the Germans and the "fit" between expectations and reality form an appropriate point of departure for this analysis. In the chaotic months before the end of the war most Germans anticipated the coming occupation with a combination of dread and hope. Allied "liberation" would at least mean the end of a Nazi tyranny which for most Germans had become simply unbearable. Many Germans fled to areas they believed would come under British or American control when or if Germany were divided up among the victorious powers. There seemed to be a general assumption that the Americans and British would be somewhere in the West, and the Russians would be in the East. This led to a flood of Germans fleeing westward in the final months of the war. There also seemed to be a general consensus that Russian rule would be harsh and vengeful, while better treatment might be expected from the British and the Americans. As one frightened German put it:

> We hoped and prayed for an end to the killing and bombing. We knew that what was to come after the Nazi defeat would be a time of great trial and suffering. But we secretly hoped that we would somehow end up under American control. We were afraid the Russians and the French would brutalize us terribly, and we suspected that the Americans would be none too kind. Still, we believed and we hoped that the Americans would not terrorize us or treat us as sub-human beings. They had a reputation for kindness and civility. We thought that, even as a defeated people, they would allow us to retain our dignity.[26]

German expectations of the Americans were probably higher than their expectations of the other allies. As a stable, prosperous, democratic nation, the United States would be expected to rule in an enlightened manner, with empathy and humanitarianism.

The conception of what ought to be done as military occupiers of Germany was rather hazy to most American soldiers. They had enlisted or had been drafted to win a war, yet that goal had already been accomplished. They were fighting men without a battle. In addition, they were suddenly thrust into an unfamiliar cultural environment where fear and deprivation were pervasive. Lack of clarity in U.S. occupation policy also caused a certain amount of insecurity. On the one hand, local MG's searched for reliable Germans to serve as advisors; on the other hand, nonfraternization with Germans was the order of the day. Most soldiers never remained in one place long enough to make significant contact with the Germans. Massive withdrawal of troops from Germany to the United States caused constant movement from place to place. In addition, military government regulations stipulated that no man, except at the higher ranks, remain in a position for longer than one year. In Marburg, for instance, there was a new military governor approximately every four months for the first few years of the occupation.[27]

The devastated German economy produced an environment ripe for entrepreneurial activity. Cigarettes, candy, and army clothing could be bartered for a vast array of goods and services. John Spanier captures the situation as follows:

The measure of Germany's collapse was indicated by the fact that the cigarette had replaced money as the prevailing unit of exchange. Cigarettes could buy almost anything. The black market flourished. Even as late as 1947, a package of cigarettes was equivalent to a working man's entire wages for a month; one cigarette had twice the purchasing power of the salary a man could earn in Berlin after a hard day's work clearing rubble.[28]

Many Germans had to pay exorbitant prices for necessary items; minor luxuries could be enjoyed only by bartering away personal treasures or human dignity. The black market was a way of life, and American soldiers were often tempted to take advantage.

The clash between German expectations and the realities of the occupation naturally caused some disillusionment. Why were troops representing the idealistic dreams Germans had of America racketeering and taking advantage of their privileged position in this wartorn country? The sheer abrasiveness of military rule in some communities also caused the Germans to wonder what kind of society a democracy was supposed to be. At the same time, however, instances of brutality were rare, and most Germans were allowed to go about their business just as they wanted as long as military government regulations were not disobeyed. Though the inconsistency between American ideals and practice dimmed an otherwise positive opinion of Americans by the Germans, still the Americans accounted for themselves relatively well by dealing with the Germans without any noticeable malice.

Momentous decisions concerning the postwar future in Germany were made in Washington, at allied conferences, and at OMGUS headquarters in Berlin. Most Germans, however, remained relatively unaware of the higher echelons of decision-making or military government. It was at the local level where most Germans encountered the occupation authorities and where the impact of the occupation was felt most immediately. In the areas which have been studied intensively,[29] the impressions left behind by the American occupation authorities are vague but generally positive. Actually, not many Germans remember the military government as having had a significant impact even locally. This may be due to a kind of amnesia induced by the numbing experiences of the war; or it may be that in many places military government changed the dimensions of life much less than expected. The exception is the denazification policy, which in one way or another affected a sizeable portion of the population. In the American zone only six percent of the population was directly or personally affected. At the same time, however, as noted by Gimbel, "since it applied almost exclusively to persons in prominent social, political, and economic positions, its effects were felt and observed much more widely than the statistics seem to indicate."[30]

Peterson describes the course of a typical American military government as beginning with a highly disruptive phase, characterized by fast and efficient American entry into the town, round-up of all prominent Nazis, requisitioning of houses, and establishment of the military government in the power vacuum left by the disintegration of the Nazi regime. Following the disruptive phase, the community usually settled into a pattern of life broadly similar to that before the occupation. A semblance of normality occurred through the early election of local officials, who were then usually the only ones required to deal with the military government officials. The rapid withdrawal of troops from Germany, together with the gradual relocation of remaining troops to the larger cities, meant that the size of the local MG was small and its level of activity modest. In smaller cities such as Eichstaett and Friedburg, local military government was virtually nonexistent by the end of 1947. In the larger cities the level of activity of the local military government was higher, and the decline in size and impact occurred more slowly. In some cities, such as Frankfurt, Heidelberg, Stuttgart, and Nuremberg, American troops never completely disappeared, though by 1950 there were fewer than 75,000 American troops remaining in West Germany. There were, of course, exceptions to these general patterns. Marburg, with an acute shortage of housing and a huge influx of displaced persons, remained the seat of a local MG which was fairly strong and active throughout the entire occupation period. Augsburg and Nuremberg, as larger cities, also had active military governments virtually the entire period.

Other factors which heavily influenced the character of the occupation and left an imprint on the German memory were the personality of the local military governor and the manner in which authority was exercised. The local commander in Eichstaett, Captain Raymond Towle, left a mark on the town as an unyielding tyrant long after his departure in January, 1947.[31] In Nuremberg, by contrast, the local military government delegated much of its work to the German staff, in particular Dr. Heinz Levie, who more or less ran the city as a kind of mayor-city manager combined with the usually friendly support of the MG.[32] A similar situation prevailed in Friedburg.

Regardless of the manner in which authority was exercised, the American troops as individuals seem to have left favorable impressions with the Germans. Professor Gimbel recorded some of the impressions as follows:

> Marburgers think Americans are energetic. They approached their duties with a zeal that could have been based only upon hope of realizing a high ideal. They provided an example of efficiency and practical know-how by their reconstruction work during the early phase of the occupation... American officers and men gave a practical lesson in equality by their mutual respect... They impressed the Marburgers by their individualism, both in acts of kindness and in crime and corruption. Above all, Americans seemed to get things done... They cleaned up the city... They attacked problems as they arose and solved them without delaying to achieve perfection.[33]

The lasting impact of the occupation on the German social order exists in the realm of intangibles. Most importantly, the Germans gained a better understanding of Americans as a people and a nation. The Americans immediately began the task of reconstruction. They treated the Germans by and large with a generous measure of magnanimity. They displayed such traits as individualism, respect, pragmatism, and willingness to compromise for all to see. They propagated the values of equality, democracy, and diversity even as conquerors and occupiers. Though they at times displayed poor judgment and behavior for all to see, they still portrayed the image of a people of great energy and imagination, the emissaries of a free society. The occupation was short. By and large it was exceedingly lenient. Even political sovereignty was returned to the German people within a relatively short time.

The Americans did not succeed in completely remolding German society. They did not, in fact, really try. The purge of Nazis from positions of authority and the discrediting of Nazi ideology was an achievement which can only partially be credited to the Americans. Much of the process would probably have taken place even without a military occupation. Despite the changes wrought by the occupation, in the political realm Germany experienced a continuity of ideas and forms that began with the Weimar Republic and ended with the Bonn Constitution. The U.S. military presence played the role of temporary guardian, rooting out the iniquity of Naziism, but allowing the Germans to construct a new social and political order of their own choosing. U.S. influence never reached the point where it could change the Germans fundamentally, but it did provide time and opportunity for the Germans to use their own genius in the creation of a new and better social order.

Some programs initiated during the occupation remained permanently, such as the America Houses, which still serve as centers of cross cultural exchange and are maintained by the German government. Many American cultural forms were adopted by the Germans, though these are the veneer of a society, not the essence. American sports such as basketball and baseball became enormously popular with German youth. American music and fashions became and remain the trendsetters for entire industries. These forms are, however, only the most recent stratum placed upon the fundamental structure of a rich and proud cultural heritage.

The most important legacy of the occupation is the mutual respect the Americans and the Germans gained for each other. The Americans surely would not have allowed the construction of a new political sovereignty if they had not gained confidence that a new German state would emerge as a vibrant, democratic, and peaceful society. For their part, the Germans decided to accept a longterm security dependency upon the United States. Trust is the only foundation on which such a relationship can be built. The most profound result of the occupation is that the Germans and the Americans decided that they are really quite fond of each other. Viewed from this perspective the occupation was a smashing success. The essence of a viable alliance relationship rests upon this firm foundation.

Notes

[1] See Daniel J. Nelson, Wartime Origins of the Berlin Dilemma (University, Ala.: University of Alabama Press, 1978), pp.101-131.

[2] John Gimbel, A German Community Under Occupation: Marburg, 1945-1952, (Stanford: Stanford University Press, 1961), p. 32.

[3] Quoted in John Gimbel, The American Occupation of Germany: Politics and the Military, 1945-1949 (Stanford: Stanford University Press, 1968), p.6

[4] Quoted in Roger Morgan, The United States and West Germany, 1945-1973 (New York: Oxford University Press, 1974), p.20.

[5] Harold Zink, The United States in Germany 1944-1945 (Princeton: D. Van Nostrand Company, Inc., 1957), p.147.

[6] Quoted in Zink, p. 95.

[7] Quoted in Franklin M. Davis, Jr., Come as a Conqueror: The United States Army's Occupation of Germany, 1945-1949 (New York: Macmillan Co., 1967), p. 143.

[8] See John Gimbel, Marburg, p. 153.

[9] Zink, p.265.

[10] Zink, p. 160.

[11] John Spanier, American Foreign Policy Since World War II (New York:

Praeger Publishers, 1971, fourth rev. ed.), pp. 44-45.

[12] Gimbel, Marburg, p. 128.

[13] Davis, p. 189.

[14] Gimbel, American Occupation, p. 35.

[15] Gimbel, American Occupation, p. 157.

[16] Zink, p. 298.

[17] Zink, p. 198.

[18] Edward N. Peterson, The American Occupation of Germany: Retreat to Victory (Detroit: Wayne State University Press, 1977), p. 161.

[19] Quoted in Zink, p. 205.

[20] Gimbel, American Occupation, p. 246.

[21] Peterson, p. 292.

[22] See Elmer Plischke, Contemporary Government of Germany (Boston: Houghton Mifflin Company, 1961), p.16.

[23] Plischke, pp. 16-17.

[24] Plischke, pp. 19-20.

[25] Gimbel, American Occupation, pp. 210-211; Plischke, pp. 21-22.

[26] Statement by Helmut Schuler. Bonn, September 20, 1982.

[27] Gimbel, Marburg, p. 40.

[28] Spanier, p. 45

[29] See especially Peterson's Retreat to Victory, and Gimbel's Marburg.

[30] Gimbel, Marburg, p. 143.

[31] Peterson, pp. 306-314.

[32] Peterson, pp. 314-322.

[33] Gimbel, Marburg, p. 210.

2

SEMI-SOVEREIGNTY
1949-1955

Transition from Occupation to Partnership

The Basic Law of the Federal Republic of Germany and the Occupation Statute entered into force simultaneously in 1949. Under the Occupation Statute the newly created Allied High Commission was the organ through which the allies exercised their residual authority over West Germany. The potential authority of the allies under the Occupation Statute was formidable. It included all the powers "necessary to ensure the fulfillment of the basic purposes of the occupation," and it provided for a resumption of the full power of government by the military governors in the event of an emergency threatening security, or if required to secure compliance with the federal or Land constitutions or the Occupation Statute.[1] The Occupation Statute provided for the maintenance of American, British, and French forces on German soil. It helped to allay general European fears that Germany's reconstruction would not lead to expansion or aggression. The strong terminology of the Statute also accounts in large measure for French acceptance of even a semi-sovereign status for Germany.

As Professor Golay has pointed out, "The real interest of the Statute lies not in its formal provisions, but in the manner in which it was applied during the first three years of relations between the Allied High Commission and the government of the Federal Republic."[2] The Allied High Commission used the powers with restraint during the entire three year period and tended to fade more and more into the background as time progressed. It maintained a watchful eye on the activities of the German government, but it rarely interfered and never attempted to dictate policy.

The U.S. component of the Allied High Commission was the U.S. High Commission for Germany (HICOG). Initially HICOG maintained a structure similar to OMGUS, and many of the OMGUS personnel remained after the conversion. In 1951, however, as negotiations for the rearmament of Germany gained momentum, HICOG was slowly reorganized to resemble an embassy, and the branch offices of HICOG (the Offices of the Kreis Resident Officers) were closed. In 1953 the reorganized HICOG structure became the U.S. Embassy in West Germany.

The first U.S. High Commissioner for Germany was John J. McCloy, the former Assistant Secretary of War. Thoroughly acquainted with German history and culture and fluent in German, McCloy established a close rapport with German political leaders and set the tone for HICOG's work. McCloy's successor, Walter J. Donnelly, assumed the position in 1952, but remained in office only a few months. James B. Conant replaced Donnelly in early 1953. A former president of Harvard University, Conant was widely respected but did not have the close rapport with German leaders McCloy had enjoyed. Conant remained in Germany after the dissolution of HICOG to become the First U.S. Ambassador to the Federal Republic of Germany.

The semi-sovereign period was a period of transition from allied occupation to full NATO partnership. During the period the political institutions of the Federal Republic were consolidated and the new state began to take small steps on the stage of world politics. In the security sphere the most important developments were the establishment of the NATO alliance, the U.S. decision to station American troops in Germany for defense purposes, the proposal and failure of the European Defense Community plan, the full integration of West Germany into NATO, and the decision to rebuild the German armed forces within the integrated NATO structure.

Under the leadership of the first chancellor, Dr. Konrad Adenauer, Germany pursued a set of ambitious goals. These included the complete termination of the occupation status and allied control, recovery of influence in international affairs and restoration of confidence in Germany by the major powers, enhancement of Germany's security through arrangements with the western powers or through NATO membership, reconciliation with France, particularly within a European framework of cooperation or integration, and, if possible, the reunification of Germany.[3] Not all of the goals were possible; some conflicted with others as the cold war deepened. Nevertheless, Germany managed to achieve many of its major goals with a speed that hardly could have been predicted.

Germany's success in gaining status and recognition is only partially attributable to astute leadership and wise policy. Much more profoundly it came as a result of developments in world politics. More than anything else it stemmed from the deepening cold war between the Soviet Union and the western powers. The United States' perception of Germany changed dramatically from erstwhile enemy to necessary ally. The Soviet Union continued to harbor a frantic fear of any kind of German resurgence and worked diligently to upset all plans for Germany's reemergence as a major power. The French also feared German resurgence, and although France cooperated closely with the western allies, the goal was French dominance of a reconstructed Germany, not German equality. With the cold war gathering momentum, the realignment of Europe took place. As the Soviet Union consolidated its sphere of control in Eastern Europe, the countries of Western Europe opted to enter into a security relationship with the United States.

The first organization established was the Western European Union (WEU). Founded in 1948, WEU was a collective defense organization which included Britain, France, and the Benelux countries (Belgium, The Netherlands, and Luxembourg). With the the horrors of World War II still a fresh memory and with fear of German resurgence pervasive among European leaders, WEU was intended to meet the danger of possible German as well as Russian aggression.[4]

The Establishment of NATO

The major milestone in the establishment of the western security system was the founding of the North Atlantic Treaty Organization (NATO) in 1949. According to the *NATO Handbook*, "The North Atlantic Treaty is the framework for a military alliance designed to prevent aggression or to repel it, should it occur. It also provides for continuous cooperation and consultation in political, economic, and other non-military fields. It is of indefinite duration."[5] NATO gradually superseded the WEU both in size (15 countries) and strength (with the inclusion of the United States). As the structure of NATO continued to develop, the need for WEU decreased. In the early 1950s most of its organs were merged with those of NATO. West Germany was not, of course, an original member of NATO. The country was not yet fully sovereign, and the question if its rearmanent was far from settled. Nevertheless, the establishment of NATO clearly showed that the eastern line of defense for NATO was the Elbe River, not the Rhine.

The timing of NATO's establishment was no accident. Two events in 1949 set the stage for a major escalation of cold war tension. First, the Soviet Union exploded a nuclear device, thus ending the U.S. monopoly on the possession of nuclear weapons.

Second, the nationalist government government of China was defeated by Mao Zedong's Peoples' Army, giving the communists control of all of mainland China. For the first time, the possibility of a Soviet invasion of Western Europe became a gripping fear in the minds of both Europeans and Americans. The Soviets could no longer be deterred from aggression by the threat of nuclear weapons dropped from American bombers. Deterrence in the form of conventional forces ready to fight in Western Europe would now be necessary. And, given the perception of a Sino-Soviet axis stretching from Moscow to Peking in the minds of western statesmen, the Soviets now had a powerful ally to assist them in their designs for world conquest. Thus the stage was set for the events of the period 1949-1955.

The Decision to Bring U.S. Troops to Europe

Communist aggression occurred much sooner than leaders in Europe and America expected. Rather than in Europe, however, it occurred on the other side of the globe in Korea. In June, 1950, North Korean forces mounted a massive attack on South Korea. The invasion confirmed the aggressive nature of the worldwide communist conspiracy in the minds of western statesmen. Though the North Koreans were the aggressors, it appeared likely that the attack had the full support of, and may even have been planned by the communist ringleaders in Moscow and Peking. President Truman never wavered a moment in his conviction that the aggression in Korea had to be countered and defeated. The United States quickly dispatched forces to Korea and mobilized support for the operation in the United Nations.

The parallel between Asia and Europe presented itself immediately to western policymakers. What would happen if a communist aggression were to occur in Europe? The aggressive, expansionist nature of communism having been displayed unmistakably in Korea, it was now clearly necessary to fortify Europe against a new onslaught. As plans were developed to send combat forces to Korea, officials in the State and Defense departments also set in motion the planning process for strengthening the defense of Western Europe. More specifically, the goal was to prepare some kind of plan for presentation to the NATO Council meeting in the fall.

During the months of July and August, 1950, intense bargaining took place between planning staffs in the state and defense departments. The draft plans produced by the two departments, though similar in broad outline, differed with respect to several essential features, leading to a standoff lasting for several weeks. Finally, however, a compromise was devised which satisfied the minimal interests of both departments and was presented to President Truman in early September.[6] Truman approved the "package deal," as it came to be known, on September 9, and announced the decision to the nation in a radio broadcast on the same day:

> On the basis of recommendations of the Joint Chiefs of Staff, concurred in by the Secretaries of State and Defense, I have today approved substantial increases in the strength of United States forces to be stationed in Western Europe in the interest of the defense of that area... A basic element in the implementation of this decision is the degree to which our friends match our actions in this regard. Firm programs for the development of their forces will be expected to keep full step with the dispatch of additional United States forces to Europe. Our plans are based on the sincere expectation that our efforts will be met with similar action of their part. The purpose of this measure is to increase the effectiveness of our collective defense efforts and thereby insure the maintenance of peace.[7]

Though Truman found the decision one of the most difficult of his presidency, he believed he had no choice. As Coral Bell wrote:

> This was one of the most courageous and radical of all Truman's decisions; radical in its break with the past, courageous in that it was bound to evoke a great wave of political feeling.[8]

Three days after Truman's announcement, Secretary of State Dean Acheson explained the "package deal" to a meeting of the Big Three Foreign Ministers (French Foreign Minister Robert Schuman, British Foreign Minister Ernest Bevin, and Acheson) in New York. The United States would be willing to send four troop divisions to Europe and to supply NATO with a supreme commander, if the Europeans would agree to the rearmament of Germany. Acheson had little room to maneuver in the negotiations with the French and the British, since his instructions were that the provisions of the package deal had to be strictly adhered to. In the afternoon of September 12 Acheson "dropped what was referred to by a member of one of the delegations as 'the bomb in the Waldorf.' The 'bomb' was the German rearmament portion of the 'package deal'."[9] Negotiations became deadlocked at the Foreign Ministers

Meeting. Acheson wrote to Truman on September 15, "...the discussion ended with one situation quite clear: That they (the British and French) were prepared to accept what we offered but they were not prepared to accept what we asked."[10]

The French fear of any kind of German rearmament was so strong that it could not be easily overcome. Schuman argued that German military units should not be formed until all of the allies had been fully equipped with military necessities. He also insisted that the construction of the NATO defense system should be much more advanced before Germany were included. Acheson countered with the argument that if the European allies were unwilling or unable to increase manpower substantially, there was no other way to get NATO forces up to strength except by including German manpower. Schuman said the French government feared that bringing Germans into the pool of NATO manpower would increase the danger of a preventive war unleashed by the Russians. Acheson's reply was that bringing Germany into NATO was no more threatening to the Russians than a major increase in NATO strength itself. Schuman's final objection was that the western powers should not appear as supplicants to the Germans by asking their former enemy to help defend them. Why had such enormous sacrifices been made only a few years earlier to destroy the German war machine? Acheson countered that rather than dealing with the Germans as supplicants, the western powers should firmly let the Germans know that they also had obligations for the common defense of the West. Also, all the western powers needed to do was to accept Adenauer's offer of a German military contribution, which had been extended on more than one occasion.

An impasse had been reached. The British seemed to be generally in favor of the American proposal, though they had some misgivings. The other members of NATO in general backed the U.S. position as well. France, however, refused to budge.

Acheson then presented the package to a meeting of the North Atlantic Council on September 15. He hoped that a full discussion of the plan by all the allies would help to persuade the French that the plan was in the best interests of western defense. His hope was only partially realized. The French did seem to be more flexible on the issue, and they seemed to accept the principle that West Germany should make some kind of contribution to western defense. They could not agree, however, that Germany should be rearmed as called for in the American proposal. The Council meeting did crystallize agreement on a number of issues. In the communique issued at the end of the first round of meetings on September 19, 1950, the foreign ministers announced agreement on seven points concerning the Federal Republic of Germany: (1) the three Occupying Powers -

the U.S., Britain, and France - agreed that they would "increase and reinforce their forces in Germany," including West Berlin; (2) the three Occupying Powers would "treat any attack against the Federal Republic or Berlin from any quarter as an attack upon themselves"; (3) the three governments authorized West Germany to form "mobile police formations" based on the *Laender* but which would be subject to call up by the Federal government in emergencies; (4) the Occupying Powers agreed to terminate the state of war between themselves and Germany; (5) they agreed to amend the Occupation Statute; (6) they agreed to enable the Federal Republic to conduct its own diplomatic relations, but representatives could be sent only to posts approved by the Allied High Commissioners; and (7) there would be a reduction of a number of internal controls within Germany.[11]

At the conclusion of the second round of discussions a second communique was issued on September 26. It expressed the Council's agreement on "the establishment, at the earliest possible date, of an integrated force under centralized command, which shall be adequate to deter aggression and to ensure the defense of Western Europe." The force would be organized within NATO, and would have a Supreme Commander supported by an international staff. On the German question the communique remained vague by stating only that Germany should "be enabled to contribute." The question of a German contribution was referred to a committee for further recommendations.[12]

Though progress had been made on several important issues concerning NATO, the matter of German rearmament remained unresolved. When it was taken up again at a meeting of the NATO Defense Committee in late October, the U.S. delegation made it clear that if the German question were not soon resolved satisfactorily, i.e., in accordance with the American proposals, the United States might not participate in the proposed integrated force and command, thereby making it a dead letter. "This faced France with a most unwelcome choice," wrote Anthony Eden. "Somehow means must be found to meet the American demand, which was too serious to be shrugged off. This had to be done while avoiding the dangers, equally vivid for many, of a German national army."[13] Fortunately, for all concerned, the French responded with an imaginative proposal, the Pleven Plan, which began a whole new process of negotiation.

The Europeans readily accepted the augmented role of the United States in European affairs. To European policymakers U.S. troops in Europe and U.S. leadership in NATO were prerequisites for the success of NATO and the defense of Europe against Soviet expansion. To Americans, however, the notion of U.S. involvement in Europe in peacetime had never before been considered on such a grand scale. The decision to triple U.S.

military personnel in Europe was far more controversial than the rearmament of Germany, as Americans tended to trust the Germans as much as the French as a major ally in the revised European order.

The troops to Europe decision faced a major obstacle in the U.S. Congress. It could not be implemented until Congress approved the funds, and isolationist sentiment was by no means dead in Congress despite the bipartisan consensus which had been forged on the U.S. role in the postwar order. The Congressional hearings took place over a three month period from January to April, 1951. The major challenge came from a group of conservative Republicans in the Senate. At the conclusion of the "great debate," as it came to be known subsequently, Congress upheld the President's decision by fairly wide margins, but not until all of its implications had been fully explored. The troops decision won Congressional approval for perhaps eight major reasons, six of them fairly explicit, and two of them implicit. As summarized by Wesley B. Truitt, the six explicit reasons include: (1) the reassurance to Europe that, despite U.S. involvement in Korea, U.S. ties with Europe remained of paramount importance; (2) the increased deterrent to Soviet adventures in Europe which U.S. troops would represent in the period after the loss of the American nuclear monopoly; (3) the assurance that if Soviet aggression had to be countered, the battle would not take place on American soil but in Europe with U.S. troops; (4) only the United States could provide the requisite military strength and leadership to insure the success of the NATO alliance; (5) U.S. troops would serve to bolster European morale and determination in the face of the Soviet challenge; (6) U.S. occupation forces in Germany were too few and ill-equipped to counter a Russian attack and needed the reinforcement of additional troops. The two implicit reasons for Congressional approval of the troops decision were vitally linked, even though they were perhaps mutually contradictory. They were: (7) that U.S. troops would allay French fears of a rearmed Germany; and (8) the assumption that U.S. troops would provide security for West Germany and Europe while the military integration process in NATO took place--it was hoped that the forces would be required only temporarily until the Europeans could defend themselves.[14]

General Dwight D. Eisenhower was appointed Supreme Commander, Europe (SACEUR) on December 18, 1950, by the North Atlantic Council on the nomination of President Truman. Eisenhower went to Europe on January 6, 1951 on a brief inspection tour of the member countries, and on April 2, 1951, he signed General Order No. 1, which activated Supreme Headquarters, Allied Powers Europe (SHAPE) as an operational

Table 2.1.   Total Number of Assigned Military
             Personnel in U.S. European Command
             (USEUCOM) by Year, 1945-1955

Predecessors of USEUCOM
1945 - 2,613,000
1946 - 278,042
1947 - 103,749
1948 - 91,535
1949 - 82,492
1950 - 79,495
1951 - 121,566
USEUCOM
1952 - 256,557
1953 - 243,842
1954 - 352,644
1955 - 356,787

Source: From data provided by Truman Strobridge,
         Command Historian, U.S. European Command
         Headquarters, Stuttgart, Germany.

command with headquarters in Paris. In early 1951 there were only two American divisions in Germany. The new decisions provided that four additional American divisions would be deployed in Germany. The first units arrived in Germany in May, 1951; by the end of the year most of the deployment had been completed. In late 1951 General Matthew Ridgway succeeded Eisenhower as SACEUR. In 1952 the American component of NATO was reorganized with the establishment of a new senior European command known as the United States European Command (USEUCOM). The number of troops in the European Command during the early 1950s is shown in Table 2.1. Not all of these forces were in Germany, though the great bulk of them were. The figure for 1951 does not include all of the reinforcements which had arrived by December. The table shows the substantial buildup which occurred in 1951-52 as a result of the troops to Europe decision. Another substantial buildup occurred in 1953-54. The number of troops then remained at over 300,000 until 1968.

By 1951 the United States had made an irrevocable commitment to the defense of Western Europe. In the U.S. view, however, an increase in the number of American troops would not be enough. The Europeans would also have to increase their defense efforts, and there would have to be a major contribution from the Federal Republic of Germany. The burden was thus shifted to the Europeans to provide a set of concrete proposals for the next steps.

The Issue of German Rearmament

Though the French government attempted to delay German rearmament as long as possible, it also produced the most imaginative and far-reaching proposals for the integration of Western Europe into a stronger entity for economic, military, and political purposes. The Schuman Plan, proposed in May, 1950, was a harbinger of subsequent French proposals which were even more ambitious. The Schuman Plan envisioned a process of economic integration which would eventually bring about a complete Franco-German rapprochement. Integration of the coal and steel industries with the creation of a European Coal and Steel Community (ECSC) would provide the impetus for further functional integration of the major European economies. The ultimate objective of the plan, according to Schuman, was the elimination of all risk of war between France and Germany, and "the substitution for a ruinous rivalry of an association founded upon common interest and the joining in a permanent work of peace two nations which for centuries had faced each other in bloody rivalries."[15]

Although there had been informal discussions of some form of German rearmament by mid-1950, no country had publicly supported the idea. In an interview with an American newspaper in December, 1949, Chancellor Adenauer had said that he was opposed to Germany's rearmament "in principle," but "he would be prepared to consider it, provided German forces were brought into the Western alliance as fully equal partners."[16] The idea of German rearmament seemed ever more viable in the minds of American policymakers as the cold war with the Soviet Union intensified. The Russians had authorized the establishment of an East German police force as early as the fall of 1948, which American military leaders feared was the beginning of a Soviet-supported East German army. The Soviet nuclear explosion in 1949 also tended to raise the issue higher on the diplomatic agenda. Field Marshall Viscount Montgomery, as military commander of the Western European Union, gave credence to the idea in November, 1949, by declaring that "the forces planned (to be deployed in Europe under WEU) at the moment were totally incapable of holding the Rhine, much less the Elbe, and that the only plausible solution lay in the use of German manpower."[17] General Clay, the ex-Military Governor of the American zone in

Germany, and John J. McCloy, the American High
Commissioner for Germany, both came out mildly in favor of
German rearmament in late 1949--Clay backing "a limited
German contribution to a composite European force," and McCloy
supporting "a strong federal police to counter the para-military
police force which East Germany was building."[18] The invasion of
South Korea by communist forces in mid-1950 forced all the
western governments to face up to the need for an increased
defense capability in Western Europe. In early September, 1950,
President Truman announced his decision to increase
substantially the size of U.S. forces stationed in Europe. The
French government responded soon thereafter.

The Rise and Demise of the EDC Plan

The French response came in the form of the Pleven Plan for
an integrated European army. The plan called for the
incorporation of small military units from the West European
countries, including West Germany, into a European army under
a European Defense Minister. The Plan was approved by the
French National Assembly on October 26, and presented to the
NATO Defense Committee on October 28, 1950. Truitt notes that
the French proposal "had the same effect on the Defense
Committee's meeting that the American proposals had had a
month earlier on the NATO Council's meeting. Each was a
momentous proposal, presented to an Alliance meeting with little
advance warning and with no prior consultation. Each was
considered a 'bomb,' and each proposal deadlocked the
meeting."[19] Conceptually, the Pleven Plan added an additional
layer to the Schuman Plan for the creation of a unified Europe.
Though its provisions were not radically different from the
American plan in that neither would have permitted Germany
an armaments industry or a general staff, the Pleven Plan sought
to delay German rearmament until after the political unification
of Europe had been accomplished.[20]

Following two months of intense bargaining among the
NATO allies, a settlement known as the Spofford Compromise
emerged, named after the American chairman of the NATO
Council of Deputies.[21] Gradual changes in perception seemed
evident. The United States ceased to cling tenaciously to the
package deal as originally presented by Acheson, realizing that it
simply could not be forced upon the Europeans without some
alteration. The French seemed to become more flexible by
agreeing at least in principle to the idea of German rearmament.
Truitt describes the Spofford Compromise as follows:

(It) provided for a West German troop contribution to NATO, but it also stipulated that German forces would be introduced into NATO in units no larger than regimental combat teams (not over 6,000 men) and would have no heavy guns; also, there was to be no West German general staff or defense minister. This plan, then, was a compromise between the original American proposal for German divisions and the Pleven Plan for German soldiers to be taken into a European Army in small units; the Spofford plan provided for German units large enough to meet the American requirement that they be effective and the French insistence that they not constitute an independent force and that they not be too large to cause French misgivings.[22]

The Spofford Compromise was approved at a meeting of the NATO Council in Brussels on December 19, 1950. The structure of NATO then gradually began to take shape under Eisenhower's direction in 1951. Though the Spofford Compromise represented some progress in the settlement of the German question, the French still continued to advocate the Pleven Plan as the proper form of the final solution. No further progress was registered until a surprising shift in the American position occurred in the summer of 1951. On July 3, General Eisenhower, in a speech at the Guild Hall in London, announced his support of the Pleven Plan.[23] Eisenhower's change of heart probably emanated from a feeling that the only way to proceed with getting German troops outfitted was through the French plan. By treating French proposals seriously, there could at least be some movement on the question.[24] In any case, support for the French plan increased among the major policymakers in Washington following Eisenhower's announcement. As Truitt notes, "This was its turning point; after Eisenhower's endorsement, generals and ambassadors rather than lieutenant colonels began arguing over the Plan's fine points."[25]

Substantive negotiations among the NATO allies began again with a renewed sense of purpose. During several months of hard bargaining the outlines of a treaty establishing a European Defense Community (EDC) emerged. The principle of German rearmament had been accepted, but the issue had now broadened into a plan for a unified Europe which included integrated armed forces. Mistrust of a rearmed Germany still persisted. The French insisted that the German government must be bound by allied guarantees to any defense treaty negotiated; no German withdrawal from the collective forces could be allowed. The

Benelux countries supported the French in arguing that the plan for integration must be thorough. Economic and political integration must at least accompany, if not precede, military integration. For the French, of course, there were deeper psychological objections to arming a traditional enemy without ironclad safeguards.

The United States attempted to allay French fears with assurances of a subdued Germany thoroughly embedded in an EDC from which there could be no escape. The Americans also stressed the absolute necessity of including the Germans in any European defense framework which could serve as a deterrent to the Russians. Actually, the American negotiators hoped that the incorporation of German troops into the defense forces might allow the U.S. to recall most of the U.S. forces recently pledged to Europe, a point the French did not fail to recognize. The Americans also often stressed the threat of imminent world war, hoping that European fears of the Russians would quicken the decision-making process.

The subject of all the discussion was, of course, the emerging German state. Chancellor Adenauer, naturally, stoutly resisted any kind of second class status for a rearmed Germany. Since his primary interest lay in a complete restoration of German political sovereignty, he adroitly used the rearmament debate as a means for West Germany to gain political equality. Adenauer also realized that the more extended the bargaining process was, the more powerful his position became. Eventually, he believed, the United States would get more or less what it wanted, if necessary by unilateral action. Hence, he could afford to monitor the negotiations with great patience. "The more often German troops were proclaimed indispensable to western defense, the more certain the Federal Republic became that it could insist on full equality.[26]

An initial draft of the EDC treaty was completed in time for a meeting of the NATO Council held at Lisbon, February 20-25, 1952. The military structure of the Community was practically complete. Troop sizes, integration of the air units, and a command structure had all been tentatively agreed upon. At Lisbon agreement appeared to emerge on the principles which would govern the relationship between NATO and the EDC. As expressed in the final conference communique:

> The NATO Council found that the principles underlying the treaty to establish the European Defense Community conformed to the interests of the parties to the North Atlantic Treaty. It also agreed on the principles which should govern the relationship between the proposed community and

the North Atlantic Treaty Organization. The North Atlantic Council agreed to propose to its members and the the European Defense Community reciprocal security undertakings between the members of the two organizations....[27]

The Lisbon agreement produced a wave of optimism in reference to the EDC plan. Acheson "felt that the agreements at Lisbon had 'brought us to the dawn of a new day in Europe.'"[28] Averell Harriman agreed, saying that he saw the end of a bloody rivalry happening "in a split second of history."[29] Such optimism was unfortunately premature. What the Lisbon meeting did not do was make any progress on the political side of the European unification effort. The French goal of a European political union to accompany or precede military integration was ignored, leaving it unclear as to how the militarily integrated EDC was to be governed politically.

Negotiations on the final draft of the EDC treaty proceeded apace during the next few months, though not without interference from the East. On March 10, 1952, the Soviet government sent a note to the western governments suggesting that the time had come for Germany to be reunified as a neutral state. If the neutrality of Germany were guaranteed, not only would reunification be possible, but even a limited form of remilitarization could be contemplated. The Soviets were, of course, attempting to stall negotiations for the EDC. They hoped that by dangling the prospects of neutrality and reunification for all Germany, they might be able to slow down the process of European unification and preclude the rearmament of West Germany. The offer also made a certain amount of sense from the Soviet point of view. A neutral Germany would at some point have to lean either eastward or westward for political and military support. With the advantage of proximity to Germany on the Continent, the Russians calculated that they would have an advantage over the West, the U.S. in particular, in being able to exert influence over the new German state. Whatever the Soviet motives may have been been, the western powers explored the Soviet proposal only half-heartedly. After brief discussions the western governments issued a firm rejection.

The negotiations among the six Western European states were concluded on May 9, 1952, when the draft treaty for the European Defense Community was initialed. Debate on the merits of the treaty began soon thereafter in the six national capitals. In Paris disenchantment was expressed very quickly by major French politicians and news commentators. What seemed to bother French critics was how different the EDC treaty was from the original Pleven Plan.[30] By late May the French government was already requesting additional assurances from the U.S. and British governments in reference to the rebuilding of German forces. The French still feared that Germany might not be kept militarily in a secondary position on the Continent. As French military commitments to Indo-China increased, French fears of a resurgent Germany grew stronger. In an effort to calm the fears and convince the French of the wisdom of ratifying the EDC treaty, the British and American governments issued a joint declaration of intent which affirmed that:

> The United States and Britain would regard as a threat to their own security any action, from whatever quarter, which threatened the unity or integrity of the EDC, and in such case would act in accordance with Article 4 of the North Atlantic Treaty, which provided for consultation.[31]

Some objections to the treaty were also raised in Bonn. Critics claimed that by giving up the right to build a German general staff and by not achieving full NATO membership the Germans had indeed been relegated to permanent second class status in Europe. The German objections required another round of consultations and another set of allied assurances that Germany's best interests lay in ratification of the EDC treaty. The finished product, then, after another month of discussion was "a vast number of accords which together comprised a web of agreements emerging from discussions among the EDC six; the EDC states and Britain; the Six and NATO, and the occupying powers and the Federal Republic."[32]

During the last half of 1952 and the first half of 1953 debate on the ratification of the accords took place in the various European capitals. Though vigorous criticism of the EDC plan was heard everywhere, the strongest, most trenchant protests were heard in Paris. The French government delayed submitting the accords to the French National Assembly, hoping that informed debate and persuasive efforts by major public figures would eventually sway sentiment in the legislature toward the treaties. The passage of time, however, had the opposite effect. As the battle for the treaties was being won in other European capitals, it was being lost in Paris. The United States ratified the accords quickly, in July of 1952. Eventually, all of the other prospective EDC members also ratified the accords, except France. Acheson's last act as Truman's secretary of state in December, 1952, was an urgent appeal to France to proceed with the building of the new Europe. The French National Assembly finally began the ratification debate in early 1953. As the months ticked by, prospects for the treaties became gloomier.

The final blow came on August 30, 1954, when the treaties were defeated in the French parliament by a vote of 319 to 264.[33] The French action shut the door on the plan for a European army once and for all.

The fundamental problem with the May accords was that they were never really able to bridge the conflicting aspirations of the French and the Germans. The only party really satisfied with the accords was, in fact, the United States, which had developed an overarching interest in the unification of Europe but was unable to allay French fears or satisfy German yearnings. The French were convinced that the accords had simply strayed too far from the original Pleven Plan. In the final analysis they were unable to accept rebuilt German forces even within the EDC structure without a preeminent commitment to a unified European political organization. Only then could Germany be kept securely in the French shadow.

There was also a noticeable decline in the United States' ability to exert leadership in Europe in the early 1950s. The two men who had the most influence among European statesmen were back in the United States. Eisenhower had returned in 1952 to run for the presidency. John J. McCloy, the former U.S. High Commissioner in Germany, had also returned to private life as chairman of the board at the Chase Manhattan Bank. The U.S. presidential election turned America's energy inward, making it less possible to exert leadership in European affairs. Acheson believed that if the American elections had been held a year later, "the United States would have had a good chance of helping Schuman get the European Defense Community through the French National Assembly."[34]

There were broader reasons for the failure of the EDC rooted in the structure of international politics. There was a general decrease in the level of East-West tension in the early 1950s. Stalin's death in 1953 sharply decreased the fear of Soviet aggression in Europe, making the EDC plan seem less pressing. The end of the Korean War in the summer of 1953 also eased East-West tension and seemed to signal a halt to the global expansion of communism. The French involvement in Indo-China drained away much of France's military vitality, thereby raising the level of suspicion of the traditional enemy to the North. Unless there were ironclad guarantees in reference to the rearmament of Germany, France wanted no part of it. Finally, there was a perceptible shift in the military posture of the United States. When Eisenhower assumed the presidency in 1953, the Department of Defense seemed to lose some interest in the deterrent value of conventional forces and place more emphasis on nuclear weapons as the major component of deterrence strategy. This was the beginning of the strategic doctrine known as "massive retaliation." Though Eisenhower had originally championed the idea of the EDC when he served as Supreme Commander in Europe, as president of the United States he did not put forth a major diplomatic effort to ensure that the EDC treaty was ratified by European legislatures.

German Entry into NATO

With the French defeat of the EDC the effort to augment NATO's defense capability with German troops was moved back to square one on the diplomatic chessboard. At the same time, however, the French action created a new impetus to find an alternative solution as soon as possible. The American government, impatient that no real progress on the German question had been made since 1950, threatened to take unilateral action very soon if a new agreement could not be worked out. As it happened, a new settlement was agreed upon with astonishing speed. The British foreign minister, Anthony Eden, took the lead in suggesting a new departure. The Eden Plan called for the resurrection of the 1948 Western European Union (WEU) as the vehicle for accomplishing German rearmament with appropriate controls. The WEU would connect Germany indirectly with NATO, since the greater part of the WEU structure had been incorporated into NATO in 1951. The treaty also contained various provisions for the control of the member nations' arms. With the Eden Plan France would at least be able to place some controls on the German military establishment, while the Americans were now threatening the rearmament of Germany with or without French consent.

In a series of meetings in London and Paris in September and October,1954, representives of the NATO countries drafted the treaties which ended the occupation regime and integrated West Germany into the western alliance structure. The London and Paris Agreements were officially signed in Paris on October 23, 1954. For West Germany it was a momentous occasion. The Occupation Statute was abolished, the Allied High Commission was dissolved, and the Federal Republic was accorded the rights and duties of a fully sovereign state, subject only to allied reservations concerning Berlin and the reunification of Germany. West Germany became a full member of the WEU, and hence an associate member of NATO. The Federal Republic agreed, in turn, to allow French, British, and American troops to remain in Germany as the first line of NATO defense in Western Europe. The troops of other NATO members could also be stationed on German soil.

The London and Paris Agreements entered into force legally on May 5, 1955. On that date the restoration of West Germany's sovereignty became an accomplished fact. The French, although no better off than they would have been with the EDC, at least received assurances that Germany's troops would ultimately be subject to the authority of an external NATO commander, since it was agreed that the post of SACEUR would be held permanently by an American general. Not only would French troops remain in Germany, more importantly a large contingent of U.S. and British troops would also remain.

The events of 1955 enshrined two phenomena as permanent features of the relationship between West Germany and the western powers. First, Germany was fully integrated into the western security system. Second, the troops to Europe decision ensured that the United States would remain bonded to West Germany both militarily and politically for years to come. The decision to increase the U.S. military presence in Germany was seen by the Americans as stabilizing for western and American security, by the Germans as a sign of genuine German-American solidarity and cooperation, and by the French as necessary restraint on German militarism. The decision was viewed by all as proof of a profound and longterm American commitment to Europe.

Relationships Between Germans and American Military Personnel

It remains for us to survey briefly the developments in relations between Germans and American military personnel from 1949 to 1955. The surveys conducted by the office of the American High Commissioner in Germany (HICOG) during the period are highly revealing. In one of the early surveys made in December, 1949, it is interesting to note that a majority of the Germans in the American zone had little or no contact with American troops. "Six in ten (59%) of the AMZON (American Zone) population and 53% of the West Berliners interviewed said they did not see any American troops during the course of an average day."[35] The population as a whole, however, seemed to have a generally favorable impression of the troops. "Majorities in all areas surveyed described the conduct of American occupation troops as good, with an additional six percent in AMZON saying they thought it was very good."[36] Of the Germans who saw an average of ten or more soldiers a day, only 11% complained of bad behavior. Evidently, increased exposure to the troops did not lead to more negative impressions. There was, however, ambivalence on the issue of military patronage of public establishments, probably as a residue of the earlier policy of nonfraternization. Although "half of the AMZON population approved of American soldiers patronizing German cafes," the other half did not or expressed some kind of reservation. "Most of those opposed to the presence of soldiers in German establishments, when asked why they did so, responded that it led to fights (no statistics recorded)."[37]

In a survey taken in November and December, 1951, the Germans were asked various questions about the purpose of the troops' presence and whether they should remain or be withdrawn. A majority of 58% of the respondents believed that the purpose of the troops' presence was to safeguard German security. Only 22% thought they should be withdrawn, though "when asked what the advantages were of the troops' presence, a third of the respondents could think of none at all." In the same survey the troops again scored high marks for behavior. "Fifty-five percent of the residents said the behavior of American troops was good, 20% called it fair, and only 8% termed it bad." Sixty-five percent likened the behavior of U.S. troops to the behavior they would have expected from their own army. A substantial majority of the respondents believed that more public contact between Germans and American military personnel would be a good thing, but private or intimate contact with soldiers was not strongly encouraged. The survey also gives early evidence of a tendency to discriminate against black soldiers more than whites. "Asked whether or not they would be willing to invite soldiers into their homes, a majority (55%) of the respondents said yes......Only 23 percent would do so if the soldier were a negro."[38]

As the troop buildup continued as a result of the Truman administration's troops to Europe decision, HICOG instituted new programs in 1952 to improve troop behavior through increased cultural awareness and to increase the level of personal contact between American troops and the German population. The programs seem to have had positive results. In a survey taken by HICOG in January, 1953, more than a third of the respondents (36%) in all areas and 44% in AMZON said that they had noticed an improvement in troop conduct. The percentage who perceived the purpose of U.S. troops as protection from external threats increased to 67% (up from 58% in late 1951). Only 19% believed that American troops should be withdrawn. The subjective impressions Germans had of the troops' characteristics are also most interesting. The major strengths and weaknesses of U.S. soldiers were described as follows:

The most frequently mentioned strength of the American soldier was his high-quality material and equipment (47%), although his character and intelligence (9%), physical health (9%), and high standard of living (9%) were also mentioned. But at the same time, American soldiers were regarded as not particularly brave (12%), soft (12%), undisciplined (9%), pampered (6%), and poorly trained (5%).[39]

Russian soldiers, by contrast were viewed as "tougher and more brutal (17%) and more easily satisfied (11%) than American soldiers."[40]

The final HICOG poll of German public opinion taken in June, 1955, continued the pattern of improving German-American relations. "...A clear majority of Germans said there was nothing in particular that they did not like about American soldiers..... Even of those who said the troops behaved badly and those who found nothing pleasing about the soldiers' appearance or manners, majorities said that rapport between the two groups had improved." The U.S. soldier was characterized in general as a "healthy, nice person, strongly supported by technological achievements, but lacking in toughness and aggressiveness." The Russians, by contrast, were described in terms of "endurance, simplicity of demands, the discipline involved by communism, and their disregard for life (no statistics recorded)."[41]

The final poll indicates increased ambivalence about the purpose of American troops in Germany. The reasons are not clear, especially in view of the fact that Germany's sovereignty had been recovered only a short time earlier. 45% of the respondents perceived U.S. troops as present for security from external threats, 30% considered the troops to be occupation troops, and 13% thought the troops were present for both reasons. It may be that many Germans thought that the recovery of full sovereignty would mean the removal of all foreign troops from German soil; or the results may reflect ambivalence in reference to Germany's entry into NATO; or the diminished perception of the Soviet threat after Stalin's death might also have had some influence.

The general pattern which emerges from the HICOG surveys is one of steadily improving relations between the Germans and American troops during the period of semi-sovereignty. It is not difficult to imagine that the Germans might have experienced some confusion over the purpose of the American military presence during these years. In 1949, when the fledgling Federal Republic was established with limited sovereignty, there were fewer than 82,000 U.S. troops in Germany. The occupation period was coming to an end, and American troops were returning home as the Germans began their new life in the context of a thoroughly reformed social and political order. A year later, in 1950, there were fewer than 79,000 troops remaining in Germany. In 1951, however, U.S. troops began to return to Germany in large numbers as a result of the Truman administration's troops to Europe decision. Was the occupation really over or wasn't it? The answer to that question was certainly by no means clear to many Germans. Whether the Germans really understood or approved of the return of American troops to the country depends, in the final analysis, upon how well they understood the rationale for the construction of the NATO alliance and what view they had of the Soviet threat. The surveys show that by early 1953 two-thirds of surveyed population believed that the troops were in Germany as protection from external threats. Only one-fifth of the respondents believed the troops should be withdrawn. Hence, there seems to have been a broad understanding of the reasons for the burgeoning American military presence even in the early 1950s.

There are, of course, some clear reasons why the West Germans did not have great difficulty accepting the enlarged American presence. A vivid object lesson in the reality of Soviet intentions existed next door in the other half of the country. The German Democratic Republic, previously the Soviet zone of occupation, was emerging as one of the most thorough, brutally regimented political systems in the world. No one had any illusions that the GDR, under the infamous tyrant Walter Ulbricht, was anything but a Soviet puppet state. The Soviet acquisition of nuclear weapons in 1949 and the outbreak of the Korean War in 1950 left little doubt that the threat of communist expansion was very real. The only thing which might preclude a Soviet thrust into Western Europe was an American guarantee of the country's security. The guarantee came in the form of the NATO alliance and the return of American troops. With a large number of American troops on German soil, there could be no doubt that if the Soviets tried to threaten West Germany militarily, they would be countered by the entire military force of the United States. The HICOG surveys seem to show that, despite some understandable ambivalence on the issue, a substantial majority of the West Germans broadly understood the nature of the security dilemma and accepted the necessity of American troops. There was really very little choice for the West Germans, unless Western Europe was to be surrendered by the United States to unrelenting Soviet pressure. The important point is that the West Germans made their choice freely and openly through the institutions of a democratic state and by popularly elected officials. And the choice they made was crystal clear. They preferred the West over the East; they preferred American protection over communist encroachment.

As for the U.S. troops in Germany, the available evidence seems to show that they were generally a positive factor in German-American relations during the period. For most West Germans, the troops served a vital security purpose without impinging much upon their daily lives. As a denser network of contacts developed between the Germans and the troops over the years, there was also more approval of the troops' presence.

Notes

[1] See John Ford Golay, The Founding of the Federal Republic of Germany (Chicago: University of Chicago Press, 1958), pp. 23-24. For the text of the Occupation Statute see Beate Ruhm von Oppen, Documents on Germany Under Occupation, 1945-1949 (London: Oxford University Press, 1955), pp. 375-377.

[2] Golay, p. 23.

[3] See Robert McGeehan, The German Rearmament Question (Chicago: University of Illinois Press, 1971), pp. 17-18.

[4] Laurence W. Martin, "The American Decision to Rearm Germany," in Harold Stein, ed., American Civil-Military Decisions: A Book of Case Studies (University, Ala.: University of Alabama Press, 1963), p. 646.

[5] NATO Handbook (Brussels: NATO Information Service, 1980), p. 17.

[6] An analysis of the decision-making process in reference to the "package deal" and other aspects of the troops to Europe decision can be found in Wesley Byron Truitt, The Troops to Europe Decision: The Process, Politics, and Diplomacy of a Strategic Commitment, Doctoral Dissertation, Columbia University, 1968, pp. 172-253.

[7] For the text of the announcement see Public Papers of the Presidents of the United States, Harry S. Truman, 1950 (Washington: Government Printing Office, 1965), p. 626, or see The New York Times, September 10, 1950, p. 1. The text is also reproduced in Truitt, p. 211.

[8] Coral Bell, Negotiation from Strength (New York: Alfred A. Knopf, 1963), p. 53.

[9] Truitt, pp. 265-266.

[10] Quoted in Truitt, pp. 271-272.

[11] The communique is summarized and quoted in Truitt, pp. 279-280.

[12] The communique is summarized and quoted in Truitt, pp. 287-288.

[13] Anthony Eden, The Memoirs of Anthony Eden: Full Circle (Boston: Houghton Mifflin, 1960), p. 34. Also quoted in Truitt, pp. 293-294.

[14] The Congressional hearings are summarized in Truitt, Chapter 6, pp. 331-430. The reasons for Congressional approval are summarized in pp. 85-114.

[15] Quoted in McGeehan, p. 16.

[16] Statement by Chancellor Konrad Adenauer in the Cleveland Plain Dealer, December 4, 1949, as quoted in Morgan, p. 44.

[17] Quoted in Martin, p. 642.

[18] Both quoted in Martin, p. 647.

[19] Truitt, pp. 294-295.

[20] McGeehan, p. 42

[21] The Council of Deputies, as implied by its name, was comprised of deputy ministers from the NATO members. Its function was to discuss issues and prepare draft proposals for submission to the NATO Council, which made the final decisions at the level of foreign ministers.

[22] Truitt, p. 315

[23] McGeehan, p. 129.

[24] Truitt, p. 473.

[25] Truitt, p. 472.

[26] McGeehan, p. 179.

[27] Quoted in McGeehan, p. 192.

[28] Quoted in McGeehan, p. 195.

[29] Quoted in McGeehan, p. 196.

[30] McGeehan, p. 206.

[31] Quoted in McGeehan, p. 207.

[32] McGeehan, p. 208.

[33] Truitt, p. 474.

[34] Quoted in McGeehan, p. 216.

[35] Anna J. Merritt and Richard L. Merritt, Public Opinion in Semisovereign Germany (Urbana: University of Illinois Press, 1980), p. 58.

[36] Ibid.

[37] Ibid.

[38] Merritt, pp. 151-152.

[39] Merritt, p. 207.

[40] Ibid.

[41] Merritt, pp. 238-239.

3

CONSOLIDATION AND NORMALCY
1955-1967

West Germany as Alliance Partner

The third period in this historical study is one during which West Germany's relationship of security dependency upon the United States became fully consolidated and widely accepted by the Germans. It was, as suggested in the chapter title, a period of consolidation and relative normalcy, a period in which a number of important security issues were debated, negotiated, and settled. In the years from 1955 to 1967 the Federal Republic successfully consolidated its political institutions and made rapid economic advances. The gross national product rose continuously until 1966. The German armed forces were reconstructed, and the Federal Republic became a strategic NATO ally, even gaining entry into NATO's Nuclear Planning Group in 1966. Even as the strength of the German forces increased, however, the Federal Republic's reliance upon the American security guarantee intensified. The German government over the years became more firmly convinced that the country's security required both the American nuclear umbrella and the presence of a large contingent of American forces. In order to ensure that the forces would remain in Germany, the German government negotiated a series of offset payment agreements with the United States beginning in 1961.

The U.S. government during the period also became firmly wedded to the conviction that the viability of NATO depended upon a strong German contribution. Without a Federal Republic strongly committed to the West, the stability of Western Europe could not be guaranteed. At the same time, however, the U.S. became more insistent that the West Germans assume a greater portion of the common defense effort. As the United States became more heavily involved in the Vietnam War toward the end of the period, the maintenance of troops in Germany became a more quarrelsome issue. At the same time, serious deficiencies in troop morale and readiness in Germany became apparent.

A plethora of issues arose in U.S.-German relations during the period. By focusing on a few of the more important ones in the security issue area, we shall perhaps cover the period with greater coherence, though at the risk of oversimplification and loss of the rich variety of nuance. Chronological purity has also been sacrificed in the interest of covering the major issues topically.

The Security of West Berlin

Located 110 miles inside East Germany, the former capital of the German Reich became a sensitive barometer of East-West relations in the postwar period.[1] The Soviet attempt to consolidate its hold on East Germany by ousting the western powers from their sectors of control in Berlin failed miserably in 1948-49. The Berlin blockade was given up because of the resolute determination of the West shown in the Berlin Airlift. With the establishment of the Federal Republic in 1949, the western powers had been careful not to accord legal sovereignty over Berlin to the West German state. Though the actual administration of West Berlin was progressively taken over by the West German government, the western powers maintained the status of allied occupation in the city. This was done to ensure that if the Soviets put pressure on the city or tried to block the access routes, they would be forced to negotiate with the major western powers, not the West Germans. They would also face the threat of allied, rather than West German military retaliation. The wisdom of this course of action became apparent in the period from 1955 to 1967.

In November, 1958, Khrushchev announced a new Soviet proposal for settlement of the Berlin question. The justification for the Soviet initiative was alleged western violations of the Potsdam Agreements. West Berlin, he suggested, should be made an independent political unit, a "free city" without any political connection to any existing state. The territory of the "free city" should be completely demilitarized through the removal of all foreign military forces from both parts of the city. Though the "correct and natural way to solve the problem would be for the western part of Berlin.....to be reunited with its eastern part and for Berlin to become a unified city with the state whose territory it is situated," nevertheless the Berlin question could be settled for the forseeable future through conversion into a demilitarized free city.²

The Soviet proposal appeared to be in the form of an ultimatum. The Russians threatened to sign a peace treaty with the German Democratic Republic which would give the GDR government authority over all matters concerning access to West Berlin. Such a treaty would be signed within six months, if a satisfactory solution had not been found. The East Germans would then control all passage to Berlin and the western powers, according to Soviet logic, would be forced to negotiate with the GDR for access rights to West Berlin.

The U.S. response was swift and angry. The first U.S. note, on December 20, refuted the Soviet legal argument by pointing out that western rights in Berlin were not derived from the Potsdam Agreements but from the conquest of Germany and the division of the country approved at Yalta. The second note, on December 31, reaffirmed the American commitment to the western sectors of Berlin and warned the Soviets that the western powers would not surrender their rights to a threat of force.³ The Soviet reply to the American notes was considerably toned down. Though the Soviet government said that it still considered the November proposal a healthy basis for agreement, there was no mention of time limits.

The Geneva Foreign Ministers Conference convened in May, 1959, and lasted through August. The original date of the ultimatum, May 27, passed without fanfare. Though the conference ended in total deadlock, a restoration of high tension was avoided by Eisenhower's invitation to Khrushchev to attend a summit meeting at Camp David the following month. The Camp David meeting, in September, 1959, also failed to resolve the issue, though, in Khrushchev's words: "We agreed indeed that talks on the Berlin question should be resumed, that no time limit whatsoever is to be established for them, but that they should also not be dragged out for an indefinite time."⁴ This formula meant that ultimatums had been shelved, though not the issue itself. A new summit meeting was set for May, 1960, in Paris.

The Paris summit abruptly ended the first day when an American pilot's U-2 aircraft was shot down over Soviet territory. Khrushchev declared that he would wait for the next president before beginning negotiations again. When President Kennedy met with Khrushchev in Vienna in June, 1961, it was in the shadow of the abortive Bay of Pigs episode. Tension was only heightened when the two statesmen conducted a dialogue of confrontation through the international press. Khrushchev on Moscow television the next week said: "We ask everyone to understand us correctly: the conclusion of a peace treaty with

Germany (ending western rights) cannot be postponed any longer. A peaceful settlement in Europe must be attained this year."[5] In July, Kennedy announced an impending call-up of reservists. On television he said: "The solemn vow each of us gave to West Berlin in time of peace will not be broken in time of danger. If we do not meet our commitments to Berlin, where will we later stand....?"[6]

The Soviet response to the impasse came on August 13, 1961, when all traffic between East and West Berlin was halted, all checkpoints were sealed, and the construction of the infamous Berlin Wall began. The Soviets did not carry through on the threat to assign authority over Berlin access to the East Germans. Instead they gave the East Germans the green light to stop the massive hemorrhage of human talent from East to West Germany. For years Berlin, with its relatively unfortified border between the eastern and western portions of the city, had been the major escape route for East Germans who decamped to West Germany. From 1949 to early 1961 the refugee flow had averaged 230,000 annually. In the first twelve days of August more than 22,000 East Germans fled to West Berlin.[7] The Wall put an end to the drain on the lifeblood of the East German regime. The U.S. response, though militarily prudent, was an enormous disappointment to most West Germans. Tanks were rolled up to the wall, strong statements were issued by the White House, but no action was taken to rebuff the Russians. Significantly, however, allied forces in West Berlin were heavily reinforced for a short period of time, and limited changes were undertaken to strengthen the U.S. ground posture in Europe. Mako describes the changes as follows:

> About 42,000 troops were sent to Europe, mostly to provide the U.S. Army in Europe with the combat and support units necessary for sustained conventional operations that had been lacking since the Army's 1956 reorganization for nuclear combat. The three infantry divisions in West Germany were mechanized and additional heavy divisions in the United States were activated, so that the ratio of heavy to light divisions in the ground forces was substantially increased.....To facilitate the deployment of U.S.-based heavy formations, the equipment for two divisions was also prepositioned in Europe.[8]

The Cuban missile crisis in October, 1962, was accompanied by renewed pressure on Berlin, though the Soviets did not hazard another confrontation. A Soviet note in early 1963, following the

Cuban debacle, significantly ommitted new threats on Berlin. The Soviets were content for the time being to delay allied military convoys on the Berlin autobahn from time to time. When in June, 1964, the Soviets finally did sign a new treaty with the GDR, it did not purport to terminate western access rights to Berlin. The reinforcement of American forces in Berlin which occurred following the wall episode did not last for any protracted length of time. The buildup of 1961-62 was followed by a builddown of similar magnitude in 1963-64, as can be seen in Tables 3.1 and 3.2. The situation remained a quiet stalemate until 1971, when a new Quadripartite Treaty on Berlin effected a new set of understandings between the Soviets and the western powers.

Nuclear Weapons Issues

The military strategy pursued by various administrations in Washington has always had a heavy influence on decisions made in reference to U.S. forces in Germany. More specifically, the role of nuclear weapons in strategy, and the relationship between nuclear weapons and ground forces are issues which have been a constantly troubling element in U.S.-German politico-military relations since 1955. In this section we review the major issues which arose from the debates and decisions on nuclear weapons questions. Though the debate on the Multilateral Force (MLF) is a logical component of this issue area, it is helpful to trace its rise and demise separately, as we do in the following section.

The London and Paris Agreements of 1955 included a pledge by the Federal Republic not to build or acquire nuclear weapons. The renunciation of nuclear weapons did not mean, however, a renunciation of nuclear defense. The decision to deploy U.S. nuclear weapons in Europe was taken at a meeting of the NATO Council in 1952. Two years later, in 1954, U.S. atomic legislation was revised to facilitate deployment of weapons to NATO allies (and also to permit the dissemination of nuclear information in the context of the Atoms for Peace proposal).[9] The first tactical nuclear weapons were deployed in Germany in 1955 under the command of SACEUR, with final authority in the hands of the U.S. president. The number of such weapons continued to increase during the 1950s.

The first overt indication that nuclear weapons were included as a component of NATO's defense of Germany came in June, 1955, when NATO held its first combat drill of that year. The exercise, named Carte Blanche, was designed to probe the problems of air defense in the event of a Soviet attack with tactical nuclear weapons and to test the link between tactical nuclear weapons and conventional ground forces. The editors of *Congressional Quarterly* note that:

> Tactical nuclear weapons, for all practical purposes, were indistinguishable from strategic nuclear weapons when they were first deployed. In theory, they were earmarked for battlefield use, but in a densely populated country such as West Germany, it would be difficult or impossible to save cities from their effects, even if Soviet forces abstained from nuclear retaliation.[10]

The NATO exercise assumed that 300 tactical nuclear warheads had exploded between Hamburg and Munich, an area about the size of Pennsylvania. Press reports carried the simulated results in bold headlines, with figures such as 1.7 million Germans dead and 3.5 million wounded.[11] The result was a political firestorm in West Germany. The idea of Germany as a battlefield was anathema to the enormous number of Germans who remembered the horrors of World War II. Pacifist and anti-nuclear groups quickly formed. Newspaper columnists such as Adelbert Weinstein argued that German attempts to meet NATO force goals would only drain money away from more pressing needs such as a civil defense program. The Social Democratic Party, chief political opposition to the incumbent Christian Democratic government, launched an attack on government policies calculated to persuade the German public that Adenauer's policies would inevitably lead Germany to nuclear self-destruction.

The CDU government did its best to downplay the results of Carte Blanche. Government spokesmen insisted that the objective of such maneuvers was not only defense against Soviet aggression but also deterrence of Soviet military adventures and that in case of war, the Federal Republic could only be saved by immediate activation of the American nuclear guarantee.[12] Adenauer's success in pacifying the opposition led him in fact to an absolute majority victory in the general elections of 1957. Unencumbered by a coalition government, and with Franz Josef Strauss as his defense minister, Adenauer openly endorsed security policies which would strengthen the German army to the maximum extent possible and which clearly included American tactical nuclear weapons as a component of Germany's defense.

Concurrent with the German debates on the role of nuclear weapons in defense was the appearance of the Rapacki Plan. In a speech to the United Nations General Assembly in October, 1957, and subsequently in a memorandum to the major powers in

February, 1958, the Polish foreign minister, Adam Rapacki, proposed a nuclear free zone in central Europe which would include both German states plus Poland and Czechoslovakia.[13] The plan met with an immediate barrage of criticism from most Nato members. In the opinion of the western governments, not only did it fail to provide necessary verification procedures, it was simply an idea calculated to give the Soviet Union an inherent political and military advantage over Europe. It would preserve the Soviet Union's advantage of proximity to central Europe while removing the threat of western retaliation with tactical nuclear weapons in the event of aggression. Given the imbalance between Warsaw Pact and NATO divisions on the ground in Europe,[14] NATO planners never gave serious consideration to the Rapacki Plan. It was met with polite but resolute rejection.

In March, 1958, the German Bundestag authorized a sweeping modernization program designed to integrate the Bundeswehr (the German army) more fully into NATO force structures.[15] At the same time another debate took place in the Bundestag on tactical nuclear warfare. Shortly following the debate the SPD launched an extra-parliamentary grassroots campaign called the "Kampf dem Atomtod" or battle against atomic death. In the Land (state) elections of 1959 the SPD lost soundly, dampening somewhat the anti-nuclear thrust in the party. A more conservative leadership then took over the party and persuaded the SPD to back the policy of rearming West Germany within the framework of NATO. The party also softened its Marxist tone and broadened its platform with the adoption of a pragmatic program. Nevertheless, the Kampf den Atomtod left behind a permanent, vociferous, and well organized anti-nuclear movement in West Germany which in subsequent years became firmly rooted.

In 1959 the U.S. began the installation of Thor and Jupiter missiles in Britain, Italy, and Turkey. This action changed the nature of the nuclear debate, since these were intermediate-range nuclear missiles (IRBM's) which were capable of striking Soviet territory from their European bases.[16] The missiles remained in Europe only for a two-year period, however. They were withdrawn in 1961 as a "result of a deliberate political decision not to have missiles of such range based in Europe; presumably they could make escalation to the strategic level too rapid or too easy."[17] The Thor-Jupiter episode is best understood in the context of the shift in military strategy from the Eisenhower to the Kennedy administrations in the early 1960s. During the Eisenhower years the nuclear strategy for NATO was "massive retaliation," as noted in the previous chapter. This was a deterrence strategy which assumed that the exposed position of West Germany, together with the imbalance in NATO-Warsaw

Pact forces, made western defense impossible without strong nuclear forces as a backdrop for conventional forces. The rationale of massive retaliation is succinctly described by William Mako:

> Increased American reliance on nuclear weapons was the key feature of the New Look. In late 1953, dismissing the possibility that another sizable conflict would be fought with conventional weapons alone, the Eisenhower administration authorized the services to plan on using nuclear weapons whenever deemed militarily feasible. Its main intention was to forestall Army formulation of large manpower and materiel requirements based on preparations for a repeat of World War II or Korea. This decision set the stage for unprecedented public emphasis on America's readiness to retaliate-massively or otherwise-with nuclear weapons against any communist aggression. And the threat amounted to more than just a bluff. By 1954, the U.S. deployment of tactical nuclear weapons had begun, and plans for Western Europe's defense had been altered to give strategic air power the decisive role. The greater emphasis on strategic air power reflected official support for 'collective balanced forces.' Although it never intended to respond with nuclear weapons to every minor encounter, the administration-not wanting to see America progressively weakened by a series of Koreas-was determined to use nuclear weapons 'in a wider range of contingencies than those for which the previous administration had firmly planned.'"[18]

Massive retaliation involved the use of tactical weapons by conventional forces as well as the use of the strategic deterrent. Applied to Europe, it meant placing conventional forces as near to the East German border as feasible to repel any attack not substantial enough to inflict serious damage or make a quick breakthrough. There would be a rapid escalation to the use of tactical nuclear weapons if the forward forces began to fall. If a major loss were unavoidable, the strategic deterrent might be brought to bear.

The advent of the Kennedy administration in 1961 brought a major change in military strategy. Known as "flexible response," the strategy was designed to counter Moscow's rapid advances in nuclear arms. It required a strengthening of conventional forces in Europe, since escalation to the nuclear level would occur only if the Soviets escalated first or if the attack on Europe were so overwhelming that NATO's forces would be quickly decimated. By countering a conventional attack primarily with conventional forces, NATO raised the nuclear threshold and allowed more time to consider the use of nuclear weapons with greater forethought.[19] The flexible response strategy was also designed to be more sensitive to European fears of nuclear holocaust at the first sign of aggression. The Kennedy administration also adopted a "two-and-a-half war" strategy which required enough forces to wage, simultaneously, a three-month conventional forward defense of Western Europe, a defense of South Korea or Southeast Asia against a full-scale Chinese attack, and a minor operation somewhere else. Steps were also taken to improve U.S. capabilities in waging a limited war.[20] It is against this background that the removal of the Thor and Jupiter missiles from Europe in 1961 must be seen. At the same time, however, a new generation of more powerful tactical weapons was deployed in West Germany as well as Mace cruise missiles.

Concomitant with the flexible response strategy the administration began consideration of a dual-basing plan whereby military units in the United States would be designated for service in Europe as reinforcements on short notice. Dual-basing would require a massive airlift of troops from the U.S. to Europe in the event of an attack on the forces stationed in Germany. The first such exercise in continent-to-continent reinforcement took place in 1963 with the "Big Lift" operation. Big Lift was an airlift of 14,983 men and 116 tons of equipment to Europe in 63 hours.[21] This demonstration of U.S. technology and commitment to Europe was a well-timed boost to German morale, though the dual-basing plan became increasingly worrisome to the Germans in later years when it was used as a rationale for removing forces stationed in Europe back to bases in the United States.

With the deployment of thousands of tactical nuclear weapons on German soil in the early 1960s, the Germans began to exert a greater effort to be included in the nuclear decision-making process. The Kennedy approach to superpower politics, despite good intentions, often left the Germans waiting in the wings for news of major policy decisions. The U.S.-Soviet Nuclear Test Ban Treaty of 1963 surprised the German government by an almost total lack of prior consultation. The Germans were also becoming more skeptical about the depth of the U.S. commitment to Europe.

With the Soviet Union beginning to deploy nuclear-armed long-range missiles, West Germans were beginning to wonder whether U.S. leaders could be counted on to sacrifice American cities to defend Hamburg, Frankfurt, or Munich. West Germans, in short, did not know what to be more afraid of: that the United States would respond to a Soviet attack with nuclear weapons, or that it would not.[22]

The German rapproachment with France can be viewed partially in terms of a search for alternative security arrangements. The Franco-German Friendship Alliance of 1963 was both the culmination of negotiations which had been in process for several years and the beginning of a much longer-term rapproachment between two former arch-enemies. Though the treaty began a major program of bilateral cooperation, France remained unsure of what kind of nuclear commitment she wished to make to the Federal Republic. France wanted to make a contribution to German security, but not at the price of draining away French military resources or giving the Germans access to nuclear weapons. French reticence, combined with U.S. wooing of Germany with the MLF plan, served to keep Germany firmly in the NATO camp with a pronounced American preference. Nuclear weapons in NATO thus remained firmly under unilateral American control, though their placement on German soil was naturally subject to the host country's assent. German efforts to achieve some kind of joint control over nuclear weapons, either in partnership with France or in the NATO context, failed to produce results.

The Rise and Demise of the MLF Plan

The plan for a Multilateral Force (MLF) was the major effort during the period to cope with the problem of shared or joint control over nuclear weapons in Europe. The EDC plan for a European army had been defeated by the French parliament in 1954,[23] but by 1957 Soviet nuclear capability called for a reassessment of the deterrent posture of NATO. U.S. tactical nuclear weapons were brought to Europe in 1955, as noted previously. In 1957 the Soviets demonstrated their new proficiency with rocketry by sending the first Sputnik satellite into space, leaving no doubt that the Soviets possessed the capability for launching both intercontinental-range ballistic missiles (ICBM's) and intermediate-range ballistic missiles (IRBM's). Faced with this frightening reality, the European NATO members needed reassurance that NATO's nuclear deterrent was still credible. The situation also seemed to demand a rethinking of the whole question of nuclear control. If

European-based nuclear weapons were to be used for defense of European territory, unilateral American decisions about their use hardly seemed an appropriate mode of operation.

The first faint shadow of the MLF idea came from Senator Henry Jackson. In May, 1957, shortly before the Sputnik launching, Jackson presented to the Senate his idea for a "Fourth Dimension in Warfare." The idea entailed constructing launching pads for IRBM's on submarines, thus combining naval power and rocketry in a deadly new combination. NATO firepower could be increased and at the same time made more invulnerable by making nuclear launchers a moving target under water.[24] Though the Jackson proposal was not addressed directly to the problem of control over nuclear weapons, the idea can be seen as an early precursor of the MLF in the sense that most of the MLF proposals were based on some version of a sea-based nuclear deterrent for NATO.

The issue of control over nuclear weapons was addressed more directly by President De Gaulle of France in September, 1958. De Gaulle suggested that a Directorate of the Atlantic powers (the United States, Britain, and France) be established to exercise control over NATO nuclear forces. The idea was not presented in any detail and was not further explained in De Gaulle's subsequent statements. Whether the Directorate was to be a tripartite supercouncil for all NATO decision-making or whether it was meant simply as a mechanism for consultation and cooperation on nuclear matters was never made clear. At any rate the proposal was rejected rather quickly by President Eisenhower on the grounds that a tripartite body would not provide an adequate means of influencing alliance policy for the other NATO members. In his final comment on the proposal Eisenhower said: "We cannot afford to adopt any system which would give our other allies, or other free world countries, the impression that basic decisions affecting their own vital interests are being made without their participation."[25]

Discussion of the control issue was continued among NATO foreign ministers at the semiannual meeting of the NATO Council in December, 1958. No progress was made, as there was no proposal on the table which did not meet with objections from one or more members of the alliance. At the time there seemed to be no practicable alternative to sole American control over the weapons in Europe. The final communique of the meeting simply said that "the existing machinery of NATO is well suited to the needs of the Alliance" and that "problems (would be) inevitably created by the widening of political consultation."[26]

The deployment of Thor and Jupiter intermediate-range missiles in three NATO countries in 1959 imparted a new urgency to the control issue. The MLF idea appeared in several configurations from several diverse sources. Two of the more significant plans were the Gates Plan and the Norstad Dyadic suggestion, both of which were unveiled in 1960. Secretary of Defense Thomas Gates proposed in March, 1960, that the MLF should consist of 300 Polaris-type missiles deployed on "rail, river, and road sites." The sites could be moved from place to place and would be manned by international NATO units. The force would be under the command of SACEUR, but final authority to launch the missiles would remain with the U.S. president. The Gates proposal, interestingly, was a land-based version of the MLF (or, as some have suggested, an early precursor of some of the MX basing proposals). Though the idea of mixed international units manning the missile sites was intriguing, the proposal still did not address the central issue, i.e., how strategic decisions for the force would be made. Final authority still rested in the hands of the American president, which, according to critics, was a situation of no progress at all. The Gates Plan was ultimately withdrawn, though it did generate considerable interest on the part of both the Europeans and the Americans.

General Lauris Norstad, the Supreme Commander of NATO forces, presented his Dyadic Suggestion to a meeting of the NATO Parliamentarians in November, 1960. The first part of the proposal called for "the creation of an IRBM force deployed on both land and sea.... and assigned to SACEUR," with final authority resting with the U.S. president. The second part called for the creation of a pool of atomic weapons which would remain under the control of all nations in the alliance equally.[27] The proposal suffered from the problem of attempting to accomplish everything at once. An IRBM force would be both land-based and sea-based under SACEUR's control. The new departure was the pool of atomic weapons under some kind of multilateral control. There were, however, many questions left unanswered. What was the structure or nature of such multilateral control? Why have one IRBM force under the sole control of the U.S. president and a parallel force under multilateral control? How could the two forces be coordinated?

Following intensive discussions in Washington the Norstad proposal emerged in revised form as the major American MLF proposal. Secretary of State Christian Herter presented it to a meeting of the NATO Council in Paris in December, 1960. The first part of the proposal remained essentially unchanged, that is, there would be an IRBM force of undefined size under the command of SACEUR, subject to the final authority of the U.S. president. In reference to the second part of the proposal, the American government was ready to make a concrete offer. The United States would contribute 5 nuclear submarines and 80

Polaris missiles on the condition that the other alliance members contribute enough funds to purchase 180 additional Polaris missiles from the U.S. for the multilateral force. The missile force could be deployed on either land or sea, as eventually decided by NATO planners. In effect, the Herter proposal reversed the bargaining scenario by placing the onus of producing a plan for strategic and political control of the MLF in the hands of the Europeans. "The crucial aspect of the proposal was that, before the United States contributed the five submarines, the members of NATO were to work out the method by which political control would be exercised over the force."[28]

The German defense minister, Franz Josef Strauss, was quick to endorse the Herter proposal and press for its acceptance. Several other governments expressed a measure of support or, at least, interest. Like the others before it, however, the proposal was eventually abandoned. The Europeans were no more successful than the Americans in producing a plan with both wide appeal and political feasibility. In addition, the timing of the American offer was unfortunate. The Kennedy administration, which took office in early 1961, was not inclined to endorse a plan produced by the Eisenhower administration. Kennedy wanted a full-scale review of the military balance between the United States and the Soviet Union, especially the prevailing nuclear balance, before making any commitments to new plans for weapons in Europe. As the perceived "missile gap" from the period of Kennedy's candidacy disappeared, the administration tended to express less and less interest in any kind of MLF plan.

Partially in response to European pressure, the Kennedy administration did produce its own version of an MLF plan in mid-1962. As presented by the U.S. ambassador to NATO, Thomas Finletter, the proposal called for the creation of a fleet of twenty-five missile carrying surface vessels...."truly multilateral in manning, finance, and control."[29] The ships would carry 200 intermediate-range ballistic missiles and would be manned by crews of mixed nationality. The decision to launch the missiles would be made "jointly by the United States and the other participants in the project."[30]

The Kennedy plan, like the others, addressed certain questions clearly while leaving others entirely murky. Why were the Americans now back to the idea of surface vessels rather than submarines? Why would the fleet have only 200 missiles, if the Soviet Union had a much larger number of IRBM's capable of reaching targets in Western Europe? Would all IRBM's in or near Europe be within the framework of the MLF, or would there be other missiles under the sole authority of the American president? What was the nature of decisions made jointly by the

United States and other NATO members? Efforts to provide answers to these questions became mired down in conflicting diplomatic crosscurrents during the next year.

The proposal seemed to give rise to considerable uncertainty in West Germany. The Adenauer government, a shaky coalition in its last year (1963), vacillated between its special relationship with France and its basic American orientation. Strong endorsement of the American proposal, in the face of French opposition, risked a loss of French political and military support, while rejection of the American proposal risked a reduction of the American security guarantee. Many German officials came to Washington for briefings on the proposal, and many more were supplied with technical background papers by the navy and the defense department.

When Ludwig Erhard succeeded Adenauer as chancellor in late 1963, the German government finally made up its mind. Since Erhard and his foreign minister, Gerhard Schroeder, both shared a strong American orientation as well as a conviction that the American security guarantee must be preserved at all cost, the German government officially endorsed the Kennedy proposal. The commitment was made in good faith, since Erhard believed he had a close personal relationship with President Johnson.

Again, however, a change in leadership in Washington contributed to the demise of a proposal which seemed to be reaching the stage of serious negotiations. Johnson had never been enthusiastic about the Kennedy plan or any other MLF proposal. After his election to the presidency in 1964, he made only passing references to the MLF as a plan under continued study; negotiations were in fact suspended, pending the review. In 1965 all mention of the MLF plan ceased. There were several reasons for the Johnson administration's tacit rejection of the MLF plan. In high-level NATO circles the MLF had never aroused any real enthusiasm. France had expressed resolute opposition to the plan from the outset. In late 1965 Britain elected a new Labor government which also opposed the formation of the MLF. One of Johnson's goals was to begin a new round of nuclear arms reduction talks with the Soviet Union. Clearly, the idea of the United States sharing control over nuclear weapons with its NATO partners, particularly the West Germans, would have been detrimental to such negotiations. Domestically, Johnson found little support for the MLF in Congress, which further reduced the impetus to press the issue. "Liberal Senators opposed the sharing of nuclear secrets with Germany, and conservatives opposed sharing them with anyone."[31]

Chancellor Erhard was thus left without U.S. support at a time when his popularity at home was already declining. The German government continued to support the MLF idea from time to time for the duration of Erhard's term as chancellor. In 1966, however, the Grand Coalition government headed by Kurt Georg Kiesinger replaced Erhard. For Kiesinger the MLF was a dead issue; it had been tossed aside before his ascendance to power. The German government received some mollification by inclusion as a full member of the NATO Nuclear Planning Group established in November, 1965. The new body's task was to discuss alliance strategy and tactics involving nuclear weapons, thus giving the Europeans at least some sense of participation in nuclear decision-making.

The demise of the MLF left NATO back at the starting gate in the effort to create mechanisms for greater European participation in NATO defense. The failure of the EDC plan in 1954 doomed the far-sighted project of establishing a multinational European army. The demise of the MLF plan in 1965 effectively shut out the Europeans from the highest councils of decision-making in reference to nuclear weapons in Europe. In the final analysis, the MLF foundered on the failure to resolve the central issue of power-sharing. No formula could be devised which resolved the conflicting security needs of the Americans and the Europeans. The Europeans were unwilling to participate in a scheme which created only an illusion of decision-making competence in reference to the use of nuclear weapons. The Americans were unwilling to give up the final, ultimate authority to decide upon the strategy and usage of American nuclear weapons based in or near Europe. It is possible that the very complexity of the question precluded the formulation of an answer suitable to all. How can control of a nation's nuclear arsenal, or even a portion of it, be shared with other states? If a decision to fire nuclear weapons actually had to be made, who would make it and by what procedures? If such an awesome decision had to be made within the timespan of a few minutes, who, besides the American president, could make it? What possible procedures or mechanisms could be devised to share decision-making in a worst case scenario? Neither the Europeans nor the Americans could invent a formula to answer these profound questions. Consequently, NATO was left with the situation which still prevails today. The final authority over American nuclear weapons based in Europe, and hence the decisions which mean the difference between life and death for hundreds of millions of people on the old continent, remain in the hands of the U.S. president. The dilemma of working out satisfactory arrangements for basing new generations of weapons in Europe in the late 1980s and beyond lies therein.

The Offset Payments Issue

Until the late 1950s U.S. expenditures for stationing troops abroad did not cause any particular controversy. The mild deficits in the U.S. balance of payments were not a matter of concern, and the benefits of stationing troops abroad, such as enhanced security and greater political leverage, seemed greater than the costs. Mendershausen notes that, "Every dollar spent to foreigners on housing and supplying American troops was a dollar earned by them to alleviate their 'dollar shortage.' There was no thought of negotiating 'offsets' to these expenditures. The general flow of liquidity from the United States also....helped create a favorable international financial position for the Federal Republic."[32]

In 1958 the convertibility of the major West European currencies, long a goal of American foreign economic policy, was achieved. This, in conjunction with greater flows of American investment capital and increased American purchases abroad, rapidly increased the growth of the deficit in the balance of payments. By 1960 the U.S. payments deficit seemed to show an alarming rate of growth. Mendershausen describes the situation as follows:

> During the three years of 1958 to 1960, the cumulative deficit was higher ($11.2 billion) than in the seven preceding years ($6.5 billion).....During these three years, notably, the U.S. gold reserves diminished by about five billion dollars through international transactions, while the gold reserves of the German Bundesbank rose by $2.6 billion. In 1960, for the first time in the postwar period, the international financial position of the United States was considered in trouble, and a reduction of the balance of payments deficit, and specifically of the 'gold flow,' became a government objective.[33]

Inevitably, the stationing of U.S. troops abroad became enveloped in the controversy over the balance of payments deficit. Since the largest contingent of troops abroad was in West Germany, and since the West German economy seemed to be glowing with prosperity, it seemed logical that the Germans should pay more for the defense afforded them by the presence of American troops. The Eisenhower administration calculated that the foreign exchange costs of stationing troops in Germany amounted to about $600 million. In November, 1960, President Eisenhower dispatched treasury secretary Robert Anderson and under-secretary Douglas Dillon to Bonn to propose that the

Federal Republic pay out of its budget about $650 million per year in support of U.S. troop costs. The Adenauer government was quick to reject the proposal since it smacked of "occupation cost" payments and would probably require a tax increase, both of which were unacceptable. Though Anderson returned to Washington virtually empty-handed, he did gain a promise from the German government to consider large military procurement purchases in the United States and to increase the German share of NATO infrastructure costs from 14 to 20 percent. This promise opened the way to the offset arrangement consummated under the Kennedy administration.[34]

In the fall of 1961 Roswell Gilpatrick, Kennedy's deputy secretary of defense, and Franz Josef Strauss, the German defense minister, completed the negotiations for the first offset payment agreement. The agreement, which was to run for two years, "provided for German procurement of new equipment from the United States, American supply and maintenance support for the existing equipment of the Bundeswehr, the use by the Bundeswehr of American training facilities, and a number of research and development projects with shared costs."[35] Agreement was facilitated by the tension arising from the Berlin crisis. There were, however, other convergent U.S. and German interests which contributed to a successful outcome of the negotiations. The Germans would be able to equip their growing army with necessary supplies and equipment compatible with that of other NATO allies. For the United States, the agreement provided assured sales to the German client. "The U.S. Defense Department looked favorably on the exports of arms to a NATO ally, and on a commitment of that ally to buy and service arms from American rather than other sources.[36]

The offset agreement not only served the interests of both countries, it worked out well in actual practice. The United States was satisfied that the "gold flow" problem, insofar as it seemed attributable to troop stationing in Germany, was taken care of. The Germans were satisfied that the equipment and logistics needs of the Bundeswehr were being met. Procurements by the Federal Republic seemed roughly equivalent to U.S. military outlays in Germany. Consequently, a second offset payments agreement was negotiated for the years 1963 to 1965 and a third agreement for 1965-1967. The amounts are shown in the following table:[37]

Period	Amount
mid-1961 to mid 1963	DM 5.7 billion ($1.42 bl.)
mid-1963 to mid-1965	DM 5.6 billion ($1.40 bl.)
mid-1965 to mid-1967	DM 5.4 billion ($1.35 bl.)

According to Franz Josef Strauss, finance minister of the grand coalition government, there was an almost precise equivalence between U.S. military expenditures and German offset payments during the period of the three agreements. The claim was never contested by the U.S. government, nor was there any suggestion that the Germans were not covering the foreign exchange costs of the American troops.[38] The agreements were also helpful to the Kennedy and Johnson administrations in resisting the pressures in Congress for a reduction of U.S. forces in Germany.

As time progressed the procurements program began to run out of steam. The German Bundeswehr became overstocked with certain types of equipment, while others seemed superfluous. German doubts about the reliability of some of the acquisitions were also heightened by the Starlighter jet fiasco. The Starlighters were supposed to become the cornerstone of Germany's new air force, but by the end of 1966 there had been 66 crashes and 38 deaths.[39] Morgan notes that by 1966, "the German armed forces were...... reasonably well equipped with the standard weapons America had provided, and were less than enthusiastic to purchase the long-distance troop transport aircraft and the new helicopters which McNamara and his advisors pressed on them."[40] In addition, the German economy, which had been surging relentlessly forward for years, began to show signs of a recession. In 1966 the German GNP failed to rise for the first time since the birth of the Federal Republic. The federal budget also threatened to go into deficit.

In early 1966 Chancellor Erhard traveled to Washington to plead with Johnson for a release from complete fulfillment of the procurement commitment. Unfortunately, Johnson was in no mood to compromise. Since the Vietnam War was beginning to strain the U.S. military budget to the outer limit, any German shortfall in offset payments would serve to increase the U.S. balance of payments deficit. Johnson was adamant that the terms of the third offset payment agreement must be fulfilled to the letter. When Erhard returned to Bonn, he had little choice but to ask the Bundestag for a tax increase. The request, together with other political blunders, undermined Erhard's coalition and led to his replacement by Kurt Georg Kiesinger a few months later.

Although the new grand coalition government managed to appropriate the funds to complete the third offset agreement, Kiesinger made it quite clear that the German government would not consider military procurement an appropriate method of offset payments in the future. The payments arrangements between the Germans and the British were also a cause of grave concern to both governments at the time. The British government, with severe balance of payments problems of its own, suggested that offset payments negotiations for future years should begin early, this time on a trilateral basis. The negotiations began in November, 1966, and lasted until May, 1967. With pressure mounting in both Britain and the United States for troop withdrawals as a partial cure for chronic balance of payments deficits, the trilateral negotiations established a link between the size of troop contingents in Germany and the amount of offset payments the FRG would have to pay in return for the troops' presence.

The trilateral negotiations involved weeks of hard bargaining. The German government insisted that the balance between NATO forces and Warsaw Pact forces ought to be the only consideration in determining the size of troop contingents in Germany. The British and American governments countered with the argument that size, cost, and balance of payments problems were interwoven elements in determining troop contingents. The German government pointed out the precariousness of its financial position. Economic growth was nil, budget deficits loomed, and the treasury was barely managing to meet the terms of the 1965-67 offset agreement. The U.S. and British governments, in reply, pointed to their mounting balance of payments deficits, portions of which were directly attributable to forces stationed in Germany. The U.S. was safeguarding the security of the West by financing a growing war in Vietnam at the same time. A reduction of troops in Germany would be a useful test of Soviet intentions, and the Soviets might possibly follow suit with troop reductions of their own in Eastern Europe.

A series of compromises brought the negotiations to a successful conclusion by the late spring of 1967. The German government agreed, unenthusiastically, not to oppose modest British and American troop withdrawals as a means of cutting overseas expenses and reducing balance of payments deficits. Subsequently, in late 1967 and 1968, Britain withdrew 6,000 troops from Germany, and the United States withdrew 35,000. As a novel type of offset payment the German government agreed to purchase $500 million worth of medium term U.S. treasury certificates, coupled with an explicit promise not to convert dollar holdings to gold.

Troop Strength and the Mansfield Initiative

A review of the size of the U.S. troop contingent in Germany from 1955 to 1967 serves as a useful shorthand summary of the period. As noted previously, this was a period of relative normalcy, a period when the security relationship between West Germany and the United States was consolidated and strengthened. Following the Truman administration's troops to Europe decision in 1950 there occurred a steady buildup of U.S. troop strength in Germany, so that by the time the Federal Republic regained full political sovereignty in 1955 just over a quarter million U.S. soldiers were stationed in Germany as the forward defense of the West. Even at the start of the normalcy period, however, there was an incident regarding troop strength which shook the U.S.-German relationship. In July, 1956, Admiral Arthur Radford, Chairman of the Joint Chiefs of Staff, proposed a major manpower cut in U.S. forces with major implications for troop strength in Germany. The Radford Plan advocated a manpower reduction in U.S. forces overall of 800,000 men. The army would be reduced by 450,000 men, with a major share of the reduction coming from forces stationed overseas.[41]

The proposal came as a shock to the West German government, especially since Adenauer had just expended considerable political capital to achieve an expansion of the German Bundeswehr. German defense specialists were nearly unanimous in their opposition to the Radford plan, since they believed that a reduction of U.S. forces in Germany would compromise the American security guarantee, make West Germany more vulnerable to Soviet political or military pressure, and lower the nuclear threshhold in case of war. Fortunately, the Radford plan never got off the ground. Though it was discussed briefly by the president's major security advisers, it was promptly scrapped when it became evident that President Eisenhower and large majorities in Congress were strongly opposed. Not until a decade later did the matter of troop withdrawals emerge again as a major issue.

Tables 3.1 and 3.2 record American troop strengths in Europe and Germany respectively from 1955 to 1967. Table 3.1 shows U.S. military strength in Europe as a whole, including naval personnel of the Sixth Fleet in the Mediterranean and the Persian Gulf. Table 3.2 shows approximate American troop strength in Germany from 1955 to 1968. We see that at the beginning of the period in 1955 there were 261,000 troops in Germany. The figure was reduced somewhat in the period 1957-58, so that the low figure of 235,000 troops was reached in 1958. In 1962 there was a sizeable increase in troop strength as a result of the Berlin crisis, bringing the figure to approximately 280,000 men. This proved only temporary, however, so that by 1965 a figure closer to the average for the period was again established. Between 1966 and 1968 a major reduction in troop strength occurred as a result of the Mansfield initiative. In general, there was considerable stability in troop strength for the

Table 3.1. Total Number of Assigned Military
Personnel in U.S. European Command
(USEUCOM) by Year, 1955-1967

USEUCOM
1955 - 356,787
1956 - 345,218
1957 - 346,176
1958 - 329,911
1959 - 326,964
1960 - 322,908
1961 - 339,024
1962 - 370,170
1963 - 337,305
1964 - 318,628
1965 - 325,089
1966 - 306,807
1967 - 303,565

Source: From data provided by Truman Strobridge,
Command Historian, U.S. European Command
Headquarters, Stuttgart, Germany.

Table 3.2. Approximate U.S. Military Strength
in Germany, 1955-1968 (in thousands)

Year	
1955	261
1956	262
1957	250
1958	235
1959	240
1960	237
1961	242
1962	280
1963	265
1964	263
1965	262
1966	237
1967	N/A
1968	210

Source: Horst Mendershausen, Troop Stationing in
Germany: Value and Cost, Memorandum
RM-5881-PR, (Santa Monica, Calif., Rand
Corporation for U.S. Air Force, December
1968), p. 52

period. An average figure of about 260,000 men prevailed, with increases or decreases not more than 25,000. The continuation of the cold war assured that approximately a quarter million U.S. troops remained in Germany for the duration of the period. The Federal Republic, having tied its national security to the U.S. troop commitment as well as the U.S. nuclear umbrella, lobbied constantly for the maintenance of both. As the period progressed, developments in East-West relations and Congressional budget restraints required the Germans to lobby ever more intensively for the maintenance of the troop commitment to Germany.

Until the mid-1960s U.S. forces were maintained in Germany with minimal dissent in the United States. East-West relations had reached a peak of intensity in 1961-62 when the Russians encouraged the construction of the Berlin Wall and attempted to install intermediate-range missiles in Cuba. The U.S. faced the Russians head-on in the Cuban crisis. U.S. troops in Germany were reinforced to show NATO solidarity and to demonstrate American willingness to defend its interests in Europe. The rise in tension was followed, however, by a period of deescalation and general relaxation. Negotiations between the U.S. and the Soviet Union resulted in a Nuclear Test Ban Treaty in 1963. Discussions for a Nuclear Nonproliferation Treaty began in 1966. More importantly, however, the United States faced a deepening involvement in Vietnam. As a result, the necessity of maintaining a large contingent of troops in West Germany became increasingly open to question.

It was Senator Mike Mansfield who, more than anyone else, crystallized American opposition to troops in Germany toward the end of this period. Mansfield had always vigorously opposed the maintenance of a large garrison of U.S. troops in Europe. As early as 1959, during the Berlin crisis occasioned by Khrushchev's "free city" proposal, Mansfield had proposed a replacement of allied forces in Berlin with either West German or United Nations forces.[42] Not until the mid-1960s, however, under the pressure of the Vietnam War and the increasingly serious nature of balance of payments problems, was Mansfield able to build isolated dissent into an organized movement in Congress. In August, 1966, Mansfield introduced a Sense of the Senate Resolution calling for a substantial reduction in U.S. forces stationed in Europe. The reasons he cited, over and above references to unequal burden-sharing in the alliance, were a reduction in antagonism between East and West and improvements in reinforcement capability in the event of a crisis.[43] Mansfield knew that the resolution did not have enough support to pass. It was introduced primarily as a scare tactic to force the Germans to make greater concessions in the offset payments negotiations. Mansfield was not about to give up, however. With dogged determination he continued to insist that there were too many U.S. troops in Europe and to garner support for at least a limited withdrawal. His persistence was in fact rewarded with larger German concessions in offset negotiations and with a troop withdrawal of 35,000 men in 1967-68. Though the drawdown was not large, it was enough to claim a moral victory for the validity of his views. Both the offset payments negotiations and the Mansfield effort to withdraw troops from Germany continued to be highly controversial matters in the years to follow.

Effects of the Vietnam War

As the period drew to a close the Vietnam War cast an increasingly dark shadow over the American military presence in West Germany. The Johnson administration committed American combat forces to Vietnam in 1965. The massive troop buildup in Vietnam during the next two years inevitably had an adverse effect upon U.S. troops stationed in Germany. Not only was troop strength reduced, but the quality of the forces in Germany also diminished. The most experienced and best trained officers and troops were needed in the hot war in Vietnam, not the cold war in Germany. The officers and men transferred from Europe to Asia, or those who would have been sent to Germany if the buildup in Vietnam had not occurred, were replaced in Germany by officers and men with much less experience and training. The high turnover in the forces in Germany had pernicious consequences. As German commentator Gerhard Baumann noted in 1968, "the U.S. Seventh Army in Germany lacks 50% of the majors (it needs), more than 37% of the lieutenants and captains, and more than 22% of the specialists in the noncommissioned ranks, so that the combat readiness (of the forces) in case of crisis is diminished."[44]

U.S. forces in Germany suffered many other spillover effects from the Vietnam conflict with pernicious consequences. As problems of drug abuse began to have noticeable effects on combat readiness and troop morale in Vietnam, the same problems began to appear in the forces in Germany somewhat later. The problem of racial strife, barely contained in Vietnam because of the desperate struggle for survival, appeared in Germany with a fury never before witnessed. Disciplinary problems swelled to alarming proportions. Crime rates soared.

By 1967 the deterioration of force morale and force readiness in Germany was a cause of major concern in the Pentagon, even though the Vietnam War continued to occupy the time and energy of top officials. The problems were also becoming evident to larger numbers of Germans in both public and private life. German analysts of the Vietnam War began to draw more frequent comparisons between the problems of U.S. forces in Vietnam and the problems in Germany. The German press in general began to be more critical of problems in Germany which seemed to be getting worse with each passing month. The massive dissent against the war in the United States also appeared in Germany, though its form and content were different since the country was not actively involved in the fighting. Inevitably, disillusionment with the Vietnam imbroglio translated into a higher level of dislike and distrust of U.S. forces stationed in Germany, especially on the part of youthful dissenters.

By 1967 the readiness and the morale of U.S. forces in Germany were definitely declining, but the problems were not yet of such dimensions that they directly influenced the basic nature of the German-American politico-military relationship. The German government was worried that the Mansfield initiative in Congress might gain ground. If it did, the future commitment of a large contingent of American forces to Germany might be endangered. There was dissent against the Vietnam War in Germany, but it was not directed against U.S. forces in Germany whose mission was entirely different. Morale problems were becoming more noticeable, but they were not yet a matter of general public concern in Germany. The basic security relationship between the United States and Germany seemed generally vibrant and healthy, certainly much stronger than it had been a decade earlier. German public approval of the U.S. presence was not seriously in question. Nevertheless, the stormclouds on the horizon seemed threatening. The readiness and morale of U.S. forces in Germany were declining, and public awareness of such problems seemed to be increasing. An erosion of German confidence in the U.S. military presence had in fact begun.

Notes

[1] For a discussion of the division of Berlin into sectors of occupation and the history of agreements concerning access to the city from the western occupation zones see Daniel J. Nelson, Wartime Origins of the Berlin Dilemma (University, Ala.: University of Alabama Press, 1978), chapters 4-6.

[2] For the text of the "free city" proposal see Frederick H. Hartmann, Germany Between East and West: The Reunification Problem (Englewood Cliffs, N.J.: Prentice-Hall, Inc., 1965), p. 97.

[3] Hartmann, p. 99.

[4] Quoted in Frederick H. Hartmann, The Relations of Nations (New York: Macmillan Publishing Co., Inc., 6th ed., 1983), p. 495.

[5] Hartmann, Relations of Nations, p. 495.

[6] Ibid.

[7] Hartmann, Germany Between East and West, p. 124.

[8] William P. Mako, U.S. Ground Forces and the Defense of Central Europe (Washington: The Brookings Institution, 1983), pp. 17-18.

[9] William Sweet, The Nuclear Age: Power, Proliferation, and the Arms Race (Washington: Congressional Quarterly, Inc., 1983), p. 107.

[10] Sweet, p. 107.

[11] Catherine Kelleher, Germany and the Politics of Nuclear Weapons (New York: Columbia University Press, 1975), p. 36

[12] Kelleher, p. 39.

[13] Kelleher, p. 118; See also David P. Calleo, The Atlantic Fantasy: The U.S., NATO, and Europe. (Baltimore: Johns Hopkins University Press, 1970), p. 130.

[14] In 1958, western forces in central Europe comprised fewer than 20 effective divisions. Official NATO estimates showed 175 Soviet divisions, of which 140 were combat ready. These included 22 divisions in East Germany and Poland and about 80 in western Russia and the rest of Eastern Europe. The Warsaw Pact also had a capability for mobilizing approximately 400 divisions in thirty days. See Robert E. Osgood, NATO: The Entangling Alliance (Chicago: University of Chicago Press, 1962), pp. 28-30.

[15] Kelleher, p. 97.

[16] Thomas C. Wiegle, "The Origins of the MLF Concept, 1957-1960," Orbis, Vol. 12, No. 2 (Summer, 1968), p. 476.

[17] Andrew J. Pierre, ed., in Introduction to Nuclear Weapons In Europe (New York: Council on Foreign Relations, 1984), p. 5.

[18] Mako, pp. 13-14. Mako quotes Glenn H. Snyder.

[19] Josef Joffe, "Germany and the Atlantic Alliance: The Politics of Dependence, 1961-68," in W.C. Cromwell, et. al., Political Problems of Alliance Partnership (Brüges: College of Europe, 1969), pp. 407-408.

[20] Mako, pp. 16-19.

[21] Harlan Cleveland, NATO: The Transatlantic Bargain (New York: Harper and Row Publishers, 1970), p. 125.

[22] Sweet, The Nuclear Age, p. 109.

[23] A discussion of the EDC plan can be found in Chapter 2.

[24] Wiegele, p.466.

[25] Quoted in Wiegele, p. 475.

[26] Quoted in Wiegele, p. 486.

[27] Wiegele, p. 477.

[28] Wiegele, pp. 483-484.

[29] Kelleher, p. 190.

[30] Wiegele, p. 465n

[31] Morgan, pp. 150-151.

[32] Horst Mendershausen, Troop Stationing in Germany: Value and Cost, Memorandum RM-5881-PR (Santa Monica, Calif.: Rand Corporation for the U.S. Air Force, December, 1968), p. 68.

[33] Mendershausen, p. 69.

[34] Mendershausen, p. 73.

[35] Morgan, p. 105.

[36] Mendershausen, p. 74

[37] Gerhard Baumann, "Devisenausgleich und Sicherheit," Wehrkunde, Vol. 17, No. 5 (1968), pp. 245-251. See also Elke Thiel, Dollar-Dominanz, Lastenteilung und Amerikanische Truppenpräsenz in Europa, (Baden-Baden: Nomos Verlagsgesellschaft, 1979), p. 67.

[38] Mendershausen, p. 76.

[39] Gregory F. Treverton, The Dollar Drain and American Forces in Germany (Athens, Ohio: Ohio University Press, 1978), p. 65.

[40] Morgan, p. 147.

[41] For a brief discussion of the Radford plan see Mako, p. 14.

[42] Mike Mansfield, "Policies Respecting Germany," Vital Speeches of the Day, Vol. 25, No. 11 (March 15, 1959), pp. 338-339.

[43] Helga Haftendorn, "Future of U.S. Military Presence in Europe," The German Tribune Political Affairs Review, No. 46 (March 4, 1984), p.1; The original German version is in Europa-Archiv, No. 20, 1983.

[44] Baumann, p. 249 (author's translation).

4

DETERIORATION
1967-1973

The gathering stormclouds noted in the previous chapter erupted into a number of fierce downpours in the period 1967-1973. This fourth period in our somewhat arbitrarily dated schematic plan became, unfortunately, the most dismal period for the stationing of U.S. forces in Germany, producing multiple complications in the structure of the U.S.-German security relationship. Indeed a number of processes were set in motion which might have substantially undermined the viability of the relationship had they not been arrested in the later period after 1973. Two major elements delineate or animate this period. First, it was the period of the predicament created by the Vietnam War, which spilled political venom far beyond the boundaries of Southeast Asia and vitally affected bilateral American relationships around the world, including Europe. Second, it was the period of transition from U.S. military forces based on conscription to those based on the principle of the All Volunteer Force (AVF). The first of these elements, the spillover effects from Vietnam, not only adversely affected the capabilities of American forces in Germany in practically every way imaginable, but also began a longterm process of undermining German respect for the security relationship based upon the presence of these forces on German soil. The second element, the transition from conscription to the AVF, increased the level of uncertainty by raising an entirely new set of questions concerning the future effects of this policy leap into the dark. What would the new American military be like in terms of demography, training, and capability? Would it be as adequate to carry out the twin purposes of deterrence and defense as the previous conscript forces which had been stationed in Germany since World War II?

Congressional Decisions in 1967

We begin the discussion of this period in 1967 primarily because of two decisions by the American Congress that year which set the stage for major longterm changes in the structure and character of American forces and hence the effects of stationing the forces in Europe. The first decision changed the operation of the military compensation system. Before 1967 every general increase in military pay since World War II had required separate action by Congress. The Military Pay Bill of 1967 not only increased the basic pay of all service members; more importantly, it altered the basic pay procedure by providing automatic military pay raises indexed to changes in the General Schedule (GS) salaries of government employees in the federal civil service. Military personnel would receive pay raises automatically unless Congress specifically blocked the military pay raises. In turn, General Schedule salaries were linked (since 1962) to white-collar pay levels in the private sector as measured by the annual survey of Professional, Administrative, Technical and Clerical Workers (PATC), a provision intended to ensure comparability between federal and private wages. This latter linkage was not automatic, however, since the President could propose to Congress a GS pay raise either higher or lower than the change in the PATC index. Military pay *levels* could be higher or lower than either private sector or GS pay levels. The law required only that GS and military pay *raises* each year be the same percentage. The section of the 1967 law that provided automatic military pay increases linked to GS increases is known as the Rivers Amendment, named for its sponsor L. Mendel Rivers (D-SC), who used his influence as chairman of the House Armed Services Committee to enact the amendment over objections from the Department of Defense and the Johnson Administration. The Rivers Amendment not only granted across-the-board increases in basic pay, it also boosted re-enlistment bonuses, reserve drill pay, and retirement pay. It also provided disproportionate pay increases in the upper grades since basic pay makes up a greater part of the total compensation of high-grade officers. An important effect of the Rivers Amendment is that whenever the President or Congress decides to effect budgetary savings by holding GS salary increases below the rise in the PATC index, military pay raises are thereby automatically depressed.[1]

Another Congressional decision in 1967 which vitally affected the future of U.S. forces in Germany was a decision to reduce permanently the level of forces based in that country. In this case Congress fully supported a compromise solution which had been reached within the Johnson Administration, largely as a response to the difficulties in Germany created by the Vietnam War, specifically the chronic shortages of junior officers and senior NCO's. Against the opposition of the State Department and the Joint Chiefs of Staff, Secretary of Defense McNamara had argued for a 75,000-man reduction. After much wrangling a compromise figure of 35,000 was finally agreed upon. In effect two-thirds of a division was returned from Germany to bases in the United States, although the units remained under the command of the U.S. Army, Europe. In addition, 28,000 military dependents were returned to the U.S. with a savings of $75 million in foreign exchange.[2]

The Acceptance of Dual-Basing

Both of these Congressional actions in 1967 impacted heavily upon the future development of the U.S. military presence in Germany. The changes in the military compensation system, though probably not intended at the time, helped to set the stage for the transition from conscription to the AVF a few years later. Both by granting long overdue raises in basic military pay and by moving in the direction of a labor market environment for military manpower, Congress moved the nation two squares closer on the social policy chessboard to the conditions necessary for serious consideration of an all volunteer force structure. Even though the catalysts were not yet present in the form of Nixon's campaign promise and violent demonstrations against the Vietnam War, it could be asserted with some credibility that the initial steps leading to the AVF were actually taken in 1967. In reference to Europe specifically, however, the second of the Congressional actions has greater relevance. The withdrawal of two-thirds of a division from Germany to the United States was brought about primarily by the force hemorrhages in Germany caused by the Vietnam War, especially the severe shortages of officers and senior NCO's. Nevertheless, the Administration had to attempt to placate the German Government and mitigate popular fears of massive withdrawal by offering the best justification possible. The new military strategy which emerged as a result of these political and military realities was the policy of dual-basing. The policy was not altogether new in the sense that the American military deterrent had always relied upon massive force reinforcements from the United States in the case of a conventional attack upon Western Europe by the Warsaw Pact. What was new, however, was the element of dual-basing, the idea that specific units in the United States would remain under the command of the U.S. Army, Europe, would return periodically to Europe on deployment exercises, and would be available permanently for rapid deployment to Europe in case of hostilities. The U.S. Government argued strenuously, of course, that the dual-basing concept would not weaken the combat power of American forces in Europe. The German Government had little choice but to accept the proferred assurances and repeat them in turn to the German people. Seen in retrospect, however, there can be little doubt that in terms of overall combat capability and readiness to engage in actual war, the decision weakened the U.S. Seventh Army in Europe. As Hanson Baldwin wisely noted, "Dual-basing is no substitute for troops on the scene ready to fight instantly."[3] Similar observations were made by numerous qualified observers, including the assertion by Kenneth Coffey that, "while the dual-basing concept provides an assurance of additional combat units in relatively short order, the decision clearly weakened the Seventh Army's ground combat capabilities."[4] The decision marked, in fact, the beginning of a period of attrition in the combat strength level of U.S. forces in Germany which lasted well into the 1970s. As a part of this process, and as a direct result of the drawdown in Germany, the annual Reforger Exercises for rapid return of U.S. based units to Germany were begun in 1968 and the program to warehouse in Germany sets of equipment for the returning forces, known as POMCUS (Prepositioned Organizational Material Configured in Unit Sets), was begun. These circumstances made all but inevitable the invention of the Total Force Policy by the Department of Defense in 1970.

Detente and the Total Force Policy

The progressive development of U.S.-Soviet detente in the late 1960s and early 1970s represents an important element in the tapestry of American foreign relations upon which an understanding of German-American relations must be based. Detente was certainly not a radical new departure in American policy; indeed many observers trace the real beginnings of detente to the aftermath of the Cuban missile crisis during the Kennedy Administration in 1962. Beginning in 1969, however, President Nixon and Secretary of State Kissinger began a series of initiatives which not only redefined and reinvigorated detente but make it the new master principle of American foreign policy. At the same time, the contraction of the Vietnam War effort became official policy. These two circumstances together produced a new milieu in which a redefinition of American policy toward NATO in general and Germany in particular could be undertaken. In 1970 the new policy was ennunciated by Defense Secretary Melvin Laird. Known as the "Total Force" policy, it acknowledged that the lower force levels which had come about in Europe during the previous three years had in fact become permanent force levels. Hence, in the case of an attack by the Warsaw Pact on NATO, the period during which the active on-site forces of the NATO allies would be have to hold the line, the short-war phase, had necessarily been attenuated. Much more now depended upon rapid reinforcements airlifted to Europe from the United States to sustain combat beyond the first few days. In essence the total force concept shifted a greater portion of the defense burden in Europe from active on-site forces to units, both active and reserve, based in the United States. Mobilization of U.S. based units and rapid deployment to Europe were the keys to the viability of the total force policy.

The policy made a certain amount of sense, of course, in the environment of the early 1970s. It was by this time a foregone conclusion that the draft would be abandoned and the nation would move to the All Volunteer Force structure. Since the AVF would probably not be able to attract enough people to maintain the pre-Vietnam active force levels, a new role must be devised for the reserve forces in cases of emergency. In addition, the dawning of the new period of detente in East-West relations implied a lower level Soviet threat to Europe, so that a reduced level of American forces in Germany need not be viewed as dangerous. Indeed, the policies of detente politically and total force militarily seemed to be highly complementary. In addition, the total force policy emerged logically from the developments of the previous three years and anticipated the new environment of the 1970s.

Substantial benefits were in fact realized from the total force policy, according to a number of careful observers. Lawrence Korb noted that the policy grew partially out of a need to assure Reserve Components, which had for years been treated as a second-rate echelon of the military, that they would play an important role in national security.[5] Such a role in fact was realized in large measure during the next decade. Not only were the reserves able to gain a clearer sense of mission; equipment inventories were replenished and modernized, training was improved, and volunteers replaced the draft-motivated enlistees of the Vietnam era. On the other hand, the price that was paid for these improvements was not insubstantial. Manpower levels in the reserves have usually failed to meet stated requirements, transportation requirements for deployment to Europe have remained severely inadequate, and problems with equipment and supply have often seemed insoluble. One careful observer concludes that, "the result has been a steady deterioration of the army's mobilization and war-sustaining capabilities, serious weaknesses which provide the basis for questioning the appropriateness of continuing the total force policy."[6]

Another event of the late 1960s which must catch our attention at this point is the installation in Germany of a new generation of American tactical nuclear missiles, namely the Pershing I missiles. The precise time when these missiles became operational in Germany remains classified information, though the year 1969 is suggested in a number of informed sources.[7] It is, at any rate, clear that the detente policy of the Nixon Administration coincided with a dawning awareness that the era of clear American nuclear superiority over the Soviet Union was ending and was being replaced by a situation of general overall parity. The beginning of the SALT talks is explained partially by this new awareness, as is the origin of detente itself. As a hedge against the uncertain future, and probably in anticipation of a stronger form of nuclear deterrence needed to lend credibility to the forthcoming total force policy, the new Pershing missiles were brought to Germany quietly in the late 1960s. The Pershings did not represent a completely new policy departure. Even then it was common knowledge that the U.S. had maintained certain types of tactical nuclear weapons on German soil since the mid-1950s. As with any new weapon, however, the Pershing I escalated the stakes in the psychological equations of deterrence. And since the deterrent based on conventional forces had weakened somewhat in the previous several years, the deficit had to be made up with a stronger nuclear deterrent. Given the developing situation of strategic nuclear parity between the United States and the Soviet Union, a state of the art tactical or battlefield nuclear weapon in the form of the Pershing I seemed tailored to the defense situation in Germany. Inevitably, the German Government worried that an increased nuclear capability in Germany might lead to a decoupling of Europe from the larger American strategic deterrent. The American answer to these fears was the enunciation of the total force policy in 1970, which was designed to convince the Germans that both the American conventional capability in Europe and its linkage to the American strategic deterrent remained in full force.

Genesis of the All Volunteer Force

The second half of the period we are considering in this chapter, namely the years from 1970 to 1973, saw the most momentous change in the character and structure of American ground capability in Germany since World War II. This was the period of transition from conscription forces to the All Volunteer Force. The idea for the AVF had been floating around for many years. What gave the concept greater currency and urgency was the disillusionment with the gross inequities of the draft during the Vietnam War. The disruption of the lives of millions of young men, the high casualty rates brought home with intensity each evening by television newscasts, the growing unpopularity of the war as witnessed by huge draft card burning rallies all combined to undermine public support for a draft which so unequally spread its burdens on American youth. It struck many Americans as capricious that millions of poor and minority youth were shipped off to the jungles of Vietnam, while large numbers of white, upwardly mobile or college men escaped the draft by gaining deferments, moving to Canada, claiming conscientious objector status, or otherwise defrauding the selective service system. In the heated presidential campaign of 1968 Richard Nixon introduced a major campaign platform in his promise to abolish the draft in a speech in March. He elaborated his views on the subject in an address on the CBS Radio Network on October 17, 1968:

> I have looked into this question very carefully. And this is my belief: once our involvement in the Vietnam War is behind us, we move toward an all-volunteer force......For many years since World War II, I believed that, even in peacetime, only through the draft could we get enough servicemen to defend our nation and meet our heavy commitments abroad......But conditions have changed, and our needs have changed too......What we can do-and what we should do now-is to commit ourselves to the goal of building an all-volunteer armed force.[8]

Soon after assuming office in 1969 President Nixon submitted a set of draft reform proposals to Congress. The proposals included a lottery system to select men for induction, changing the order of call from an oldest-first to a youngest-first basis, and an end to student, occupational, and fatherhood deferments. Though all the reforms were eventually enacted, the President had already clearly committed the nation to an end to the draft entirely. In March, 1969, Nixon appointed the President's Commission on an All-Volunteer Armed Force, popularly referred to as the Gates Commission after its chairman, former Secretary of Defense Thomas S. Gates, Jr. The Commission's task patently was not to debate the merits of the AVF concept, in view of the President's clear commitments, but to recommend a plan for the implementation of the volunteer force structure. There were no major surprises then when the Gates Commission issued its long awaited report in the spring of 1970.[9] Three major policy changes would be needed, it asserted. First, basic pay for recruits would have to be increased by 75 percent in order to create credible market conditions to attract military manpower. The commission thus recommended that pay for junior military personnel be raised to a level commensurate with that earned by their peers in civilian employment. Second, major improvements in the conditions of military life and in recruiting would have to be made. Third, a standby draft system would have to be established which could be activated by joint resolution of Congress upon request of the president for cases of national emergency. The "Debate" section of the Report restated the rationale for the AVF, then identified and dismissed one by one all major objections which had been raised in public debate over the course of the last many months. The Commission confidently concluded that: (1) the costs of such a force could well be afforded by the nation; (2) the force would have the flexibility to expand rapidly in times of sudden crisis, if a standby draft law were put into effect by Congress; (3) patriotism would not be undermined even though a general duty to serve would not be recognized; (4) a separate military ethos would not develop to pose a threat to civilian authority or democratic institutions; (5) the composition of the force, especially its racial demography, would not change greatly; (6) there need be no fear that an AVF would be manned primarily by mercenaries animated by money and adventure rather than patriotism; (7) an all volunteer force would not foster an irresponsible foreign policy or decrease civilian concern about the use of military force; (8) the prestige and dignity of military service would not decline due to the recruitment of less qualified youths; (9) there would not be a deterioration of the nation's overall military posture due to inadequate funding of the necessarily higher defense budgets.[10]

The philosophical underpinnings of the Gates Commission Report were anchored solidly in a *laissez faire* version of marketplace economics. Milton Friedman, a leading member of the Gates Commission, stated one vital aspect of this ideology in a debate in 1979: "...though there is a real problem in the case of the Army, a large part of that problem arises out of the unwillingness of Congress to implement the pay scales that were recommended by the Gates Commission..... The present issue is that, so far as the armed forces are concerned, it is the same as in every other occupation in this country: low-paid people are doing low-paid jobs; high-paid people are doing high-paid jobs."[11] Since conservative economics served as the foundational philosophy of the Commission's work, not much attention was paid to strategic and political considerations. Two omissions, in particular, have been cited as glaring blindspots in the Commission's vision: the lack of attention paid to the impact of the AVF upon the nation's longterm strategic capabilities, and the failure to investigate thoroughly the AVF's impact upon the reserve forces, as well as the relationship of reserve to active forces. While the

Commission made cost projections for a volunteer active force of up to 3 million members, its working hypothesis was that the AVF active force would approximate the size of the pre-Vietnam draft force of approximately 2.6 million men. Since the AVF presumably would not have a rapid mobilization capability, many observers argued that the shift to an AVF argued for a larger standing force in peacetime. Though the commission had no clear answer, the assumption seemed to be that force augmentation would somehow be provided for by the reserves and a standby draft. In addition, one element of the analysis which was either superficial or completely specious, as will be discussed later, was the Commission's treatment of the demographic changes likely to take place in the AVF. By the time the Commission's Report was issued in 1970 opposition to the Vietnam War and to the draft which supported it had reached the level of a deafening roar. Though Congress was divided on the issue, public support for the AVF concept was rapidly gaining ground and the number of Congressional supporters was growing. Since the battle lines between pro-draft and anti-draft forces were already clearly drawn, the national debate on the Report resembled more a shouting match than a reasoned discussion. It was, however, widely debated in practically every public forum, from the mass media to small discussion groups.

Finally, in November, 1971, Congress passed the major military pay increase which represented the largest plank in the bridge from the conscription military to the AVF. Since pay in all of the higher military grades had been linked to federal civilian GS salaries since 1967, the new legislation completed the process for the lower grades. The emphasis was on raising the compensation of junior enlisted men to the level of their peers in civilian employment, thus making military service competitive in the national labor market for enlisted volunteers. For a private in the army, for instance, basic monthly pay was increased more than 50 percent.[12] Average increases were in the range from 35 to 40 percent. Two other decisions by Congress in 1971 also provided for a transition to the AVF. The draft law was amended to provide for a standby selective service system, though the President was precluded from resuming inductions without the consent of Congress. Finally, the President's draft-induction authority was extended for only two years, rather than the customary four years. This action was taken in the face of enormous, powerfully driven efforts to abolish the draft immediately, which might have succeeded had not President Nixon reiterated repeatedly that the draft could not be ended until the armed forces had been completely withdrawn from Vietnam and had reached a peacetime manning level; his goal for zero draft calls was 1973. As the drawdown in Vietnam continued during 1972, the President announced during his reelection campaign that the last draft calls would be issued in December 1972, six months before the expiration of the induction authority. The promise was kept. The last draft call was issued in late December, 1972. Though the President's induction authority did not expire until July 1, 1973, we may say that as of January, 1973, the United States had effectively completed the transition to the All Volunteer Force. A dramatic new era in American military history had begun.

The Shift in Strategic Doctrine

During the transition period from conscription to AVF the Nixon Administration in 1971 announced a major shift in strategic doctrine, which revolutionized the military's view of its global objectives. The shift was from a two-and-a-half war strategy to a one-and-a-half war strategy as part and parcel of the new Nixon Doctrine. As elaborated by the president in his 1971 foreign policy message, the Nixon Doctrine anticipated a reduced commitment to fight wars or deploy American forces in the Asian theater, combined with a much greater American effort to assist Asian allies to strengthen their own defense capabilities against internal and external threats. Secretary of Defense Melvin Laird elaborated upon the priorities in his 1971 report to Congress on the defense program for 1972-1976: "With regard to U.S. force capabilities in Asia, we do not plan for the long term to maintain separate large U.S. ground combat forces specifically oriented just to this theater, but we do intend to maintain strong air, naval, and support capabilities."[13] With the two-and-a-half war strategy, prior to the Nixon Doctrine, the military services worked on the assumption that they should be able to fight two major wars simultaneously, one in Europe and one in Asia, and to cope with a lesser contingency in some area of the Third World, perhaps Latin America or Africa, at the same time. Clearly the major aggressor in Europe was expected to be the Soviet Union, while the major aggressor in Asia would be the Peoples' Republic of China or one of its proxies. The Vietnam War of course reduced desire to become engaged ever again in a major land war in Asia, while the Nixon Administration's rapprochement with China reduced the perception of that country as a threat to American interests in Asia. The new one-and-a-half war strategy, which seemed much more congruent with a realistic assessment of America's global capabilities, envisioned only the ability to counter a major aggression from the Soviet Union in Europe and to handle a lesser contingency elsewhere in the world at the same time. Obviously the one-and-a-half war strategy moved Western

Europe more directly to the center of American global concerns in anticipation of the end of the Vietnam War.

Considered together, these strategic changes demonstrate how costly the Vietnam involvement had been in reference to America's protection of its global interests. And for the Europeans, the signals seemed highly conflicting. European planners might feel reassured that with the Nixon Doctrine and the one-and-a-half war strategy, Europe was now the centerpiece of American strategic thinking. On the other hand, the Total Force policy, announced by Secretary Laird in 1970, indicated the extent to which American defense capabilities in Europe had been shaken, given the new reliance on reinforcements from the United States in the case of Soviet aggression in Europe. Clearly, major changes were occurring in the global strategic balance with uncertain consequences for the credibility of the American defense guarantee of Western Europe.

The Struggle over the Mansfield Initiative

Two other major struggles of the 1967-1973 period merit brief consideration here, though both culminated at a later time and are treated at greater length in the following chapter. They are, firstly, the struggle over Senator Mansfield's efforts to withdraw American troops from Germany, and secondly, the struggle over offset payments agreements. Both struggles heated up to a boiling point in the early 1970s, threatening major disintegration of the German-American security relationship. We shall consider first the withdrawal efforts of Senator Mansfield.

The Democratic Majority Leader, Senator Mike Mansfield, began his efforts in the mid 1960s to gather support for withdrawing at least some American troops from Germany. It was not for him a capricious or unwarranted suggestion. He sincerely believed that the United States maintained in Germany a substantial number of troops in excess of what was needed for deterrence and defense, and he thought that such excess troops engendered an unnecessary drain on the U.S. balance of payments. It was not until the beginning of the period under consideration in this chapter, however, that a real debate began in the Senate over the Mansfield proposals. It was in August, 1966, when the first of a long series of resolutions on troop withdrawals was introduced in the Senate by Senator Mansfield. The timing is significant, because of the confluence of two factors in the late 1966-early 1967 period, which seemed to create a foundation for discussion of troop withdrawals. It was at this time that concern deepened measurably in public consciousness and in Congress about ballooning and seemingly uncontrollable deficits in the U.S. balance of payments; at the same time a rising tide of angry dissent over the Vietnam War was becoming clearly visible and beginning to shape the national debate over U.S. foreign policy. The link between the Vietnam War and the Mansfield initiative was endemic from beginning to end. If overcommitment of U.S. military resources had caused an untenable situation in Vietnam, so the argument went, the cycle must not be allowed to repeat itself in Europe. If our Allies in Europe were not ready to shoulder their fair share of the burden of Western defense, then the U.S. commitment should be decreased in order to force them to do so. If the U.S. were overcommitted around the world in terms of security guarantees, such guarantees must be reduced where possible, as in Europe, in order to bring commitments into line with capabilities.

The Mansfield initiative achieved a limited success in 1967, partially because of a temporary alliance between Senator Mansfield and Secretary of Defense Robert McNamara. As noted in the previous chapter, Congress agreed to the withdrawal of two-thirds of a division from Germany to the United States, about 35,000 men. Though Mansfield's objective was more to relieve pressures on the U.S. balance of payments by forcing the Europeans to assume more of the defense burden, McNamara needed to retrieve every available military unit from anywhere outside Asia for possible deployment in the Vietnam War, even though the units brought home from Germany remained under the command of the U.S. Army Europe. Once again it is clear that the German-American security relationship suffered almost inversely with the morass of the Vietnam involvement, though neither Senator Mansfield nor Secretary McNamara achieved his real objectives in this unhappy compromise. The dual-basing policy thwarted McNamara's objective, since the withdrawn units would not be available for service in Vietnam without further Congressional action, while the two-thirds of a division withdrawn represented far less than Mansfield had in mind. And even this compromise was pushed through Congress despite the objections of the State Department and the Joint Chiefs of Staff. Nevertheless, the die was cast in 1967 for several years of severe difficulties for the U.S. military in Germany. The overall force level was reduced, dual-basing of units was instituted, and the forces in Germany began to suffer severe shortfalls in junior officers and senior NCO's for the next six years.

The 1967 withdrawal represented Senator Mansfield's single modest victory, though certainly not the end of his efforts. A general Congressional awareness of major difficulties in the American military in Germany, together with a conviction that it would be unwise to compromise security interests in Europe too far for the sake of the Vietnam War prevented the Mansfield initiative from gaining much ground in the period 1967 to 1971. Undaunted, the determined Senator continued to introduce the withdrawal resolutions year after year and to propagate his message of equal security at less cost in Europe through troop withdrawals. By 1970 Mansfield decided he had gained enough support to elevate the issue to the top of the Senate agenda. In addition, he reformulated the proposal in the form of a command requiring the president to reduce the forces deployed in Europe by approximately fifty percent. Major debates on the so-called Mansfield Amendment took place in the Senate in January, 1970, and May, 1971, attracting considerable public attention and broad media coverage both in Germany and the United States. The 1971 version of the Amendment would require the president to reduce all U.S. Forces stationed in Western Europe by one half, from approximately 300,000 to 150,000. The Amendment was defeated in the Senate on May 19, 1971, by a vote of 36 in favor to 61 against. Undaunted, Senator Mansfield introduced a new amendment on August 24, requiring the withdrawal of all American forces from Germany, except for one division, which would serve the tripwire function. Through a series of maneuvers the proposal was scaled down to a withdrawal of 60,000 troops and finally defeated in the Senate on November 23 by a vote of 39 to 54. Similar amendments were defeated again in 1972, though by a slimmer margin, showing that the initiative was slowly gaining momentum. The high point in the drama was reached on September 26, 1973, when the Senate by a vote of 48 to 36 did in fact briefly and narrowly pass a new version of the Mansfield Amendment, which required a reduction of 188,000 men stationed overseas, with the great bulk of the reduction, or about 110,000 men, coming from the forces stationed in Germany. The reaction in Germany was tumultuous, resulting in near panic. The Senate was, however, overridden in conference committee a month later. As a substitute for the Mansfield amendment the conferees accepted the so-called Jackson-Nunn amendment, which required a withdrawal of American troops from NATO countries in the percentage by which a particular country failed to cover the American balance of payments deficit arising from the stationing of American troops. The 1973 votes represented the climax of the Mansfield initiative, as well as part of the conclusion to the period under review here. In 1974 the Mansfield Amendment was defeated by a much larger margin, and by 1975 discussion in the Senate concerning troop withdrawals had virtually ceased, largely as a result of the deep introspection caused by the total collapse of South Vietnam to communist control. Senator Mansfield himself retired at the end of 1976. Nevertheless, the damage done to German-American relations all during the period of the Mansfield initiative was substantial and cumulative, reaching a near breaking point at the height of the drama in 1973.

The Struggle over Offset Payments

The closely related struggle over offset payments agreements also forms an important segment of the tableau for the 1967-1973 period. (For a discussion of the issue prior to 1967, see Chapter Three). Though U.S. balance of payments problems, caused partially by the stationing of forces abroad, appeared as early as 1957, the rapidly worsening U.S. balance of payments position did not lead to offset agreements until the early 1960s. The first of the offset agreements between the German and American governments had been negotiated in 1961, to run for a two-year period until June 30, 1963. During the period of the agreement the German Government agreed to purchase 1.22 billion dollars worth of military weapons and supplies in the United States in order to offset the foreign exchange costs of U.S. forces in Germany. The first agreement was followed by two successive similar agreements, which ran from 1963 to 1965 and from 1965 to 1967 respectively. In 1967, the beginning of the period under review, the negotiations became much more difficult, indeed quite acrimonius at times, owing to ever higher American balance of payments deficits and stronger German reluctance to purchase unneeded American military equipment. In hard bargaining in the first half of 1967 the German government managed to scuttle the principle of offset through military purchases by demonstrating that the country was already awash with unnecessary American equipment and overcommitted to purchase additional equipment for which the military leaders had no use. As a substitute a new device was worked out whereby the German central bank would purchase four medium-term U.S. Treasury certificates worth a total of $500 million (each certificate worth DM 500 million, or a total of 2 billion German marks). The certificates would mature after four and one-half years. In addition the German government agreed not to convert dollar holdings into gold at the U.S. Treasury.[14] The difficulty of the negotiations was evidenced by the fact that the agreement was valid for only one year. Only a few months later negotiations had to begin all over again for the 1968-69 agreement. The perspectives of the German and American negotiators and their constituent pressure groups seemed to be growing ever more divergent. The agreement for 1968-69 was again valid for only one year. The compromise in this case involved a combination of

German central bank purchases of medium term U.S. Treasury certificates, for a total this time of 2.9 billion German marks, and German purchases of American military equipment in the amount of 400 million marks. In addition, by continuing the agreement not to exchange dollar holdings for gold the German government undertook what amounted to an obligation to help finance the U.S. balance of payments deficit whenever its own payments position was in surplus.[15] Neither side was very happy with the agreement, and, given the ever widening differences, the negotiations for the next one in the series were tougher and more prolonged than ever. Nevertheless, agreement was achieved in 1969 for another two-year agreement, which would terminate June 30, 1971. Additional inventive devices were incorporated this time, such as German purchases of longer term, ten-year U.S. government securities at approximately half the market rate of interest, plus purchase of some U.S. Export-Import Bank loans and Marshall Plans loans to other countries, these purchases substituting for purchases of medium-term securities at commercial interest rates. Major German purchases of American military equipment were also to be continued, so that the total amount of the offset would amount to 6.08 billion German marks, or slightly more than 2 billion dollars, covering 80% of the U.S. balance of payments costs.[16]

The year 1971 witnessed a major acceleration in both the struggle over troop withdrawals and the struggle over offset payments. As the Mansfield initiative began a major push toward its zenith, the offset negotiations plunged nearer the nadir. By this time the perspectives of the German and American negotiators and their constituent bureaucracies seemed so divergent as to be well nigh irreconcilable. Though the Germans were pushed to make larger concessions by the threat of troop withdrawals on the one hand, the pressure of the Mansfield initiative tended to make them more intransigent on the other. As the Americans argued ever more sharply that the Germans were not contributing their fair share to the cost of NATO defense, the Germans argued with increasing resolve that they should not be required to pay the price of American military folly in Vietnam and domestic economic mismanagement, as mirrored in the huge American balance of payments deficits. Each new nuance, threat, and posturing statement in the negotiations was given detailed coverage in the German press, often accompanied by acrid editorials. The sixth offset agreement expired on June 30, 1971, with no new agreement in sight. Finally, however, on December 10, 1971, after several more months of negotiations, the two sides managed to patch together a series of compromises and makeshift arrangements which became the seventh offset agreement to run retroactively from July, 1971, to mid-1973.

According to this agreement, the German government again agreed to offset approximately eighty percent of the foreign exchange costs of American forces, amounting to 2.034 billion dollars (6.65 billion marks, or 550 million marks more than the previous agreement). The major elements of the agreement consisted of German purchases of American military equipment and medium-term U.S. government securities, as well as longterm loans to the United States at less than market rates of interest as in previous agreements. This time, however, a new element was included, namely, a German agreement to contribute to the renovation of American barracks and other facilities in Germany.[17] This new sector of the agreement marked a recognition of the severe morale problems which by this time plagued American forces in Germany as a result of outdated facilities and the arrival in Germany of the psychological baggage of the Vietnam War. The deeper significance of the 1971 agreement lay in the fact that it signaled an acceptance by Bonn of the principle of "burden-sharing" or direct budget support. In the past, the German government had resolutely refused to commit itself to burden sharing, arguing that this kind of arrangement should be underwritten by the entire NATO alliance rather than West Germany alone. In all previous offset agreements, the Germans received something for their money, either military hardware or interest payments on their loans to the U.S. or purchases of U.S. government securities. Now, for the first time, they agreed to underwrite part of the American troop costs without any tangible return. The agreement was greeted with general discontent on both sides. Many members of Congress still believed that the Germans were being unduly tight-fisted, while major segments of the German press characterized the American Congress as rapacious, especially in the light of Nixon's efforts to overhaul the international monetary system to the advantage of the United States shortly after the agreement entered into force.

An eighth and last offset agreement was negotiated for the period 1973-1975. In 1976 the offset payments program was ended in exchange for a German agreement to contribute substantial amounts to the construction of a giant new American military base in North Germany, as discussed in the next chapter. No one was sorry to see an end to the offset negotiations, which had caused so much acrimony in the bilateral relationship every one or two years. Clearly, the deteriorating American balance payments position in the late 1960s helped to fuel an ever widening divergence between the German and American sides. The major changes in the international monetary system between 1971 and 1973, bringing a *de facto* end to the Bretton Woods system, helped to clear the air somewhat by defusing the

Table 4.1.   U.S. Military Personnel in Europe,
             1966-1973

Year	Personnel*	Personnel**
1966	366,000	306,807
1967	337,000	303,565
1968	316,000	267,538
1969	300,000	263,217
1970	296,000	246,594
1971	314,000	255,462
1972	300,000	252,535
1973	313,000	264,435

*Source: Adapted from Richard D. Lawrence and
    Jeffrey Record, U.S. Force Structure in
    NATO: An Alternative, (The Brookings
        Institution, 1974), table 8-1, p. 93.

**Source: Adapted from data provided by Truman
    Strobridge, Command Historian, U.S.
    European Command, Headquarters,
    Stuttgart, Germany.

argument that American balance of payments deficits were
caused in substantial measure by stationing troops abroad.

Declining Force Levels

It is revealing to take a look at American force levels for the
period under review in order to understand the nature of the
changing American military posture in Germany during this
period. Table 4.1 provides an overview of the drawdown of
American troops in Germany in the late 1960s. Even though the
data include military personnel stationed throughout Europe,
land-based and sea-based, the picture is accurate, since the lion's
share, or approximately three-quarters of the personnel, were
stationed in Germany at any one time. What is striking here is
the rather substantial drawdown which occurred between 1966
and 1970. As we have seen previously, the first major decrease
between 1966 and 1967 is accounted for by the 1967 decision to
return one-third of a division from Germany to the United States
in conjunction with the beginning of the program for dual-basing
of units. For the next three years, however, major attrition of
Europe-based personnel continued to occur. The principal
reason, of course, was the Vietnam War. For each of the years
from 1967 to 1969 the diminution of personnel in Europe was

rather substantial, between 15,000 and 20,000 men. The low point was reached in 1970, when military personnel in Europe fell even below the 200,000 level. The massive attrition stopped in 1970, the same year that the withdrawal from Vietnam began. A kind of stabilization seems to have been reached in 1970, though the number jumped back and forth between 296,000 and 313,000 between 1970 and 1973.

The Effects of Vietnam in West Germany

These numbers, together with other kinds of evidence, give us some idea of the pernicious effects the Vietnam War had upon the American military presence in Germany. The Germans, of course, worried that an even larger drawdown of forces might occur at any time, if the Mansfield initiative achieved success in the U.S. Senate. The initiative appeared to be perilously close to success in 1971 and again in 1973. There were, in addition, many other ways in which the Vietnam War adversely affected America's military presence in Germany. The entire period from 1967 to 1973 is, in one sense, a story of decline and decay in the quality of American's military presence in Germany. Not all of the problems can be traced to the Vietnam involvement, though many of the most important ones can. The German government, the press, and the public at large watched with feelings ranging from discomfort to despair as many of the problems of American forces in Vietnam were transferred to the European arena. By the late 1960s and early 1970s it had become clear beyond doubt that the morale, discipline, and readiness of American forces in Germany were in precipitous decline. The problems in Vietnam were reported and discussed in considerable depth by the press in Germany, often with an eye to the relationship between Vietnam and American forces in Europe. In 1971, for instance, there was a flurry of press reports that forty-five percent of American soldiers in Vietnam habitually used marijuana, hashish, or other hard drugs, and that the problems had become steadily worse ever since 1965.[18] A headline in the Berlin newspaper *Tagesspiegel* in 1973 read, "Vietnam has poisoned the U.S. Army in Europe," and attributed to the Supreme Commander, General Michael S. Davison, a statement that U.S. forces in Europe had been only an empty shell when he had assumed command in 1971. The article continued, "It is no longer a secret to anyone that the Vietnam War throughout its most intense phase has drained off the military substance of American units stationed in Europe. Experienced officers and units, especially career officers, were pulled out and shipped off to Indochina. Much of the time units in Europe and probably also the reserve units in the United States had barely half of their authorized strength and only a fraction of the readiness attributed to them. This is true of combat troops as well as support units."[19]

Problems of race relations in the U.S. military worsened measurably after the assassination of Martin Luther King, Jr. in 1968 and spread quickly to Germany. In addition, incidents of criminal behavior and drug problems multiplied steadily after 1968, so that by 1971 the problems appeared to be out of control. In mid-summer the *Stuttgarter Nachrichten* reported that the inhabitants of the garrison city of Ludwigsburg lived in a state of habitual fear because of a string of violent acts committed by American soldiers.[20] In a period of two months the local police had recorded seventeen violent incidents, ranging from destruction of a fire department callbox to rape. The incidents included four cases of severe personal injury, four cases of rape, and eight muggings. The mayor of the city lodged a demand with the local American commander that no soldiers be allowed to leave military bases at night. Though the demand was refused on the grounds that the punishment of all soldiers for the misconduct of a few would heighten tensions even further, the local commander did agree to set up additional courtesy patrol units and to work more closely with the German police.[21]

In the town of Neu-Ulm a similar situation led to a flood of protests by various German groups to American military authorities. The tense situation began in early summer when an American soldier created mass panic by throwing a tear gas cannister into a crowded beer tent at a local festival. In the ensuing weeks an increasing number of incidents of mugging, robbery, and rape took place, coupled with reports of the existence of a black power organization at one of the American bases, leading the *Stuttgarter Zeitung* to suggest that if the situation did not improve very soon, the massive criticism would lead inevitably to the American presence being viewed as a situation of occupation rather than defense. The newspaper described three recent incidents, which showed, it said, "why the population is reacting with little restraint: a fifteen year old girl was raped by a black soldier while her male companion was threatened with a knife. The automobile of a local resident was totally demolished with no provocation whatever. A resident of a home for the elderly in Neu-Ulm was assaulted by a G.I. and had her pocketbook stolen. Every week the police register incidents which, though they may not be legally serious, are morally devasting to the American presence."[22]

The anarchy at Camp Pieri in Wiesbaden was not atypical of the disorder in which the army found itself in the summer of 1971. Earlier in the year, in February, a raging fire, determined to be the work of arsonists, had consumed a substantial portion of the barracks area. In August the local commander was faced with a situation of outright insurrection. When the signal was given to begin a three-day exercise maneuver, a large group of soldiers simply refused to move out of their quarters and then began shouting and rioting. One hundred men, subsequently cited for insurrection, were awaiting trial before a military court. As one paper described it:

> Refusal to obey orders, overstepping of boundaries, and above all offensive rallies in reference to American policy in Vietnam have long been the order of the day at Camp Pieri.....One thing, however, is certain: the very mixed character of the personnel at Pieri is not conducive to discipline.....Life inside the barracks fence is monotonous. Drill and drugs preoccupy the thinking of the U.S. boys and produce all those aggressive impulses which they also occasionally display in public as unsoldierly behavior.....The fact cannot be denied: harmony between Germans and Americans is not the best in Wiesbaden.[23]

In the late summer of 1971 a team of reporters from the *Washington Post* spent several weeks in Germany collecting information on the condition of the U.S. military. The resulting series of articles published by the paper in Washington was given wide coverage by the press all over Germany. According to the *Post* the U.S. army in Germany was a mutilated army fighting for its very existence against criminality, narcotic drugs, racial conflict and rebellion against officers. At Merrell Barracks in Nuremberg, for instance, the reporters found "all components of the chaotic conditions against which the army is struggling, wherever it is stationed, in Germany, Vietnam, or at home." One officer was quoted as saying: "The barracks are a scandal for the United States....Even if we could renovate them one hundred percent, they still wouldn't be as good as they were when Hitler's troops lived in them. Why is the Nuremberg Zoo in better condition than the barracks where my men live?" The reporters concluded that narcotic drugs were the single most important cause of criminality, fear and violence among American soldiers. They described the case of a slender, fearful seventeen year old soldier, who had only been in Nuremberg one month and had already been beaten up twice by other soldiers. Another soldier showed the reporters a bayonet and said: "At night I only run around here when I have this with me." When asked about the causes of the chaos, soldiers and officers repeatedly mentioned Vietnam. "We have paid a terrible price for Vietnam," the paper quoted General Davison as saying. "The Seventh Army in Europe was destroyed" by the demand for personnel in Vietnam. The withdrawal of troops from Europe to Vietnam created a situation in which "whole batallions of the Seventh Army were left with only one first lieutenant, a captain or a major and eighteen to twenty lieutenants in command... The result was total chaos in morale, discipline, and readiness."[24]

A paper in Cologne, also drawing from the *Washington Post* series, reported that G.I.'s were constantly subjected to the tyranny of gangster squads in U.S. uniform. New recruits were often forced to smoke hashish so that the squads could win new clients. Such organized criminality created an atmosphere of fear and terror. It was not unusual for courts in the U.S. to sentence gangsters to a term in the army rather than to prison, and most of those were packed off to Germany. The disorder caused by gangster squads was closely connected to the drug trade. In a unit with 1200 soldiers a few wholesale dealers could make over 150,000 dollars within three years. Even at the lower retail levels a soldier could easily double his pay. The polarization between white and blacks was as great a matter of concern to the High Command as the gangster situation. When blacks discovered that their rights were not equal to those of the whites even in the army, they would take matters into their own hands. The situation was nothing less than explosive.[25]

Though German politicians at all levels had for some time been pressuring American authorities to improve the condition of the military forces in Germany, the attention given in the German press to the *Washington Post* series prompted a spate of protests from state and local political leaders. Bertold Kamm, an SPD deputy in the Bavarian state legislature from Nuremberg, promptly wrote a letter to the Army Supreme Commander in Heidelberg demanding immediate action:

> For many years now the Nuremberg SPD deputies have pointed out that in the case of the drug trade conducted by Americans in Germany vigorous action must be demanded from the U.S. Army. As is well known, Germans who have been arrested on drug charges are put in a grave situation when the U.S. Army lets its own members under similar charges go scot free. I have been shaken to take cognizance of the fact that racial hatred in the U.S. Army is evidently widely distributed. In the interest of the fight against criminality and the restoration of normal conditions in the Nuremberg barracks, I demand that you take the necessary measures. The people of Nuremberg

> have a right to the proper observance of security
> measures. It is disturbing to have to live in a city
> where soldiers threaten innocent citizens or
> brandish weapons often under the influence of
> drugs.....I would be grateful if you would reply as
> soon as possible about action to be taken to
> ameliorate these catastrophic circumstances.[26]

As one newspaper after the other in Germany reprinted portions of the *Washington Post* series, other papers began their own investigations of conditions in the American army in Germany. For several weeks headline after headline appeared with alarming statements to the effect that living conditions in the U.S. army were "a mixture of criminality, drugs, race conflict, and rebellion."[27] The army was described as "in the most severe crisis of its entire history," and "on the verge of complete collapse."

It is to the army's credit that the response to the press barrage was one of complete candor. The authors of the *Washington Post* series, Haynes Johnson and George C. Wilson, were respected veteran newspaper reporters. Their research had been carefully designed and meticulously carried out; hence, there could be little quarrel with the validity of their conclusions. At briefings for reporters both in Washington and in Germany the army decided to face the issues directly and to respond with a combination of probity and forcefulness. Even the Commander in Chief of the U.S. Army Europe, General Michael Davison, granted a number of interviews in which he discussed the issues with uncommon forthrightness:

> In the final analysis it's a problem of leadership.
> The rapid increase in serious criminal incidents
> such as robberies and other similar things must be
> viewed in the proper perspective, that in the past
> the Seventh Army was caught in the situation of
> having to support our troops fighting in Vietnam.
> Here in Europe we had a continuous turnover of
> personnel. Company commanders often remained
> with their units not longer than three months, and
> the companies themselves were rotated every nine
> months. Such a situation naturally reduces
> discipline. No one really bears responsibility for
> what actually takes place. And so it leads to chaotic
> circumstances, which bring with them poor morale,
> miserable troop discipline, and a whole host of
> problems in the area of misuse of drugs, racial
> tensions, and so forth.[28]

As General Davison's statement confirms, the demands of the Vietnam War on American forces, plus the general spillover of problems from Vietnam into Europe, help to account in large measure for the miseries of the U.S. army in Germany in the early 1970s. Obviously, however, the entirety of the explanation does not lie with Vietnam. The American military, as in all democratic societies, is a reflection in many ways of the larger society from which it is drawn. Massive abuse of marijuana, hashish, heroin, amphetamines, and other drugs were the order of the day among youth in America. Other forms of youth rebellion against war, the military-industrial complex, the CIA, authoritarianism in universities and other societal structures, racial injustice, poverty and other real or perceived ills of modern technological society were rampant on every hand. It could hardly be expected that the military forces would remain completely immune from this rebellion, especially since large numbers of youth were still being drafted in the early 1970s. With a certain time delay, major social movements, especially youth movements, also tend to be transferred, albeit in somewhat altered form, from the United States to Europe. Though the phenomena of drug abuse and youth rebellion were probably more severe in the United States than anywhere else, European societies were also rocked by similar disturbances. Hence, the problems in the U.S. military were by no means unique or without precedence elsewhere. Though racial disturbances in the U.S. peaked in the late 1960s after the death of Martin Luther King Jr., they were still continuing with considerable force and, with a certain time delay, were now working their way into the military apparatus with a fury. The problems of drug abuse, criminality, race conflict, and poor morale would have afflicted U.S. military forces in the early 1970s in any case. The spillover effects from Vietnam, however, accentuated them to dimensions which seemed larger than life. And, in the final analysis, there was no way in which the U.S. military in Germany could be isolated from the larger trends. In the setting of a quieter, more stable and conservative society such as West Germany, it is little wonder that there was substantial worry that the problems of the U.S. military might threaten the stability of public order. As explained by a spokesman at U.S. Army Headquarters in Heidelberg:

> The army is a mirror of American society. We have in our society profound race problems and we have not been able to come to grips yet with the problem of narcotics. In addition, we have a steep rise in the crime rate. It would be more than peculiar if all these problems stopped at the gates of the barracks.[29]

In the fall of 1971 multilevel discussions were held between the German and American governments on ways to ameliorate the severe problems of the U.S. forces. Two partial solutions were agreed upon. The German Ministry for Youth, Family, and Health reached an agreement with USAREUR Headquarters to expand significantly a program for German-American youth contact which had been begun the year before on an experimental basis. Known as the "Contact Program," the experiment had been judged a success in the three garrison cities of Würzburg, Heilbronn and Mannheim. Now it was to be expanded to fifty-five additional cities. German-American youth councils would be established, composed of youth from both countries, which could define their own goals, programs, and activities without interference from government authorities. The rationale for the program was the idea that increased contact in youth-defined common activities would lead to a decline in stereotypes and prejudices, as well as help to end the psychological isolation of American soldiers in a foreign culture. The second solution was enshrined in the offset payments agreement for 1971. In recognition of the fact that decaying, miserable physical accommodations were a decisive factor of poor troop morale, the German government agreed to accept a "burden-sharing" obligation to contribute several million marks annually for the renovation of barracks and recreational facilities. "Help is on the way for our defenders, the unloved G.I.'s," read the headline in a major newspaper.[30]

Military Race Relations in the Early 1970s

Though both agreements were a step in the right direction, neither one had much impact in the short term. Race relations in the U.S. military continued to deteriorate dramatically in late 1971. By this time a thriving underground black resistance movement had been established, replete with a flourishing underground press. A number of newspapers were published, such as "Voice of the Lumpen" in Frankfurt, "Forward," in Berlin, "About Face," in Mannheim, and "RITA (Resistance Inside The Army)" in Heidelberg. Most disturbing to military authorities was the evidence of multiple links between the black power movement and radical groups of German youth. Radical student movements had been established in Germany soon after they appeared in the United States during the student riots of 1968. Some of them appeared to be oriented more strongly to violence than radical groups in the U.S., and the natural affinity between German youth radicalism and black power in the U.S. military could only serve to make a bad situation even more hopeless. A mass rally on July 4, 1970, brought nearly 1,000 soldiers, mostly blacks, to the Heidelberg University campus, an event which tended to solidify links between black soldiers and leftist German students. There was evidence that the black underground press was subsidized, at least in part, by German students. In addition, it was known that there were at least 20 black organizations in 10 German cities with various links to German radical organizations.[31]

As part of the complex of problems associated with racism, the problem of crime among black troops had also become a particularly troublesome issue by late 1971. A report leaked to the press at an army conference on racism in early November, 1971, contained shocking statistics on black crime. Though only 14 percent of the American troops stationed in Germany were black, blacks accounted for two-thirds of all serious criminal offenses in the period from October, 1970, to September, 1971. During the period there were 2984 cases of robbery, rape, and assault committed by black troops as against 740 such cases committed by white troops. In terms of percentage of total serious crimes, the lowest and highest percentages during the period for each group were: for blacks 72% in December 1970 and 87% in June 1971, for whites 28% in December 1970 and 13% in June 1971.[32] Reported crimes of violence by blacks against white soldiers almost doubled - from 553 in the first nine months of 1970 to 1,002 in the same period of 1971. General Davison called the figures "disturbing," but challenged their validity on the grounds that many white assaults on black soldiers went unreported. The army command in Heidelberg also stressed that the report referred to the number of individual offenders, not to the total number of incidents. Since a large number of blacks were involved in certain incidents, "some statistics in the report may not give a true picture of crime in USAREUR."[33]

A three-day hearing on "Racism in the Military" was conducted by the congressional Black Caucus in September, 1971, chaired by Representatives Ron Dellums (D-CA) and Shirley Chisholm (D-NY). Unsettling testimony was offered by a number of witnesses, the most forceful of whom was Samuel Berry, a former sergeant in Heidelberg and founder of a federation of black power groups in Germany. According to Berry's testimony, organized black and white servicemen had moved from a "position of conciliation to revolutionary defensive and violent stands" because of continued racism in the armed services. Since "the level of intensity and potential for violence" had heightened in recent years, radical soldiers "are poised and ready to raise the level of the struggle to a defensive, violent stand." The cause for this set of circumstances, he asserted, was the rising level of frustrations over attempts to end racism and the feeling that "military officials will only act favorably if we act as a group in an unfavorable manner." Discrimination against blacks in promotions, assignments, housing, and recreational facilities was rampant and had to be abolished.[34]

Both the congressional hearings and the military race relations conference at Berchtesgaden in November, 1971, provide insight into the enormous problems faced by the military in reference to black soldiers during this period. Youth revolt, opposition to the Vietnam War, increasing drug usage, and student rebellions are all part of the milieu in which the military functioned at this time. The ugly phenomenon of racism, however, deeply institutionalized in American society at all levels, including the military, was a problem which had achieved a certain priority in the American political agenda. In a sense, the civil rights movement of the 1960s had finally established a new battleground in one of the major bastions of traditional, conservative values, namely the armed forces of the United States. In retrospect, we can see now that the military establishment was as afflicted with conscious and unconscious racist attitudes as most other American institutions, from corporations to universities. Those committed to an equal opportunity society, indeed to the essence of the American dream, could find no reason why racism should not be confronted and fought within the military establishment as well as in other institutions. The evidence of blatant discrimination in every aspect of military life was not difficult to document. Though blacks comprised 14.3% of enlisted men in the army in 1971, their share of the officer ranks was only 3.6%. In the air force, they represented 12.3% of the enlisted men but only 1.7% of the officers. In occupational categories in the army blacks were overrepresented proportionately in lower skills categories such as infantry and gun crews (19.0%) or service and supply handlers (22.2%) and underrepresented in higher skills categories such as communications and intelligence specialists (11.6%) or technical specialists (10.4%).[35] In other areas such as housing, promotions, and recreational programs, abundant evidence of discrimination was not hard to find. In Germany the problems of black soldiers were magnified by expressions of racism in German society and by the phenomenon of being a member of a tiny minority group in a society over 98% white. Wherever they went, black soldiers were a curiosity for Germans unused to seeing black faces. As a black military policeman expressed it, "Over here a black sticks out like a sore thumb. Whites, on the other hand, are much more difficult to identify as Americans."[36] Little wonder then that when the black civil rights movement began to rock the military, it found some of its ugliest expressions in the units stationed in Germany.

   Though the services had instituted various programs over the
years to combat racial discrimination and improve race relations,
intensified efforts were begun in late 1971 in response to
problems which now threatened massive disintegration. Earlier
in the year a black, Major General Frederic Ellis Davison, had
assumed the second highest post in the army in Germany as
Deputy Chief of Staff for Personnel. In a speech at a race
relations conference in Berchtesgaden in November he
underscored the army's determination to combat racism in all its
manifestations. "It won't be long," he asserted, "before every
cotton-picking commander knows his neck is on the line. Just
watch and see the fur fly." His words were echoed by the supreme
commander of USAREUR, General Michael Davison, who
stressed that all unit commanders would henceforth be under
close scrutiny in their handling of racial problems.[37]
   The Supreme Commander also demonstrated his
determination to combat discrimination in the administration of
military justice. The previous July a brawl between whites and
blacks in an enlisted men's club in Darmstadt and the
subsequent refusal of blacks to obey orders had led to the
celebrated case of the "Darmstadt 29." By fall the case had
become somewhat of a *cause celebre*, due to the involvement of
lawyers from the NAACP and other lawyers well-known in civil
rights circles. In late October General Davison unexpectedly
ordered all charges dropped against the black defendants and
cancelled administrative punishments already meted out. He
also ordered that all "inexcusably delayed" court-martial cases be
thrown out, that army lawyers be exempt from other duties in the
cause of swifter justice, and that applications for search warrants
be made in writing. He dismissed a number of unit commanders
for being too slow in suppressing discrimination, and sent home a
number of soldiers, both white and black, who were regarded as
troublemakers in instigating racial incidents. Few were left in
doubt about General Davison's commitment to combatting
racism. "We know how the commander in chief feels," said one of
his subordinates. "I can assure you his eye is on the spiral"
(chain of command).[38]
   Other innovations were instituted which slowly but surely
began to change traditional rules and methods as they filtered
down through the chain of command. Equal opportunity officers
were appointed throughout the command structure with explicit
instructions as to their responsibilities. In some units soldiers
were authorized to meet with their batallion commanders at any
time to appeal against what they considered an unreasonable
order or unfair or discriminatory treatment. In certain enlisted
men's clubs arrangements were even made to change the musical
fare, so that soul music would be played one night and country

and western the next. Instructions were distributed up and down the line to commanders on how to avert or defuse racial tensions.[39] To some extent the services were spurred to stronger action by the Black Caucus in Congress, which in November issued a set of ten recommendations and served notice that in legislative efforts and in meetings with the Pentagon all ten initiatives would be vigorously pursued. The recommendations included, among others, legislation which would give federal courts jurisdiction over suspected military offenders in discrimination cases, a campaign for a greater percentage of black officers in command positions, a re-evaluation of promotion policies, a review of U.S. foreign policies concerning governments that allowed discrimination against black soldiers, and initiatives to involve black political action groups in military race relations training.[40]

Slowly but surely the services' new programs began to bear fruit. A few important corners were turned in late 1971 and early 1972 which put U.S. forces in Germany on the road to recovery, though many violent storms were yet to occur. As the war in Vietnam continued to wind down in 1972, the army in Europe received higher priority in allocations of men, money, and equipment. Experienced noncommissioned officers and junior officers were no longer whisked off for duty in Vietnam, leaving inexperienced second lieutenants in command of rebellious companies. "A captain now stays at least a year with his company," stressed General Michael Davison.[41] "Battalion and brigade commanders remain eighteen months. They get to know every man in their units." The transition from conscription to the AVF continued in full swing, with a mixture of positive and negative effects. In the Seventh Army in Germany the "early out" program was instituted for the separation of draftees who had only a few months left to serve. The program was helpful in weeding out malcontents, but also tended to strip units of needed men in certain critical specialties. "There is no question," stated one unit commander, "that the Seventh Army, as a fighting force, is on its way back from the sad state of the past few years."[42]

Even in the critical area of race relations there was evidence that slow progress was being made. New human relations programs were established. All Fifth Corps officers were required to attend leadership seminars on black-white relations. A touring road show called "Who Are You Calling 'Boy,' Pig?" traveled the Fifth Corps route and hit hard at unhealthy racial attitudes, black or white. In an extensive interview with the *Christian Science Monitor* in February, 1972, Commander in Chief Michael S. Davison, with justifiable pride, pointed out some of the accomplishments. "Eighteen months ago black dissident organizations could turn out 1,500 soldiers for a demonstration. By last summer it was only 500. Now it is perhaps 150 or 160.....A year and a half ago roughly fifteen militant black organizations were operating in the Seventh Army area. Now we are down to three or four. And this is not simply the result of mergers. Total membership is down." When asked what accounted for the decline in militancy, he replied, "I think that the black soldier is beginning to believe that we really mean to eliminate discrimination. He is more ready to give us a chance." The general also cited statistics which showed a decline in the number of violent crimes. "For eighteen months we had a steady increase in the number of violent crimes, peaking in July, 1971. Since then there has been a five-month decline, despite an occasional upsurge." Less progress could be demonstrated, however, in the area of drug abuse. Since racial incidents seemed to be receding, the problem of drugs now seemed to be the army's number one problem. In this area also the army was at least attempting to confront the problem headon. A variety of drug counseling and therapeutic programs was created, designed to help a soldier solve a drug abuse problem, rather than to punish him. "We can only help those who want to be helped," stressed Col. James D. Hefner, Fifth Corps surgeon. "We now provide ways and means for a man to help himself."[43]

Problems with Drugs, Crime, and Violence

Even though the variety of new measures represented a modest turning point in the army's efforts to stem the tide of deterioration, the improved climate proved to be disappointingly short lived. The summer of 1972 was the hottest, ugliest yet experienced for U.S. forces in Germany. The activity of German terrorists had reached such a level by 1972 that it served as an important catalyst to a stiffening mood of belligerence and rebellion among U.S. troops. A wave of bomb attacks occurred in May, many of which appeared to be the work of the Baader-Meinhof gang and other similar terrorist groups. On May 11 an explosion at the Headquarters of the army's Fifth Corps in Frankfurt claimed the life of an American colonel. The most spectacular assault occurred less than two weeks later on May 24 inside the Headquarters compound of USAREUR at Campbell Barracks in Heidelberg. Double bomb blasts tore a gaping hole in the wall of a building housing data processing computers, destroyed more than a dozen automobiles and smashed windows of buildings surrounding the parking lots where the blasts occurred. Three soldiers were killed and five others seriously injured. The penetration of the Headquarters compound not only had a chilling effect on morale and security but also, as the terrorists hoped, brought about a major escalation in the climate of violence in the U.S. military.[44]

Even teenage dependents of military personnel participated in bloodcurdling acts of revenge. In Wiesbaden fifteen high school students administered a severe beating to an elderly German man working in his garden near the high school and then proceeded to attack and beat two German employees of the city utilities department. As German police intervened in an attempt to arrest the ringleaders, a group of two hundred high school age youth counterattacked the police. The police finally resorted to drawing their pistols after several of them had been beaten to the ground and stomped on, resulting in serious injuries. The mayor of Wiesbaden promptly dispatched a letter to the local American commander demanding that strong measures be taken against "the criminal behavior of students in a country where they were living as guests."[45] In order to decrease tension in the poisoned atmosphere of German-American relations a new German-American committee was established to recommend additional security measures in Wiesbaden.

As the summer wore on acts of violence continued with numbing frequency and the ugly specter of racial violence appeared again with ever more frightening dimensions. In Neu-Ulm on the 10th of July eight black soldiers kidnapped a sixteen year old girl and raped her one after the other. The following weekend the police in Ulm registered eight serious attacks by both white and black G.I.'s on German citizens walking down the street. In mid-July in Ludwigsburg fighting broke out between black and white soldiers, resulting in twenty-four injured. On August 13 about one hundred blacks armed with knives, staves, broken bottles and stones, clashed with German police for five hours, after the soldiers had attacked a local police station in Stuttgart. Ten policemen were severely injured. The battle culminated a series of complaints over three months that black soldiers had been scuffling with, robbing, and using abusive language to passers-by and tram passengers. "Harlem in Stuttgart?" asked the newspaper *Stuttgarter Zeitung*. Describing the incident as the "bloodiest pitched battle on the streets of Stuttgart since World War II," the paper editorialized that "until now we believed that this form of primitive violence was restricted to the African and the American continents."[46] The *Stuttgarter Nachrichten* concluded sadly:

> One lives dangerously in the vicinity of American garrisons. For several years the acts of violence of American soldiers have repeatedly made headlines. But the cases are becoming ever more frequent. Given the spectacular cases in recent

weeks and the newest mass battle in Stuttgart, are we now threatened with an escalation of violence by black U.S. soldiers? Robberies, stabbings, drug addiction, and pitched battles have inevitably given rise to the public perception of the "criminal American black."......Until a few years ago the U.S. Seventh Army had the reputation as the model disciplined elite army of the world. That reputation has vanished.[47]

The litany of shame continued unabated. On August 14 a German fire brigade came to the assistance of American M.P.'s attempting to extinguish a fire set by an arsonist in Neu-Ulm. Soldiers attacked the M.P.'s and firemen with stones and bottles. An iron bar wielded by a G.I. severely wounded a volunteer German fireman, resulting in a decision by the Neu-Ulm fire department no longer to respond to fires in American garrisons. On August 22 at Wharton Barracks in Heilbronn forty blacks stormed the military police station in an attempt to free two "brothers" who were being held for robbing and beating a Turkish guest worker. German police cars attempting to assist the M.P.'s were demolished with rocks and pipes. On August 27 fifteen black soldiers attacked and raped "in animalistic fashion" two young girls from Biberback who were camping on the bank of the Danube River. Countless other attacks and indignities occurred which were not reported in official statistics. In restaurants American G.I.'s often ordered German guests to pay for cigarettes. German wives and girlfriends were subjected to abusive language. On the streets women and girls were grabbed, and passers-by were frequently robbed.[48]
Inevitably a flood of letters from German political leaders at all levels inundated the offices of American military commanders. "Our patience is exhausted," wrote an SPD deputy from Neu-Ulm to Supreme Commander Davison. He suggested that the leadership of the U.S. military had completely lost control of the situation and that the U.S. army would simply sink into the twilight zone if the violence continued.[49] General Davison apologized publicly with dignity and promised to "take all necessary measures to establish and maintain an appropriate degree of discipline in military units in Germany."[50] About the same time army headquarters announced that classes would begin on September 11 at a newly established race relations school in Oberammergau in the Bavarian Alps. Patterned after the Defense Race Relations Institute at Patrick Air Force Base in Florida, each class would consist of sixteen teams and last for three weeks. Each team would be composed of an officer and an NCO, one caucasian and the other a minority group member.

The volunteer students would have outstanding records and leadership qualities and be fully aware of current social issues. By December 15 the school planned to have completed training for sixty-four two-man instructor teams. Though a program a hundred times larger was obviously needed, at least the army was again undertaking new initiatives on the race relations front.[51] Earlier in the summer the army sent out orders to all commands for the establishment of local affirmative action plans as well as an army-wide plan to curb racial complaints and violence. The plan aimed at increasing minority group participation in officer schools, in such specialized jobs as the medical corps and judge advocate corps and in specialized military occupation specialities rather than unskilled ones. It would provide educational facilities to overcome such obstacles as the language problems of some Spanish-speaking personnel, insurance of equal opportunity for career-enhancing assignments for officers and improvement of the army's image among minority group civilians.[52]

Despite the new initiatives the army's reputation in Germany plunged to a new low in October with a series of bizarre murders of Germans by American soldiers. Three murders occurred on the European express train "the Alps Express" near Göttingen in the early morning hours of October 6. A deserter being brought back to his unit managed to steal the guns of his two American guards, then shot both guards and hurled their bodies through the window of the speeding train. When he was surprised during the act by a female German rail hostess, he shot the hostess and also hurled her body from the train. That the deserter managed to get to Beirut, Lebanon, before turning himself in escaped the comprehension of both German and American authorities.[53] Later in October the drug trade between German youth and American soldiers resulted in double murder and rape in Augsburg. With the discovery of the nude body of a seventeen year old German boy, Klaus Gammel, a story of degradation so deep as to be scarcely believable unfolded. Three American soldiers, one seventeen years old and the other two eighteen years old, planned the murder of Klaus Gammel and of twenty-one year old Franz Rothmaier because the soldiers did not have enough money to pay for the hashish they had ordered from the German youths. Methodically and with cold calculation they had pulverized the German youths with rocks and then shot them repeatedly. Later the same evening the soldiers, in an effort to build an alibi, gave a ride to a twenty-year old German girl on her way home from work at the barracks, then tormented and raped her.[54] The population of Augsburg was outraged. Their anger increased with the total silence of American authorities concerning the case. Days passed and not even a letter of condolence was sent to the German parents of the slain youths by American commanders. A movement to call the Americans to full account was established by a German university professor. In addition, a major quarrel developed between German and American authorities over who had the right to jurisdiction over the accused American soldiers. Inevitably, the cry "Ami Go Home!," previously heard only sporadically from assorted leftists, spread from newspaper to newspaper in South Germany.[55]

Early German Perceptions of the AVF

By the end of 1972 the Germans also seemed increasingly worried about the possible results of the American transition from the conscription army to the all volunteer force, a move now well underway. In December data released by USAREUR Headquarters showed that 77% of the soldiers stationed in Europe were volunteers. Since the last draft calls were to go out in late 1972 the transition to the AVF would be largely complete by 1973. In an effort to placate fears widely expressed in the German press, Supreme Commander Michael Davison held a press conference in late December. The effectiveness of the U.S. forces, he said, would be enhanced by an increase in the quality of the volunteers which would be obtained by the new pay scales for military personnel fully competitive with pay scales in the civilian sector. He assured reporters that there would be no diminution of the number of U.S. forces stationed in Europe.[56] The timing for these assurances was perhaps not the best, since army headquarters released new statistics on drug abuse among troops in Europe a few days later. Though statistics issued by USAREUR had little credibility in the eyes of the German press and were thought vastly to underestimate the extent of real drug usage in the American military, even the army's own figures showed an alarming increase in the use of hard drugs during the past year. Matters were not improved by the army's effort to soften the conclusions with the explanation that some of the increased usage could be accounted for by improved detection and testing techniques. And there was a hollow ring to General Davison's insistence that the drug situation in Europe bore no relation to the problem in Vietnam because "the two situations cannot be compared."[57]

The Germans felt they had good reason to be worried about the implications of the switch to an all volunteer force, given the concern expressed in the German press about high rates of crime among American troops in general and black troops in particular. U.S. Government figures also showed that the percentage of blacks in the enlisted ranks of the U.S. forces as a whole had increased from 11.0% to 12.6% between 1970 and 1972, and in the army from 13.5% to 17.0%.[58] Throughout the year concern had been expressed by government officials and the German press that the switch to an all volunteer force would also inevitably lead to a diminution of the American military presence in Germany and hence of the American security guarantee. The Germans widely suspected that a slow, but prolonged and insidious withdrawal of American forces had been taking place for some time. Disagreements surfaced from time to time between American and German authorities about the numerical strength of American forces. In August, for example, reports circulated that although the Americans stuck by their official figure of 215,000 troops stationed in Germany, certain informed German experts had ascertained that the true figure was approximately 200,000. As one report expressed it:

> Informed circles in Bonn believe that under-the-table troop reductions have already been taking place. In the past year alone the Americans have withdrawn 5000 troops from the Federal Republic according to documents available in Bonn. American officials, when questioned about the matter by their German counterparts, emphasize that any reduction of forces only concerns administrative and support personnel, but that the fighting capability of American forces constantly increases.....Certainly the example of the British Army of the Rhine ought to show quite clearly how problematic an all volunteer army is. Limited combat situations lead to force reductions to be sure, but not to the callup of reserves as replacements......It is also possible that Italy, the Netherlands, and France might change from conscription armies to all volunteer forces.[59]

1973 – Year of Crisis and Transition

The last year of the period under review, 1973, was a good bit quieter than the previous two years in terms of race conflict and other serious problems, yet the strains caused by the Vietnam War and the transition to the AVF continued to exact a heavy toll, and the process of rebuilding and regenerating U.S. forces in Germany proved to be inordinately slow and painful. In January passions were again aroused by the brutal slaying of an American soldier in a restaurant in Bamberg. Following a serious argument the manager and twenty other German guests beat up the American soldier and tossed him out into a nearby alley. After an hour of waiting, during which many Germans refused aid, a taxi finally stopped and took him and his companion to the American hospital. But it was too late. The soldier was already dead. Though the motive of the slaying remained unclear, one newspaper captured the mood of the times in its remark that, "One can safely assume that in this case the pentup emotions against American soldiers in Bamberg gushed forth like a broken dam."[60]

The following month the army, at long last, decided that drastic measures were necessary to stem the tide of drug abuse which threatened to destroy what was left of the army's reputation in Germany. The justification given was that the problems of the drug trade had reached such dimensions that nothing less than drastic measures could now cope with the situation. In essence, all constitutional rights would be suspended for any American soldier suspected of being involved in drug abuse or the drug trade. The new measures included checks of automobiles and personal belongings without previous warning, extensive checks before granting approval for any trips outside Germany, cancellation of drivers' licenses and other privileges for offenders, new regulations requiring that military uniforms be worn in off-duty hours, and fines for maintaining unapproved quarters off base. Reasonable grounds for suspicion, rather than concrete proof, would suffice to bring the measures into force for any soldier suspected of drug abuse or sales. Any soldier under suspicion of drug usage could be immediately interrogated by an officer and examined by a physician. In the barracks no doors could be closed without authorization, no partitions erected, and no candles burned. In every barracks building a drug watch would be established which could investigate soldiers or guests without warning. "Black lists" would be prepared of soldiers suspected of being drug abusers or traders for every commander. Proof of drug abuse would henceforth be reason for dishonorable discharge from military service and severe additional penalties. Though the constitutionality of some of the measures was perhaps highly questionable, the army left little doubt that all out war had been declared on the army's most debilitating problem and that the army meant, at all costs, to rectify the situation.

In March the Headquarters of the United States Air Force, Europe (USAFE) moved from the centrally located resort city of Wiesbaden to the more remote location at Ramstein in southwest Germany. According to a local newspaper the move was "widely applauded" by the people of Wiesbaden,[61] even though local officials were highly displeased that the move had been announced with little lead time only a few months earlier. As usual with such movements of American military units, German officials expressed resentment on two counts: the displacement of German employees and inadequate consultations on the matter between German and American authorities. As usual, one report noted, the plan to move a major installation had actually been decided upon many months ago, but no meaningful consultations had been held and the move was simply announced to the Germans as a "fait accompli."[62] At the official ceremony to mark the occasion on March 13, the deputy mayor of Wiesbaden expressed the hope that the friendship and sympathy between Americans and Germans "would not be changed by some of the voices of recent times."[63]

Also in March a report was issued by the General Accounting Office which again confirmed the deleterious longer term effects of the Vietnam War on U.S. forces in Germany. According to the report a substantial proportion of the material stored in Europe for use by forces returning from the United States for the Reforger maneuvers was defective, could not be located, or was fully unusable. The most serious deficiencies concerned tanks, vehicles, and weapons, though severe problems extended to most of the army's equipment in Europe. As one German newspaper reported the story:

> It is an open secret that the fighting ability, readiness of reserve forces, and condition of equipment of the Seventh Army in Europe badly need to be overhauled. These ground troops, which are the most important for the Americans in the NATO alliance, have been disadvantaged for years in terms of manpower and material by the consequences of the Vietnam War.[64]

The summer of 1973 was another hot, unpleasant period for U.S. forces, though considerably less gruesome than the previous two summers in terms of racial disturbances and criminal behavior. A series of incidents shook the Bamberg area in July, including the stabbing of a twenty-one year old German student by a black G.I., and the rape of a fourteen year old girl at gunpoint by two soldiers. The leadership of the local union wrote letters to the local American commander demanding an end to "gangster activity by Americans in uniform, and an immediate order forbidding soldiers to leave base until the perpetrators were arrested." If the American commander were unwilling to take matters in hand immediately, the union would call upon the population of the city to organize self-protection of its own choosing.[65] Racial clashes and fire bombing incidents in

Bamberg became so severe in August that reinforcements of military police from Ansbach and Erlangen had to be called in to put down the disturbances.[66] In Munich incidents of rape, robbery, and mugging occurred with disturbing frequency all summer. Local politicians in September reported that excesses by American soldiers against German citizens had reached intolerable limits and called for new investigations and protests to American authorities.[67] In August and September a batch of articles and analyses, now no longer a novelty, appeared in newspapers and newsmagazines throughout Germany documenting horrendous conditions of race conflict, drug abuse, and criminality in American forces. "American Terror as Never Before," screamed the headline of one magazine. "They are supposed to protect us. But they rob, murder, and rape. American soldiers in Germany arouse naked fear. Panic-stricken mayors and police chiefs are sending new alarms to Bonn that they can no longer cope with the American terror."[68]

Despite the screaming headlines the army could take some comfort in the fact that there were fewer incidents of racial conflict and fewer serious criminal cases in the summer of 1973 than in the previous two summers. The favorable trends were discussed intensely at the fifth annual Conference on Race Relations and Equal Opportunity at Garmisch-Partenkirchen in October, attended by 450 commissioned officers, senior noncomissioned officers, and high ranking persons from the Pentagon. "The number of serious incidents has been substantially reduced," said General Davison. "I think the worst is behind us, and we have a kind of truce at present. That is not to say that racial peace has been achieved. We still have a very long way to go."[69] At the conference sessions much consideration was given to a study of ways in which the all volunteer force concept could contribute to racial harmony. By this time statistics were available showing that blacks were volunteering for military service in much higher percentages than whites and that over time the percentage of blacks in the army would continue to rise. The general theme that seemed to emerge from the conference was that the key to racial peace over the longterm lay in the achievement of genuine equal opportunity in the nation's armed forces. Many young blacks now looked to the military to give them the kind of status and opportunity not afforded to them in civilian life. Progress and renewal would be possible in the military if every person in leadership positions would make a personal commitment to the principle of equal opportunity for all.[70] Despite the many problems of the long, hot summer there was an air of encouragement and hope at the conference that the worst of the misery might indeed be over and that an era of progress and renewal had begun.

Signs of Poverty and Ghettoization

The closing year of the period under review is important in another very different respect. For the first time unmistakable signs of economic poverty began to appear among American troops in Germany. Major changes in the international monetary system had been instituted by President Nixon in 1971 when the dollar's international convertability to gold was suspended. Between 1971 and 1973 the Bretton Woods international monetary system had collapsed almost entirely, and beginning in 1973 currency exchange rates were floating rather than pegged by governmental agreement. The new situation meant that the strength of the dollar in terms of its exchange rate to other major currencies depended on the competitive strength of the American economy in international trade and finance. Since the dollar had long been a chronically overvalued currency, its exposure to international market forces meant that its value against the German mark began a precipitous slide in late 1972. According to one report, the cost of living on the German economy increased 23% for American G.I.'s between January and July, 1973.[71] Hence, despite the increased pay scales in effect for the AVF, enlisted G.I.'s in Germany found their paycheck rapidly losing ground for purchases they made on the German economy. Especially hard hit were soldiers who rented living quarters off base. For the first time since World War II American soldiers in Germany had a difficult time making ends meet.

The effect of the weaker dollar was magnified by the fact that the transition to the all volunteer force brought many more married soldiers and their dependents to Germany than had been the case during the draft years. Single men living in the barracks and buying most of the necessities of life on base could mitigate the effects of the dollar's declining purchasing power much more easily than married soldiers living off base with dependents. One important effect, consequently, of the lowered military standard of living was to increase the tendency of American soldiers to live either on base or in one of the housing areas adjacent to bases which were inhabited solely by military personnel. The "ghettoization" of the military, which became increasingly pervasive during the next decade, began at about this time. Naturally, the military presence had existed in the form of huge concentrations of men and material at specific locations in southern Germany ever since the war. During the 1950s and 1960s, however, the Americans tended to fan out further and further from base areas. In ways large and small many American families had integrated portions of their social and economic lives with their German neighbors. Now a definite contraction began to occur, with Americans pulling up roots from

German neighborhoods and moving back closer to base areas. The effect, of course, was to reverse the process of cultural integration which had been occurring over the years and to set in its place a slow but noticeable process of estrangement. The ghettoization of the military meant simply that fewer ties of warmth and closeness would be established between Germans and Americans and that some ties of longstanding duration would be broken. In addition, the ghetto phenomenon could not but result in an increasing tendency on the part of both Germans and American to build stereotypes of each other's societies.

Psychological Estrangement

The psychological effects of this "creeping poverty" of U.S. forces in Germany worked to create an altered picture of the American military presence for both Germans and Americans. For over twenty-five years American soldiers in Germany had represented the enormous clout not only of the world's most powerful military machine but of the world's richest and most productive economy. For years the Germans had been used to viewing G.I.'s as "rich Amis" who personified the essence of American wealth and power. Now it began to appear that the erstwhile rich Amis were becoming poor cousins to the more prosperous Europeans. The psychological impact of this changed perception, though difficult to measure, had profound consequences. For the Americans it meant that the period of exalted lordship in Germany, of being able to travel anywhere and afford anything, was coming to an end. A heightened perception of being "guests" in a strange land, of diminished status and position began to take root. For the Germans also, the appearance of mild poverty among American soldiers had the unmistakable effect of diminishing the former deference to American power. Admiration for the prosperous American way of life, for the "land of unlimited possibilities" no longer seemed as appropriate as in former times.

The point is that the first appearance of poverty in 1973 began to change the whole psychological equation surrounding the American military presence in Germany. By showing the international weakness of the American economy, it increased a tendency on the part of the Germans to reevaluate the meaning, as well as the essence, of Germany's security dependence on the United States. And as time and events proved, things would never be the same again. The image of the American soldier as a ten-foot-tall representative of the world's most powerful state began to fade. And it was never able to regain the luster of former times. In 1973 it was not clear how much the Vietnam

War and the rebellious movements it spawned had weakened America's military role in Germany, nor was it clear when or even if the former vibrance of the security relationship could be established.

Changes in the structure and texture of East-West relations in the early 1970s also had an important impact upon German public perceptions of the American military role in Germany and, more importantly, upon the base of public support on which the American presence rested. Mention was made earlier of the policy of detente which became the organizing principle of East-West relations during the Nixon administration. The German corollary was the Brandt government's Ostpolitik, viewed by both Washington and Bonn as a logical adjunct and supplement to detente in the European arena. The major concrete expressions of Ostpolitik were the two treaties signed between the Federal Republic of Germany and its eastern neighbors: the Bonn-Moscow Treaty and the Bonn-Warsaw Treaty, both signed in 1970 and ratified by the German parliament in 1972. East-West detente and Germany's Ostpolitik were joined in the Quadripartite Agreement on Berlin of 1971 and the ensuing Treaty on the Basics of Relations Between the Federal Republic of Germany and the German Democratic Republic of 1972. Both German states became members of the United Nations in 1973. The importance of detente and German Ostpolitik for our study lies in the changing perceptions both generated in Germany of the nature of the Soviet threat and the importance of the NATO alliance. The Berlin treaty led not only to better access and higher flows of people and goods between West Germany and West Berlin but also to measurable improvements in many aspects of the city's daily life. The treaty between the two German states made possible a greater flow of visitors from West to East Germany and increased human contacts of all kinds. The Bonn-Moscow and Bonn-Warsaw treaties removed some of the major points of friction between the Federal Republic and its eastern neighbors and normalized relations across a broad spectrum. Hence, in Germany as in the United States, the public began to perceive that a new age of international relations had been launched. The SALT I Treaty between the superpowers even seemed to have put a meaningful cap on the dreaded arms race. However illusory the period of detente may seem in retrospect, the fact is that, especially in Germany, detente generated a perception of a much reduced, if not benign Soviet threat to the country's security.

The importance of such altered perceptions was compounded by generational changes. By 1973 every person in Germany under the age of twenty-eight had been born after World War II. The situation of unparalleled prosperity and peace in postwar

Germany, coupled with an inadequate historical grasp of the history of the war and important postwar developments, meant that young West Germans were coming of age at a time when it seemed that the cold war was receding into the dim and misty past, if not coming to an end altogether. Given the division of Germany into two separate states linked to two vastly different social systems and military alliances, it is not surprising that a revisionist view of history seems to have struck much deeper roots in Germany than elsewhere in Europe. Many young West Germans began to take it for granted that the United States and the Soviet Union bore approximately equal responsibility for the cold war which led so catastrophically to the division of Germany. With the liquidation of the cold war at long last, the need for the NATO alliance seemed less clear. So also did the necessity for the stationing of a large number of American troops on German soil.

The policies of detente and Ostpolitik produced hopes that were left unfulfilled. They were hopes nonetheless which would not fade. What was actually begun in the early 1970s was a longterm process of diminishing or undermining that bedrock of public support upon which the NATO alliance had so firmly rested since its inception in 1949. Tragically the process was abetted and accelerated by the terrible problems of indiscipline, racial conflict, and drugs among American troops in Germany. The appearance of poverty in the early '70s served also as an important catalyst. The conjunction of all these factors meant that a process of longterm atrophy in bedrock support for NATO and the American presence was set in motion in Germany. And, as events have shown, that bedrock support could never be reproduced. The fruition of the process was shown clearly in the deeply divisive dispute over the stationing of a new generation of nuclear missiles on German soil in the 1980s.

Notes

[1] Congressional Quarterly, U.S. Defense Policy: Weapons, Strategy and Commitments, 2nd edition, (Washington: Congressional Quarterly, Inc., 1980), pp. 124, 127. See also Military Manpower Task Force: A Report to the President on the Status and Prospects of the All Volunteer Force, Department of Defense, October, 1982, pp. IV-1,2.

[2] Kenneth J. Coffey, Strategic Implications of the All-Volunteer Force: The Conventional Defense of Central Europe, (Chapel Hill: The University of North Carolina Press, 1979), pp. 116-117. See also United States Security Agreements and Commitments Abroad: United States Forces in Europe, Hearings Before the Subcommittee on United States Security Agreements and Commitments Abroad of the Committee on Foreign Relations, U.S. Senate,

1970, pp.2061-2069.

[3] Hanson W. Baldwin, Strategy for Tomorrow (New York: Harper and Row, 1970), p. 141.

[4] Kenneth J. Coffey, op. cit., p. 117.

[5] See Statement of Lawrence J. Korb, Assistant Secretary of Defense for Manpower, Reserve Affairs and Logistics, in Toward A Consensus on Military Service: Report of the Atlantic Council's Working Group on Military Service, Andrew J. Goodpaster and Lloyd H. Elliot, Jr., eds. (Elmsford, N.Y.: Pergamon Press, 1982), p. 266.

[6] Kenneth J. Coffey, op. cit., p. 136.

[7] "Playing Nuclear Poker," TIME Magazine, January 31, 1983, p. 11.

[8] Richard M. Nixon, "The All-Volunteer Force," in The Military Draft, Martin Anderson, ed. (Stanford, Calif.: Hoover Institution Press, 1982), p. 604.

[9] The President's Commission on an All-Volunteer Force, The Report of the President's Commission on an All-Volunteer Armed Force (Washington, D.C.: Government Printing Office, 1970); hereafter cited as Gates Commission Report.

[10] Gates Commission Report, 1970. The "Debate" Section of the Report is reproduced in The Military Draft, Martin Anderson, ed. (Stanford, Calif.: Hoover Institution Press, 1982), pp. 611-619.

[11] "National Service, the Draft, and Volunteers: A Debate," in Registration and the Draft, Martin Anderson, ed. (Stanford,Calif.: Hoover Institution Press, 1982), p. 190, 205-206.

[12] Congressional Record, Senate, November 9, 1979, p.S16376.

[13] Department of Defense, Defense Report on President Nixon's Strategy for Peace, Statement of Secretary of Defense Melvin R. Laird before the House Armed Services Committee on Fiscal Years 1972-1976 Defense Program and 1972 Defense Budget, March 9, 1971, p. 77.

[14] "Die deutschen Devisenausgleichs-Abkommen mit den USA," DPA Hintergrund, Archiv- und Informationsmaterial, (Hamburg: Deutsche Presse Agentur, Gmbh, 3 November, 1971), p.5. Also John Newhouse, U.S. Troops in Europe: Issues, Costs, and Choices, (Washington: The Brookings Institution, 1971), p.130.

[15] "Die deutschen Devisenausgleichs-Abkommen mit den USA," p. 5.; Newhouse, pp. 130-131.

[16] Ibid.

[17] "Der höchste Devisenausgleich, den es je gab," Wehr und Wirtschaft, Jr. 16, Nr. 1, (1972), S. 15.

[18] See Süddeutsche Zeitung (München), January 8, 1971.

[19] Der Tagesspiegel (Berlin), March 16, 1973.

[20] Stuttgarter Nachrichten, July 31, 1971.

[21] Stuttgarter Zeitung, August 7, 1931.

[22] Stuttgarter Zeitung, August 20, 1971.

[23] Vorwärts, (Bonn), August 26, 1971.

[24] Neue Württembergische Zeitung, (Göppingen), September, 14, 1971.

[25] Kölner Stadt-Anzeiger, September 14, 1971.

[26] Nürnberger Nachrichten, September 16, 1971.

[27] Stuttgarter Zeitung, September 14, 1971.

[28] Stuttgarter Zeitung, (Nr. 233), September 20, 1971.

[29] Ibid.

[30] Vorwärts, (Bonn), November 18, 1971.

[31] International Herald Tribune, (Paris), November 20, 1971.

[32] Frankfurter Rundschau, November 3, 1971.

[33] The Guardian, (London), November 12, 1971; International Herald Tribune, (Paris), November 13, 1971.

[34] International Herald Tribune, (Paris), November 20, 1971.

[35] Binkin, et. al. Blacks and the Military, Table 3-1, p. 42, and table 3-9, p. 60.

[36] International Herald Tribune, (Paris), November 13, 1971.

[37] International Herald Tribune, (Paris), November 13, 1971.

[38] International Herald Tribune, (Paris), November 13, 1971. See also The Daily Telegraph, (London), September 16, 1971, and International Herald Tribune, October 25, 1971.

[39] International Herald Tribune, (Paris), December 6, 1971.

[40] International Herald Tribune, (Paris), November 20, 1971.

[41] Possible confusion arises during this period because of two senior commanders with the same last name. The Commander in Chief of the U.S. Army Europe (USAREUR) was General Michael S. Davison. The Deputy Chief of Staff for Personnel at Headquarters, USAREUR, was General Frederic E. Davison, the highest ranking black in the U.S. Army.

[42] The Christian Science Monitor, February 3, 1972.

[43] Ibid.

[44] International Herald Tribune, (Paris), May 28, 1972.

[45] Frankfurter Rundschau, June 2, 1972.

[46] Stuttgarter Zeitung, August 15, 1972.

[47] Stuttgarter Nachrichten, August 14, 1972.

[48] See Der Spiegel, October 2, 1971; also International Herald Tribune, August 16, 1972, Stuttgarter Zeitung, August 14, 1972, Stuttgarter Zeitung, August 16, 1972, The Times, (London), August 14, 1972.

[49] Stuttgarter Zeitung, August 31, 1972.

[50] Südwest Presse, (Ulm), September 15, 1972.

[51] International Herald Tribune, August 17, 1972.

[52] International Herald Tribune, September 26, 1972.

[53] Saarbrücker Zeitung, October 28, 1972.

[54] Die Welt, October 21, 1972.

[55] Augsburger Allgemeine, October 27, 1972.

[56] Berliner Morgenpost, December 20, 1972.

[57] International Herald Tribune, December 20, 1972.

[58] Binkin, et. al., Blacks and the Military, table 3-1, p. 42.

[59] Saarbrücker Zeitung, August 5, 1973.

[60] Münchener Merkur, January 22, 1973.

[61] Wiesbadener Kurier, September 27, 1972.

[62] Allgemeine Zeitung, (Mainz), September 26, 1972.

[63] Wiesbadener Kurier, March 14, 1972.

[64] Frankfurter Allgemeine, March 14, 1972.

[65] Nürnberger Nachrichten, July 26, 1973.

[66] International Herald Tribune, August 29, 1973.
[67] Süddeutsche Zeitung, September 14, 1973.
[68] Neue Revue, August 27, 1973.
[69] Augsburger Allgemeine, October 31, 1973.
[70] Ibid.
[71] Kölnische Rundschau, July 16, 1973.

5

THE AVF
1973-1985

Hopes for Renewal and Rehabilitation

The final segment of our historical analysis of American forces in Germany treats the period from 1973 to the mid-1980s. If the preceding period from 1967 to 1973 portrays a slump into a dark canyon of problems, indeed the nadir of the American military presence, the final period is one of slow and painful reconstruction. As we have seen, American forces in 1973 were beset with gargantuan problems of morale, drug abuse, indiscipline, and shortages of manpower and equipment. At the same time, however, some new beginnings had been initiated by the Pentagon and the senior commanders in Europe, notably General Michael Davison. A sense of new hope and of renewal seemed to permeate the air. Part of the reason for the new spirit was the launching of an entirely new regime with the transition from conscript forces to the All Volunteer Force in 1973. Though the Germans as well as the Americans harbored latent fears that the new AVF regime might well produce larger problems than it solved, still a new regime always brings hope for a new day, a better future.

There were also many other encouraging signs at the beginning of this period. The Vietnam War officially ended with the signing of the Paris Agreements in 1973. The last contingent of American troops was withdrawn from Vietnam the same year, creating hope that America could now turn its full attention to clearing up the difficulties in the forces in Europe. With the Vietnam imbroglio liquidated, there was reason to believe that many of the problems in Europe which were a spinoff of the misfired Asian adventure could be positively and forthrightly corrected. The end of the antiwar movement could be expected to boost morale by liquidating the major source of youthful disillusionment. Chronic shortages of officers and senior noncommissioned officers in Europe could be rectified by the return of veterans from the Asian theater. East-West detente was securely in place, bringing hope for a new era of international relations. Not only had the SALT treaty and a series of other agreements between the superpowers been signed, Bonn was a party to a network of agreements with Moscow, Warsaw, and East Berlin in the complementary Ostpolitik structure. The Quadripartite Treaty on Berlin had normalized relations around the city that had often served as a flashpoint of East-West tension. The Mansfield initiative to withdraw substantial numbers of troops from Germany seemed to have reached its peak and to have crested with the defeat in the Senate in 1973. No doubt the redoubtable senator would try again, but meanwhile the steam seemed to have evaporated from the movement. Riots and rebellions in both Germany and the United States had largely ended, though in the case of West Germany, an egregious residue had been left behind in the form of a violent terrorist movement. With a new set of policies in place for U.S. forces, there was sanguine expectation that the worst problems of the recent past could be solved. Despite the optimism, however, there was also good reason for caution. Though the transition to the AVF held promise of improvement in the morale and readiness of U.S. forces, it also created uncertainty, since no one really knew whether or how well the AVF would succeed. For the U.S. military as well as for the German government it was a case of hoping for the best.

The Final Struggle over Offset Payments

During the first few years of the period under review the offset payments problem continued to cause severe strains in German-American relations. The seventh offset agreement, covering the two year period from mid-1971 to mid-1973, was scheduled to expire June 30, 1973. Early in the year both governments began posturing in an effort to stake out strong bargaining positions in what were expected to be exceedingly difficult negotiations. In February Paul Volcker, Undersecretary of the Treasury for Monetary Affairs, stated in an interview with German journalists that the recent devaluation of the dollar would very likely lead to American demands for a greater German contribution to offset arrangements. If the Germans wished to counter growing pressure in Congress for cutting down on foreign aid and military commitments, he said, they would be well advised to prepare for a greater assumption of the burden of the common defense.[1] The West German Finance Minister, Helmut Schmidt, attempted early on to keep American demands to a minimum. "Not a pfennig," he was quoted as having said. *TIME* Magazine reported that Schmidt was in "an unusually arrogant mood. In what may or may not be a negotiating tactic, he has told other officials that congressional sentiment in favor of the Mansfield Amendment to reduce troops does not matter, that Nixon has pledged to keep all troops in Europe and will do so even if the Germans refuse all payments."[2]

Despite Schmidt's alleged views, it was clear to both sides that there was a close connection between the offset negotiations and the Mansfield initiative to withdraw troops. As the *Christian Science Monitor* put it, "The West German Government knows full well that unless it makes an extra effort, Congress may well decide unilaterally to pull out some American troops."[3] In addition to the Mansfield movement, the American side was burdened with a constantly weakening dollar, since by the spring of 1973 international exchange rates were beginning to float freely, exposing the weakness the dollar had accumulated over the last several years. Estimates of the decline in the dollar's real value during the two years of the previous offset agreement ranged between twenty and thirty percent. Though the Germans realized that they would have little choice than to stand good for the increased dollar costs of stationing American troops in Germany, they still believed that Germany should not assume the entire burden of the American economic difficulties which had caused the dollar's slide.

Round after round of negotiations were held during the first half of 1973 at various levels, involving at various times the finance ministers, defense ministers, and foreign ministers of both governments. Even Chancellor Brandt's meeting with President Nixon in April failed to bring the two sides closer together. Given the sensitive and highly volatile nature of the negotiations, both countries attempted to shroud the talks in complete secrecy. The Germans feared that reports of a rising tide of anti-Americanism in Germany would fuel the Mansfield drive in Congress. The American negotiators feared not only the effects of the Mansfield initiative but also the effects on German public opinion of ever escalating demands on the German treasury for American troops. The press in both countries tended to portray the negotiations as a giant poker game played out in rooms hidden from public view. As with any set of delicate negotiations, however, exposure to public view would only produce grandstand tactics, hardening positions on both sides. The seventh agreement quietly expired on June 30 with no prospects of a new agreement in sight.

In mid-July it was reported that Washington would demand at least 8.2 billion marks in the next agreement, which would be 1.6 billion marks more than the previous agreement.[4] The German government's initial reaction caused no surprise. "Bonn Says the Amount is Unjustified," was the headline in one newspaper.[5] According to some accounts Washington had even demanded that West Germany must now pay the total foreign exchange costs of American forces, in contrast to the 80 percent figure which had been agreed upon in the previous agreement.[6] Complicating the negotiations was the matter of German arms purchases, which had taken up a large share of most previous offset agreements. In the German view the arsenal was overfilled already and could not be overloaded with unnecessary weapons. Delivery of the 175 Phantom jet aircraft and 50 CH-53 helicopters Germany had purchased under the previous agreement would extend well into the late 1970s, limiting the scope of future arms purchases. As far as helping the American balance of payments was concerned, officials in Bonn argued that West Germany had already made a substantial contribution by successive revaluations of the German mark in December, 1971, and March, 1973, and by piling up huge reserves of unwanted American dollars during the period of fixed exchange rates, thus helping to finance part of the American balance of payments deficits. In addition Germany had made substantial contributions to the NATO defense improvement program.

The negotiations were further strained by the Yom Kippur war in the Middle East. The German government sharply protested U.S. arms shipments to Israel from West German bases. This was answered with a stern rebuke from President Nixon and administration hints that American military and diplomatic commitments to Germany perhaps ought to be reduced. The cumulative difficulties of course increased pressure in Congress to withdraw some of the troops from Germany, the tactic always used to club the Germans into submission. As one reporter saw it, "Now, more than ever, money may have to replace America's diminishing goodwill in keeping large numbers of troops in West Germany."[7] As the negotiations dragged on interminably without results, the tone became decidedly more negative on both sides. The Germans were angered by what they considered to be unnecessary American intransigence. In an interview in which he characterized the American demands as simply beyond the pale of reality, Defense Minister Georg Leber reminded the Americans that "the presence of the U.S.A. in Europe is not a labor of love for the Europeans; it is in the Americans' own interest."[8] Chancellor Brandt was described as "just plain angry" over the exorbitant American demands.[9]

In November American leverage in the negotiations was increased when Congress passed the so-called Jackson-Nunn Amendment as part of the defense budget bill. According to the amendment American troops, beginning in 1976, must be withdrawn from European NATO countries in the same percentage that the foreign governments failed to cover the American balance of payments deficit arising from the foreign exchange costs of the stationing of American troops. If, for example, a government failed to cover 20% of the foreign exchange costs, then 20% of the troops would be withdrawn to the United States. Threatening as it was, the Jackson-Nunn Amendment culminated a successful effort to soften and hence blunt the Mansfield effort to withdraw troops in a wholesale fashion. Though the Nixon administration was strongly opposed to the provisions of the amendment, it nevertheless accepted it as a substitute for the proposed Mansfield legislation. The German government, as might be expected, resented the amendment deeply, since it presented the Germans with an all or nothing choice: agree to complete coverage of American foreign exchange costs or standby as the Americans unilaterally withdrew some of the forces. Though the amendment increased the pressure on the German negotiators substantially, there can be little doubt that resentment of the amendment increased the level of the German government's intransigence. To many observers it appeared that the Americans were prepared to use any device to force the Germans into submission for security measures which benefitted the United States fully as much as West Germany. Did the Americans believe that budgetary appropriations for foreign troops could be pulled out of a hat with no particular difficulty for the Germans? In addition, the German government was worried that the huge new bills for imported Middle East oil, the price of which had tripled in 1973, would inevitably call for greater stringency in all budget decisions. According to Defense Minister Georg Leber, "Europe's ability to pay has limits, which one in America ought to be able to see."[10]

Month after month went by with no progress in the negotiations. In February, 1974, the gaps between the two sides appeared to be as great as ever. The Americans were still demanding $3.3 billion for the two year period, while the Germans were offering $1.3 billion. The Americans argued that German contributions to NATO were entirely insufficient, since U.S. citizens afforded twice as much for defense per capita as German citizens. In addition, the Germans had for years been gaining a foreign exchange surplus from American forces which was unjustifiable and must be completely offset. The Germans pointed out that since 1961 they had paid no less than 34.5 billion marks to the American treasury for the stationing of American forces. They argued that the United States no longer had a net balance of payments deficit, partly because of dollar devaluations which adversely affected West Germany's trade with the U.S. and partly because of revaluations of the German mark which compounded the effect. Second, they argued, the West German armed forces could not absorb mass arms purchases at the time. In addition, the past practice of granting longterm bank credits to the United States no longer made sense because of the surplus in the American balance of payments.[11]

In March, 1974, a number of high level meetings were held in which the offset payments problem was one of the major topics of discussion. Secretary of State Kissinger met with Chancellor Brandt in Bonn in the early part of the month. The decisive breakthrough came in mid-March when Finance Minister Helmut Schmidt travelled to Washington for intensive consultations with Secretary of the Treasury George Schultz. The basic principles of the new agreement were drawn up, with details to be filled in by lower level negotiations in the coming weeks. Finally, in late April, the eighth offset agreement was signed in Bonn by American Ambassador Martin Hillenbrand and Minister Director Peter Hermes of the German foreign ministry. The agreement was made retroactive to July 1, 1973, when the previous agreement had expired, and extended for the two year period from 1973 until June 30, 1975. The total amount agreed upon was $2.2 billion or DM 5.92 billion, to be divided as follows: 2.75 billion marks would be used for German military purchases in the United States; 600 million marks would be applied to the program to renovate American facilities in Germany; 300 million marks would be used for civilian purchases of high technology goods or services, such as uranium processing facilities or other joint projects for scientific-technical cooperation; 20 million marks would be calculated as a contribution through German agreement to abolish landing fees and other taxes for military aircraft at German civilian airports; 2.25 billion marks would be used to purchase U.S. Government securities at preferential interest rates. Most of the devices had been used in previous agreements. The major new feature of the 1973 agreement was the provision for German purchase of civilian rather than purely military goods and services and for joint cooperation projects in high energy technology.[12] The Germans could take considerable delight in the fact that the agreement would cost them 700 million marks less than 6.65 billion marks they had paid under the previous agreement for 1971-73. And both sides could breathe a sigh of relief that the ordeal was over and an agreement had been struck. In a joint statement the two governments characterized the agreement as "a visible and convincing example of German-American cooperation within the framework of the alliance."[13]

One major reason for the smaller amount of the eighth offset agreement was the changed exchange rate between the currencies. During the negotiations Schmidt and Schultz had agreed to calculate the exchange rate at 2.67 German marks for the dollar, down from 3.5 marks two years earlier. The Americans accepted, at least partially, the German contention that the devalued dollar and revalued mark not only affected German-American trade to U.S. advantage but that the stronger mark and weaker dollar meant that the German payment would logically be less than before the currency realignments. The agreement, as expected, met with mixed reviews in the press. The *International Herald Tribune* editorialized that, "It represents a sensible, workable compromise on a delicate issue after arduous negotiation; an example of exactly the kind of cooperation that has long been lacking in the NATO alliance but that is imperative for its effectiveness and long-run survival.[14] Newspapers in Germany, the United States, and Britain wondered whether the new agreement would satisfy Congress enough to defuse the troop withdrawal agreement. According to the *London Financial Times*, "it looks as if the two sides have spent nearly nine months since the previous agreement expired working out a patchwork solution which a hostile Congress would be quite capable of tearing to pieces. The agreement may make President Nixon's task a little easier, but it looks as if Congress will take a lot of convincing." The British also tended to take a dim view of the offset payments program altogether. Huffed the *Times*, "The British recognised the potential absurdity of the position some time ago and simply abandoned the regular haggle with Bonn over offset payments. The present Anglo-German agreement runs for five years, includes only a small straight budgetary payment by the Germans to the Exchequer, and accepts that defence co-operation is a two way process of benefit to both countries.[15]

Both governments were relieved that the offset payments wrangle was over for a while. The respite was, however, uncomfortably short, since the agreement had been signed only fourteen months before it was scheduled to expire on June 30, 1975. When it did expire, new negotiations had not even begun, though the German government meanwhile had staked out a strong position. The Germans made it clear that, in their view, changed circumstances made any new offset payment superfluous and that thirty years after World War II they no longer felt obliged to buy their way into full membership in NATO or the international community. Surprisingly there was little pressure from the American side to renew the negotiations. In late June Chancellor Schmidt said that he did not consider negotiations for a new agreement "a pressing problem at the moment." Though his statement drew an immediate threat by Senator Sam Nunn to introduce legislation that could force either a new agreement or U.S. troop cuts, the Ford administration countered with a number of statements to the effect that negotiations would be entered into in due time and that reserves of good will on both sides lessened the salience of the issue.[16] Quite clearly, the controversy over the offset payments issue had to some extent been defused by changes in the international monetary system and an improved political climate for German-American relations. In addition, both governments were more anxious than usual that the potential dispute not receive much public attention nor be perceived as a major rift between the two nations. In late May President Ford sent a communication to Congress which asserted that the balance of payments cost of stationing American troops in Europe for the year 1974 had amounted to 1.99 billion dollars. Against that sum the Germans had agreed to pay $2.2 billion for 1974-75 and had already purchased $1.15 billion worth of military equipment, while other NATO allies had purchased $917 worth of equipment. The administration, consequently, was not giving any consideration to withdrawing troops from Europe.[17]

As the weeks went by with no new negotiations it became clear that the matter of a new offset agreement had in fact become moot. The reform of the international monetary system, especially the adoption of floating exchange rates, had largely halted the drain on U.S. gold reserves and helped put the U.S. balance of payments into surplus. Moreover, the balance of payments cost of U.S. troops in Germany now appeared small compared to such international capital flows as the billions of dollars flowing to the Middle East for purchase of more expensive oil or the billions of petrodollars being recycled from OPEC countries into U.S. banks. The quadrupled price of oil also meant more severe budgetary problems for Germany, a country much more dependent upon imported oil than the United States. It was obvious to both sides that, given the growing capabilities of the Warsaw Pact, NATO was faced with much more serious business than quarrels over offset payments.

Quietly the offset payments issue faded into the background. Larger issues concerning strategy and planning within NATO took precedence as time went on. Defense Secretary Schlesinger's visit to Bonn in September resulted in an unusually conciliatory communique which said only that a "satisfactory solution" to the payments problem would not be difficult and that "new mechanisms will have to be created at the highest level."[18] A few days later it became clear that the new mechanisms involved all the European NATO partners, not just West Germany, in an attempt to modernize and strengthen allied forces through the new NATO defense improvement program. In lieu of offset payments to the United States Bonn agreed to increase substantially its contributions to the common NATO defense improvement program and the infrastructure program.[19] In addition, far reaching changes in the composition of American forces, required by the Jackson-Nunn legislation of 1974 discussed below, were being drawn up by defense planners, and the first plans for German participation in the new venture were under consideration.

The matter of offset payments was finally laid to rest definitively when Chancellor Schmidt visited President Ford in Washington in mid-July, 1976. In a joint declaration the two statesmen declared that offset payments were a thing of the past and that no new payments agreement would be negotiated. The declaration also noted that Bonn had agreed to make a onetime payment of 171.2 million marks for the construction of facilities for a new American combat brigade in northern Germany. The declaration was greeted with delight, relief, and unabashed joy in headlines in newspapers all over Germany. Some commentators believed, with somewhat inflated expectations, that the end of the offset payments regime would bring about fresh new understanding between Germany and the United States on all issues relating to Western security.[20] A more sober and realistic assessment was made by the *International Herald Tribune*:

> Politically and psychologically, the offset agreements were always unfortunate, even when a necessity financially. To Germans, they resembled the occupation costs paid immediately after the war and they represented an onerous tax burden. U.S. threats to withdraw troops if offset payments were reduced made it appear that the troops were there entirely to serve German interests, rather than as part of a common NATO defense that protects U.S. security.....There was no good solution to this problem. But what has happened now, without most Americans realizing it, is that the problem has virtually disappeared.....The end of the offset era undoubtedly will benefit the political fortunes of Schmidt in the approaching West German elections. But the United States may prove the greater beneficiary in the end. The troop costs and balance of payments deficits of the past two decades have clouded thinking in the United States about the true security interests of the country.....From a budgetary point of view, it costs no more to maintain U.S. forces in Europe than in the United States-and may even cost somewhat less.[21]

No one on either side of the Atlantic mourned the demise of the offset payments issue. The final liquidation of the frustrating matter meant simply that statesmen could focus their energies on the more pressing problems of the alliance relationship. Two postscripts to the account should, however, be noted. Following the election of Jimmy Carter as U.S. president in November, 1976, a flurry of reports circulated in Germany that the new administration was giving serious consideration to a resumption of demands for offset payments. A great deal of temporary, albeit unnecessary worry was expended by the German press in late 1976 and early 1977.[22] Fortunately, nothing ever came of the matter. When no statements from the Carter administration were forthcoming on the offset payments issue, the German press quickly shifted its attention to the implications for Germany of Carter's troop withdrawals from Korea. In an altered form the payments issue reappeared in late 1980 with the appearance of the eight-point Stoessel Plan, discussed below. Embedded in the new document was a series of new American demands for various kinds of payments by Germany to the United States. The most important of these was a demand for German payments to cover the cost of moving American troop units closer to the East German and Czechoslovak borders in keeping with new strategic concepts emerging in the Pentagon. The effort, as we shall see, led to the signing of the Wartime Host Nation Support Treaty in May, 1981. The rationale of the later negotiations rested, however, on an entirely different basis than that of the offset payments program of 1961-1975.

The Final Struggle over the Mansfield Initiative

Inextricably related to the offset payments issue was the issue of troop withdrawals. Led by Senator Mike Mansfield, the majority leader, the movement to withdraw troops gained greater momentum in the Senate in 1973, the beginning of the period under discussion, than at any time before or since. Several factors converged to force a basic reassessment of America's role in the world: disillusionment with the results of nearly a decade of heavy investment in the Vietnam War, growing balance of payments deficits, a precipitous decline in the value of the dollar since 1971, endless disputes over offset payments, growing isolationist sentiment in American public opinion, and growing sensitivity in Congress over what appeared to be European unwillingness to contribute adequately to the burdens of the common defense.

It is useful at this juncture to delineate the major arguments on both sides of the troop withdrawal issue. In Mansfield's view the presence of over a half million American troops in Europe more than a quarter of a century after World War II was militarily, economically, and politically unjustifiable. If the U.S. would only withdraw its troops from Western Europe, the Soviet Union would follow suit and withdraw its troops from Eastern Europe. Mansfield believed that the governments of Western Europe preferred to encourage anxieties "for the very purpose of keeping us in Europe." He resented their talk of interdependence at the same time that they erected barriers against American trade. "If you're going to have interdependence, it doesn't work in only one area," he said.[23]

In Vienna the preliminary talks for mutual and balanced force reductions (MBFR) were underway. Having been agreed to by the United States and the Soviet Union in 1972, the first official round of talks was scheduled to begin on October 1, 1973. In Mansfield's view nothing of substance would ever emerge from the MBFR talks; they were, at best, a propaganda exercise whose major purpose was to justify further American buildups as a bargaining chip. If America were really serious about fostering greater political and military cooperation among the states of Western Europe, it might take the shock treatment of American troop withdrawals to get the Europeans moving on the right path. The continued U.S. defense of Europe served merely to psychologically weaken and discourage the Europeans from taking charge of their own defense. To the argument that U.S. reduction of forces would lower the nuclear threshhold in war because of Soviet superiority in manpower and tanks, Mansfield replied that NATO strategy relied on the use of nuclear power at the outset of a war already; hence the removal of half the American troops would hardly alter the strategy. Neither as a symbolic force nor as a tripwire were such high levels of forces useful. In addition, Mansfield believed, one of the principal consequences of a U.S. reduction would be to expose more than ever the French military contradictions and stimulate France into realistic military cooperation with its European partners. As for the West Germans, removal of U.S. troops would not cause a shift to neutral policies. The Germans, Mansfield emphasized, had contingency plans ready in case of U.S. reductions, and it would not be for a few U.S. divisions that they would rush into the arms of the Soviet Union.[24]

The German government, of course, strenuously opposed the Mansfield initiative. In Germany every chancellor, every foreign minister, and every major political party leader had, without exception since the early 1950s, opposed American troop withdrawals. Given the shattering of the proposal for a European Defense Community in the mid-1950s, West Germany had no alternative but to enjoin its security with the NATO alliance. And with the endemic military weaknesses of some twelve to fourteen separate European states, either alone or in combination, the only hope for Western Europe to protect itself from Soviet military aggression or political blackmail was through the common arrangements of the NATO alliance. For NATO as a whole as well as specifically for West Germany, the credibility of NATO rested primarily on the military might of the United States. And the military prowess of the U.S., in turn, rested squarely on the deterrent value of American forces stationed in Germany, backed up by the American nuclear umbrella. If there were too great an imbalance between Soviet and American forces in central Europe, German political leaders argued, the Soviets might be tempted to undertake an aggression against Western Europe, which would surely begin in Germany. If the Soviets believed they could not swiftly and surely win a conventional war in the first few days, they would not run the risk of military confrontation. The guarantee that such a risk could not succeed was the presence of U.S. troops in substantial numbers on West German soil. In addition, the presence of the troops was the acid guarantee that Soviet aggression would engage the entire military might of the United States. Chancellor Brandt and other leading German political leaders often repeated the arguments of the U.S. army supreme commander in Germany that reduction of U.S. troop levels would inevitably lower the nuclear threshhold. Fewer troops meant the necessity of engaging nuclear weapons at an earlier stage of the conflict, in German eyes, and given the enormous fear of nuclear devastation in densely populated Germany, the country was well served with the presence of as many American troops as the U.S. government could afford to send.

Mansfield's opponents and the German government tended also to put much more stock in a successful outcome of the Vienna MBFR talks than Senator Mansfield. The Germans believed, at any rate, that serious and intensive talks should be given every chance to succeed, and that any unilateral American withdrawal of troops from Germany outside of a mutual withdrawal formula agreed to at Vienna would doom the talks from the very beginning. Indeed, many German leaders deeply resented the Mansfield initiative for the effect they believed it would inevitably have on Soviet leaders. Why should Soviet leaders negotiate in good faith in Vienna, if they could achieve one of their major objectives, namely, a withdrawal of U.S. troops from Europe, through unilateral action by the U.S. Congress? If Mansfield would only keep quiet, the Vienna talks might indeed have a good chance to succeed. As for arguments that troop withdrawals would foster better European economic and military cooperation, German leaders, though heavily committed to the process of European integration, realized that the era of true military integration was still a long way off. There were far too many latent European suspicions of a strong role for German forces in any arrangements for European defense to hope for integrated military arrangements at present. Under such circumstances, any attempt to accelerate European unification by simply handing over to the Europeans the responsibility for their own defense, confident that their will to survive would make them overcome their difficulties, was likely to be counter-productive. As far as the French were concerned, German leaders believed that American attempts to force the French to cooperate militarily with the Germans and the British were doomed to failure. Given strong Gaullist traditions of French independence from European neighbors, even NATO, American attempts to bludgeon the French would surely backfire.

German leaders feared, perhaps more than anything else, a withdrawal of the United States into a new period of isolationism, leaving the Europeans to fend for themselves. They saw in the Mansfield program a retreat into the kind of isolationism which would be exceedingly dangerous for the world of the 1970s, since it would lead eventually to a decoupling of the Europeans from the Americans. Such a decoupling would represent for the Soviets the achievement of one of their primary diplomatic objectives since the founding of NATO. The Germans also resented Mansfield's suggestions that Germany was not bearing its fair share of the burdens of the common defense. For German political leaders the negotiation of seven offset agreements dating back to 1961 represented a substantial drain on the German treasury and a heavy political and economic burden that the Germans had carried for twelve years with precious little complaint. Though there were obvious differences on the offset issue, the Americans ought to realize that quarrels among friends about who was paying too much were not unusual. Indeed, the very fact that the Germans were willing to assume a new burden of offset payments every two years ought to be a powerful demonstration of Germany's desire for good relations with the United States and of her desire to contribute more than any other ally to the common defense. Why should Germany be penalized for her unfortunate geography? Soviet forces were not, after all, massed on the French, the Italian, the Dutch or the Danish border. They were primarily massed in East Germany, so that logically the American forces had to be stationed on West German soil. But did this geographical fact of life then mean that the Germans must alone bear the burden of paying the Americans for their military presence?

Finally, German leaders found it necessary to remind Senator Mansfield and his supporters that the stationing of

American forces on German soil was not only, or even primarily for the defense of West Germany. Their presence served, in the first instance, the national interest of the United States. Withdrawal of forces from Europe would mean that the forward defense of the United States, instead of being at the Czech and East German borders, would be the coastline of Manhattan Island. In statement after statement the German leaders emphasized that the deterrent power of NATO had been successful in keeping the peace in Europe for a quarter of a century and that the risk of diminishing this deterrent entailed enormous security risks for the United States, as well as for Germany and Europe.[25]

The German press covered the debate in the U.S. Senate with uncommon interest. With few exceptions the Mansfield efforts were portrayed in highly negative terms. "Mansfield's Childlike Faith," said the *Stuttgarter Zeitung*, could lead to a terrible disaster. "The Senate majority leader has always been unusually productive when it comes to peddling dangerous nonsense on defense matters."[26] Though the press in South Germany denounced the Mansfield initiative in stronger terms than that in other parts of the country, the commentary in the *Bayern Kurier*, under the headline "Senator Mansfield's Monotonous Melody," was far from exceptional. In the opinion of the *Kurier*:

> What would happen to a singer who year after year, for a decade or longer, performed the same simple song, perhaps with a few variations of the text, but always with the same melody and tenaciously with the same refrain? The answer to the question is not hard to figure out, for everyone who could endure such a performance would not grant to a troubador, who could think of nothing further, the chance to climb above the lowest rungs on the ladder of reputation.....Similarly, in the realm of politics,...how is it possible that month after month the NATO partners have to endure Senator Mansfield, who unflaggingly and with the monotonous rhythm of a Tibetan prayer wheel pleads for the withdrawal of troops of his country from European soil?.....Internal political strategy cannot be satisfied with the exploitation of the Watergate affair, but turns now massively to foreign strategy, where ignorance and naivete mix to produce a dangerous poison.....The consciousness of Americans, which once seemed to concentrate on the attempt to guarantee freedom to humanity, seems now to succumb to the erroneous belief that

> detente with the Soviets brings peaceful, harmonious relations not only between the U.S. and the U.S.S.R., but peace to all the world.....Thereby the lessons so painfully learned by the previous generation may simply be forgotten, that the expansionary drive of a totalitarian power cannot be assuaged by the simple recognition of its present gains.[27]

The troop withdrawal issue was debated in both houses of Congress throughout the summer and fall of 1973. In the Senate the Mansfield-Symington forces seemed to gain ground steadily. In different versions a withdrawal amendment was passed by the Armed Services Committee and the Foreign Relations Committee. Finally on September 26, 1973, the full Senate by a vote of 48 to 36 passed an amendment calling for a reduction of overseas troops by 188,000 men, of which 110,000 would come from Germany. This was the culmination of the Mansfield initiative. The victory was, however, shortlived. In the House of Representatives the sentiment for withdrawing troops from Europe never commanded anything near a majority. Despite herculean efforts by Representative Ron Dellums (D-CA) and House majority leader Thomas P. O'Neill, amendments to various bills were beaten back repeatedly during the summer and early fall. Troop reduction amendments represented a wholly new approach in the House, where attempts to cut back various weapons programs had repeatedly been defeated. With manpower costs by this time accounting for 56 percent of the defense budget, the O'Neill forces decided to concentrate this time on attempting to cut military manpower levels. Their political premise was that a House that historically had been unwilling to challenge the military judgment on weapons might be more willing to make reductions in an area that politicians felt they knew best, personnel. The two most crucial votes in the House came on July 31, when two amendments to the military procurement bill were defeated. First, by a vote of 339 to 67, the Dellums Amendment to cut all overseas troops by one-half was defeated. The critical vote came on an amendment offered by majority leader O'Neill to reduce the army and air force by one fifth, or approximately 100,000 men, with all the reduction to be made in troops stationed at overseas bases. The amendment was defeated, 242-163, as the Republicans succeeded in pushing through a substitute calling upon the House Armed Services Committee to make a study of the feasibility of maintaining forces abroad, with suggested numbers, in all parts of the world.

With the House and Senate in disagreement the two versions of the defense procurement bill went to a conference committee.

In these negotiations the Mansfield forces proved to be particularly intractable. Since the earlier Senate vote approving the troop withdrawal amendment was a victory of such historic and enormous dimensions, Senator Mansfield was determined to preserve the prize at almost any cost. The House conferees were, however, equally determined that the Senator's dangerously risky policy not be allowed to succeed. Following protracted and bitter negotiations, the logjam was finally broken on October 11 by the acceptance of a substitute amendment offered by Senators Henry Jackson (D-WA) and Sam Nunn (D-GA). The Jackson-Nunn amendment required U.S. troop levels in NATO countries to be cut proportionately to any shortfall in offsetting remittances. Thus, if offset purchases or payments should equal only 75 percent of the balance of payments deficit attributed to troop stationing in a given country, the U.S. force level in that country would be reduced to 75 percent of its present level. Though the Nixon administration strenuously opposed both the Mansfield and the Jackson-Nunn initiatives, it reluctantly accepted the Jackson-Nunn amendment as the lesser of the two evils. Quite obviously the amendment applied primarily to West Germany, though it could be applied as a sanction against any NATO country where U.S. troops were stationed.

The 1973 votes represented the culmination of the Mansfield initiative. In the ensuing months the prevailing winds began definitely to blow in another direction. The new offset payments agreement signed in spring, 1974, undercut arguments that the Germans were unwilling to pay for the upkeep of American troops. Nixon reported to Congress in May that the new offset agreement with Germany and arrangements under negotiation with other NATO countries adequately fulfilled the requirements of the Jackson-Nunn amendment and that there was consequently no reason to contemplate any troop withdrawals from Europe.[28] Secretary of State Kissinger's prestige rose to an all time high with his successes in Middle East diplomacy, and few senators were anxious to weaken his bargaining position prior to a planned trip to Moscow with Nixon. There was also considerable hope that the Moscow trip would produce some concrete progress in reference to the MBFR talks in Vienna. In addition, there seemed to be by 1974 a marked increase in congressional suspicion of the Soviet Union and the whole idea of detente.

In May the House of Representatives decisively defeated a troop withdrawal proposal by 240 to 163. Hence, when Mansfield, this time with Senator Alan Cranston of California, introduced a new troop withdrawal amendment to the military procurement bill in early June, the time seemed anything but ripe. The initiative was defeated in two separate votes on June 6.

The first proposal, which would have cut overseas forces by 125,000, failed by a vote of 54 to 35. A second amendment to reduce the number of army and air force troops overseas from 433,000 to 357,000, a 76,000 reduction during the next eighteen months, was beaten by a vote of 46 to 44. Prior to the vote Mr. Kissinger had warned in a letter to Senator John Stennis, chairman of the Armed Services Committee, that a major troop reduction overseas could undermine negotiations with the Soviet Union for mutual reductions in Vienna, as well as jeopardize efforts to achieve a permanent peace in Asia. The Secretary also pointed out that the United States already had cut its troop levels in Europe from around 400,000 in the early 1960s to about 300,00 by 1974, while in the same period Soviet forces in Eastern Europe had increased from 475,000 to 575,000.[29] Given the changing winds in the Senate, the defeat of the Mansfield initiatives this time occasioned no surprise. The final *coup de grace,* however, came in the form of new amendments offered by Senator Nunn for major restructuring of U.S. forces in Germany by abolishing a number of support units and replacing them with combat units, as explained below. By changing and refocusing the debate on U.S. forces in Europe, the substitute amendments took the remaining wind out of the sails of the Mansfield initiative. In the spring of 1975 the illusion of the Paris Peace agreements was shattered with the total collapse of South Vietnam. That event clearly sounded the death knell of the Mansfield effort, as congressional attention shifted rather swiftly from the disaster in Asia to the security situation in Europe.

Changes in the Structure of U.S. Forces

Some rather far-reaching changes in the structure of U.S. forces in Germany were undertaken in the years 1974-1977. Impetus for the changes came from both the Pentagon and Congress. At the Pentagon Defense Secretary James Schlesinger, together with certain planning staffs and senior military officers, completed work on a restructuring plan by early 1974. In Congress the changes were strongly supported, and to some extent generated by Senator Sam Nunn (D-GA). The Germans were first informed that such changes might be forthcoming in April, 1974, during an unofficial visit to Bonn by Secretary Schlesinger. Since the Germans were likely to be highly suspicious of any major changes in U.S. force posture, Schlesinger's report was coupled with strong reassurances that changes would not mean a decrease of defensive capability or a reduction of the fighting strength of U.S. forces. Following a study trip to Europe Senator Nunn in early April submitted a restructuring plan to the Senate Armed Services Committee. In

July the Brookings Institution published a book which detailed the logic and rationale of the proposed plans. Entitled *U.S. Force Structure in NATO: An Alternative*, the study was written by Colonel Richard D. Lawrence, commanding officer of the First Brigade of the First Cavalry Division at Fort Hood, Texas, and Jeffrey Record, a Brookings research associate who had previously served as a staff member in Senator Nunn's office.[30]

The Brookings study aroused major interest both in the American military policy planning community and in Germany. Many German newspapers carried summaries of the book together with commentaries suggesting that the proposed changes might indeed be translated into official policy. The study was influential in raising the debate on the structure of U.S. forces in Germany to a place high on the policy planning agenda. Not since the 1950s had there been such ferment over the subject. According to the authors, American forces in Germany were in the wrong place to fight the wrong war, using false assumptions about the duration and intensity of the war most likely to take place. The origin of this military problem, they pointed out, was political. When Germany was divided into occupation zones in the closing months of World War II, the U.S. forces were placed in southern Germany. They had simply remained there ever since and, according to NATO plans, were charged with defending the Fulda Gap and the Hof Corridor, the main invasion routes to Frankfurt and Nuremburg from the East. As Soviet and Warsaw Pact abilities expanded, this situation became more and more of an anomoly. In Lawrence and Record's analysis, Soviet armies were geared for a high-velocity offensive aimed at overrunning Western Europe before American and other NATO reserves could be mobilized. The most likely route of such a Pact invasion would be the north German plain, with its flat, open terrain and good roads. Hence, some American units should be stationed in northern Germany.

The dramatic proposals for improving the American contribution to European defense included a reorganized army of eight full-strength divisions compared with the then present 13 1/3 divisions. Six divisions of two brigades each would be deployed in Europe. Their troop strength would be only slightly less than the 4 1/3 divisions in Europe at the time. The remaining brigade of each of the six divisions would be stationed in the United States, ready to join its parent unit by air within seven days after mobilization, thus rounding out a full six-division force. The authors proposed improving preparation for meeting a Soviet conventional attack through the following additional measures:

 * moving northward two divisions then in southern Germany to balance Soviet weight in the north German plain, which most experts considered the most likely axis of Soviet attack
 * raising the ratio of combat to support troops through a series of measures, including more use of civilian resources
 * repositioning supply lines and communications to run west to east through the Netherlands and Belgium rather than north to south, paralleling the East German frontier, as they did at the time
 * insuring effective air support for ground forces and wholesale revision of air force tactical priorities and adjusting aircraft design in favor of ground support planes
 * establishing a multinational logistics command in NATO[31]

The major proposals of the Brookings study, which mirrored the thinking of both Secretary Schlesinger and Senator Nunn, were used most effectively in the two leaders' budget strategy in 1974. The idea of getting rid of "fat" in the services through elimination of support troops and headquarters units proved popular on Capitol Hill. By promising that any reduction in support troops could be converted into greater numbers of combat troops, Mr. Schlesinger also held out an incentive to the military services to go along with the proposals. At the same time, his slogan that he was "hammering fat into swords" proved to be a popular argument for persuading Congress to accept a larger defense budget and to endorse an increase from thirteen army divisions to sixteen. Senator Nunn was also able to use the ideas effectively to defuse the Mansfield initiative.

In June Congress passed into law several of the proposals as an amendment to the military procurement bill. Known as the Nunn Amendment, the provision required the military services in Europe to cut support troops by 18,000 men, with the reduction to be converted into an equal number of combat troops. The conversion of the first 6,000 must be complete by June 30, 1975, and the second conversion of 18,000 must be complete by June 30, 1976. Within the general guidelines the Pentagon could work out concrete plans for restructuring the forces in consultation with the NATO allies. Negotiations with the German government had to be undertaken with great care. As experience had demonstrated many times previously, the Germans were always worried that structural changes in U.S. forces stationed in Germany would be used mainly as a cover for a reduction of the

American commitment. In addition, if the Americans wished to alter the *status quo* in a significant way by moving American forces to the northern part of Germany where they had never been before, thoughtful and logical explanations would be necessary in order to secure German agreement.

Negotiations with the Germans continued for several months. In November, 1974, Secretary Schlesinger made his first official visit to Bonn for discussions of the Pentagon plans with German defense minister Georg Leber. A substantial meeting of the minds was achieved, though important details were left for decision at a later time. In a television interview on November 4, Schlesinger announced that the U.S. planned to reduce support troops by 18,000 men in the next two years, but that the reduction would be matched by the creation of two new combat brigades, thereby increasing American combat capability. He indicated that discussions were underway with Mr. Leber on the possible sites for the two new brigades, including consideration of a location in northern Germany. Simultaneously the German government announced that a structural reform of the *Bundeswehr* would be undertaken which would result in the creation of three additional combat brigades. In subsequent briefings German and American officials emphasized that the creation of the new American units was designed to reinforce existing forces, not replace any British, Dutch, or Belgian forces already stationed in Germany. The new American brigades would be rotated between Germany and the United States, with soldiers stationed for brief periods in Germany without dependents.[32]

Details of the restructuring plans were worked out in consultation with the German government over the next several months. In December the Pentagon announced that a 3,800 man brigade would be moved to West Germany, beginning in March of the following year. The brigade would initially be stationed at Grafenwoehr, Hohenfels, and Wildflecken, three of the army's main European training areas. A final decision would be made later on the permanent post. The movement would increase U.S. army forces in Germany by one-third of a division, to four and two-thirds divisions, the highest level since 1967, when a third of a division was pulled out due to the pressures of the Vietnam war. The brigade headquarters and a support battalion of about 660 troops would be permanently stationed in Germany with their dependents. The other brigade components, including the combat troops, would be rotated between the United States and Germany every six months without dependents. In addition, a second brigade would be moved to Germany late in 1975 or early 1976, bringing combat strength once again up to five full divisions.[33]

For many months following the announcement of the restructuring initiatives the German press engaged in a lively debate over the wisdom of the plans. Though the overwhelming majority of the reports and commentaries approved of the scheme, there were some important voices of dissent. Most newspapers tended to agree broadly with the *Sueddeutsche Zeitung* that, "The two brigades are a double political signal: to the Europeans they mean that the USA expects greater defense efforts from them as well; and to the Soviet Union they mean that the West has both the means and the will to guarantee the defense of the West."[34] On the other hand, however, a few critics agreed with the *Deutsche Zeitung* that the new plan was simply "a further step in the process of the final disengagement of the United States from Europe. The support units are by no means superfluous troops; they are rather the essential structural personnel for the air transport in connection with Big Lift and therefore cannot be relinquished. For this reason the creation of two new brigades cannot serve as a replacement."[35]

Moving to North Germany: The Garlstedt Decision

In March, 1975, when the first units of a new brigade arrived on schedule in West Germany, it was announced that the Third Brigade of the Second Tank Division from Fort Hood, Texas, would be the first of the two new brigades to be reassigned to Germany. Not until the summer of 1975 were additional aspects of the restructuring plans released to the public by the German and American governments. Quite obviously the German government attempted to prepare the way gently but surely by revealing details of the plans in a piecemeal fashion, giving public opinion time to adjust to the new strategic concept and the difficulties it would inevitably create in terms of bringing American forces into a new part of Germany. In most cases a vague general announcement, considered by careful observers and some segments of the press as a trial balloon, would be followed some weeks later by a more detailed announcement.

The first intimation that marines would somehow be involved in the new plans came in July, 1975, with the appointment of General Louis Wilson as the new commandant of the marine corps. The appointment revealed an emerging Defense Department concept that, following the Vietnam disaster, the three marine divisions should be counted as a reserve force that could be used in a war in Western Europe. Indeed one of the reasons General Wilson was selected was that he expressed a willingness and interest in refocusing the marine corps toward the Atlantic. The idea represented a major departure, since the corps had been primarily oriented toward the Pacific since World War II. In an interview on June 29, General Wilson stated that in his opinion the marine division on the East Coast could be more heavily armed for fighting in Europe, while the division on the West Coast could be reorganized to fight in either the Atlantic or Pacific theaters, and the division in the Western Pacific would remain in basically its present form as an amphibious assault force. To convert the divisions into general purpose forces that could be used in Europe, it would be necessary to equip them with additional tanks, armored personnel carriers and heavy artillery.[36]

In early August the German Defense Ministry gave additional clues as to what the population in northern Germany might expect as a result of the decision to station a new American brigade in that region. Possibly a location near the North Sea in western Lower Saxony might be chosen, though the consultations had not been concluded by the German-American commission which had been studying the matter for several months, nor had the German federal government concluded negotiations with state (Land) authorities.[37] At the same time British military authorities began to express certain reservations about the impending move. Traditionally the northern sector of Germany had been the responsibility primarily of the British Army of the Rhine. The British were worried now that the plan to bring American troops into the area would place an intolerable strain on barracks and training facilities used by the British army. In addition, the British wondered if it was a good idea to place American units in wartime under the control of NORTHAG, which was commanded by a British general, while all other American units would be commanded by CENTAG, headed by an American general.[38]

One extremely thorny problem remained to be solved. Aside from the likely resistance of local populations anywhere in northern Germany to the idea of a vast new American military installation in the immediate area, a solution could not be found without the cooperation of the Land government of Lower Saxony, since the German federal government did not own tracts of land in the state, alone or in combination, which could accommodate a large military facility. To expropriate the land merely through the right of eminent domain would be out of the question, since organized resistance by the citizenry might well make the effort politically nonviable. Only patient negotiations between the Bund (federal government) and the Land (state government) could solve the problem. By late August a location near Garlstedt, between Bremerhaven and Bremen, began to be mentioned often by federal authorities, since the government did own a relatively large tract of land there, though by no means large enough without additional acquisitions from the state of Lower Saxony.[39] Other locations remained, however, part of the discussion, with primary consideration being given to Bremerhaven, Bergen-Hohne, Walsrode, and Seedorf.

In late September, during a visit by Schlesinger to Bonn, the German Defense Ministry announced that a final decision had been reached, pending agreement between Bonn and the Land government of Lower Saxony in Hannover. The choice: Garlstedt, a small town midway between Bremerhaven and Bremen. The choice was dictated by many reasons. In the first place, the *Bundeswehr* possessed a small training area there, which could become the core of the new installation without destruction of any buildings. Aside from the loss of the training area, no units of the German army would have to be relocated. Garlstedt was also very near the major American supply depot and communications facilities at Bremerhaven. According to the announcement, twenty-five new groups of buildings would be erected at the Garlstedt location, with no expectation that any of the traditional recreation areas around Heilshorn, Garlstedt, Eggestedt, or Schwanewede would need to be disturbed. Brigade '75 was expected to be able to move into the new installation by 1978. Until then the troops would be stationed in barracks of the *Bundeswehr* at the training ground Bergen-Hohne in the Lueneberger Heath.[40] A few days later the defense ministry announced that in anticipation of the arrival of Brigade '75, American units would undertake joint maneuvers with the German army for the first time in northern Germany during the annual fall Reforger (Return of Forces to Germany) exercises. It was another section of the declaration, however, which captured the attention of the Germans, namely, an announcement that American marines would take part in the exercises, the first time that marines had set foot on German soil since the winter of 1918-1919, when they had served briefly as occupation troops after World War I.

The marines landed in Germany on October 12. The coverage in the German press accorded the occasion the aura of a landmark event in the history of the world. For various reasons the idea of American marines on German soil captured the imagination of the Germans in a poignant, powerful way. Especially intriguing was the fact that American troops operated fully under German supreme command for the first time ever in the context of NATO exercises. Though 12,000 troops of the German *Bundeswehr* and 3,500 American troops took part in the exercise, code-named Tight Reins, "the real attraction among the foreign fighters were the 1,800 men of the U.S. Marine Corps, who enjoy a legendary reputation as the 'Leathernecks.'" Continued the *Augsburger Allgemeine*:

Indeed, these Leathernecks are considered the toughest guys around. It is not without reason that America sends them as a kind a military fire brigade to all possible corners of the world. These marines, who now freeze in the heath, have previously sweat at the Panama Canal, in the Philippines, in the Hawaiian Islands, and on the islands of the Caribbean and in Vietnam. That these battle seasoned jungle fighters who, since the Second World War have drilled in primeval forests for close combat, have now been sent to the Lueneberger Heath....reflects, in the opinion of military experts, a shift of thinking in the Pentagon. After the disaster in Vietnam, the Americans have had their fill of Asia. Even in the highest military staff groups the Americans once again are thinking about Europe.[41]

The north German press was equally enthused with the new visitors:

The excellent understanding between the marines and the German soldiers as well as the civilian population surprised everyone. Just as soon as the Amis had taken up their positions the Germans offered them coffee and salami bread and tried to communicate to them in schoolboy English that we were so glad to see them here.....Certainly the Americans showed themselves as uncommonly obliging and friendly. At the sergeants mess U.S. and German officers confirmed new friendships over and over again with mutual invitations to come for a visit. Outside the men exchanged cigarettes and exchanged stories about Old Germany. All kinds of trips were organized to show the American guests a little bit of Germany.[42]

Despite the general enthusiasm a number of German critics tended to question the deeper motives of the Pentagon in sending marines to northern Germany. The move, after all, could be considered mainly a political signal, or part of an effort to convince the U.S. Senate that the marine corps could play as significant a role in the Atlantic theater as in the Pacific. A decision would have to be made concerning what to do with the third marine division, at the time stationed at Okinawa, when Okinawa was returned to Japanese sovereignty. With one marine division already stationed on the East Coast and another on the West Coast, a new location for the division returning from Okinawa would have to be found. In the face of pressure in the Senate to abolish the third marine division altogether, the marines in Germany could be seen as part of an effort by the Pentagon and General Wilson, the new marine commandant, to demonstrate to the Senate that the third marine division would be perfectly suited as a strategic reserve for the NATO alliance.[43] Such criticisms were, however, fairly isolated. For the most part, the Germans seemed delighted to have the marines on German soil once again. For the marines, one might reasonably guess that their reception in Germany on the basis of their legendary reputation was a welcome salve for the deep wounds left by Vietnam.

The arrival of Brigade '75 and the erection of the Garlstedt military base did not go unchallenged. In a densely populated country such as Germany, with a long tradition of containing urban sprawl in the interest of maintaining adequate parks and forests, every acre of land is a precious resource. Very few quiet, rural communities in any country generate much enthusiasm for a giant new military base in the midst of a nature preserve. And, given the severe social, racial, and disciplinary problems of the army only a few years previously, it should not surprise anyone that a substantial number of German citizens opposed the arrival of Brigade '75. Garlstedt, as a rural community of 713 inhabitants, was one borough of the small city of Osterholz-Scharmbeck, with a population of 24,000 inhabitants. The Garlstedt Heath, a picturesque uncultivated tract of land covered with heather, had long been considered by the citizens of Bremen and Bremerhaven as a traditional park and recreation area of undisturbed, natural beauty.

Resistance came in the form of a number of "citizens' initiatives" as well as in committees and opposition groups formed in the Lower Saxony Landtag (state legislature) and the Bremen city government. Of the plethora of citizens-initiative groups, probably the most vocal and important were the "United Citizens' Initiatives for the Protection of the Garlstedt Heath,"[44] an umbrella organization of local groups from the Osterholz-Scharmbeck area, which opposed the plans mainly on ecological or social grounds, and the "Citizens' Action for the Garlstedt Heath,"[45] headquartered in the more radical city of Bremen, which opposed any new military installations whatever on more ideological grounds, and one component of which was supported by the German Communist Party. The various protest groups began organizing in the fall of 1975 and by the spring of 1976 had gathered 40,000 signatures on various petitions to the Landtag in Hannover. The more moderate groups within the United Citizens' Initiatives organization feared primarily the consequences of an "American invasion" in rural northern Germany. The already heavily travelled Highway 6 between Bremen and Bremerhaven would become even more dangerous, claiming the lives of more children who played in the vicinity of the highway. A new pleasure industry, with military bars and prostitutes from other parts of Germany moving to the area, could hardly be avoided. The prehistoric graves on the site, which until this time had been carefully preserved and cared for by the *Bundeswehr* would not be adequately cared for by the Americans and would probably be lost altogether. And most seriously, the integrity of the Garlstedt Heath as a recreational area of unparalleled natural beauty would be destroyed with the erection of a vast new military complex based on tank regiments.[46] With the mayor of Bremen, Hans Koschnick, strongly supporting the plans of the defense ministry, the stage was set for massive protest demonstrations in Bremen, which occurred in the spring of 1976. In May 75,000 to 100,000 demonstrators formed a human chain around the proposed site. Though the protests and demonstrations did manage to delay the beginning of construction of the complex for several months, largely by necessitating repeated legislative reconsideration, actual construction finally got underway in the summer of 1976.

Previous to the beginning of construction, however, the German defense ministry announced that NATO plans had changed rather substantially for the stationing plans at Garlstedt. The original plan had been that the brigade staff and one support unit would be located in Bremerhaven, with the rest of the troops stationed at Garlstedt. The troops at Garlstedt, without dependents, would be rotated between the United States and Germany every six months. According to the new plan, announced in mid-May, the entire brigade would be permanently stationed at Garlstedt. Hence, instead of the 680 dwelling units required for the staff in Bremerhaven, most of which the German government had already made available, the installation would now need 1,707 dwelling units in the Osterholz-Scharmbeck and Garlstedt areas for the approximately 6000 dependents of the staff and at least a portion of the married soldiers. In addition, the Americans now intended to strengthen the military presence in northern Germany by stationing 400 officers of an air force reconnaissance wing in Bremerhaven. As might be expected, the new plans occasioned a new storm of protest. The more radical groups figured, perhaps not without reason, that the new plan in actuality had been the real plan all along. In order to soften the impact of a massive new American presence in northern Germany, both the German and American defense ministries had probably packaged the plan in the softer version of the rotation principle and location in two places in order to create the illusion that the new presence would be smaller and less overwhelming that it was now turning out to be.[47] Whatever the merits of the protestors' suspicions, Herr von Friederichs, Oberkreisdirektor (chief county manager) of the county surrounding Osterholz-Scharmbeck, felt compelled to laud the revised plan as a major step forward in civilian-military planning and a "joint success of the county and the county seat."[48]

Another thorny problem surrounding the Pentagon's plans to carry out the Nunn Amendment by moving U.S. troops to northern Germany concerned the matter of finance. Who would pay for the large installation which would arise in the midst of the Garlstedt Heath? The problem had been the subject of negotiation since the original plan to station two new combat brigades in Germany was announced in November, 1974. Only with the expiration of the eighth offset payments agreement in June, 1975, however, did the negotiations gain a sense of urgency. With Schmidt's view having been clearly articulated early on that the era of offset payments was over because of changes in the international monetary system, the assumption in both Bonn and Washington from early 1975 was that offset payments agreements would be replaced in some form or other by a substantial German contribution to the construction of new facilities for the combat brigade to be brought to northern Germany. From mid 1975 on the negotiations were also pursued within the framework of NATO, since Bonn and Washington were agreed that the costs of any restructuring arrangement involving troops and facilities that would strengthen the military capability of the alliance as a whole should be shared by all the NATO allies, not the U.S. and Germany alone.

In late 1975 a plan was proposed whereby Germany, the United States, and NATO would each pay for one-third of the costs of building the base at Garlstedt. Despite strong lobbying for the plan by the German and American governments, it proved to be unacceptable to the other NATO allies.[49] The money would be taken, logically, from the NATO infrastructure fund. Since most of the fund was aleady committed to other purposes, however, the allies were reluctant to undertake a commitment for a major replenishment, since all were facing difficult budgetary problems domestically. They also argued that arrangements dictated by the American Congress and involving American troops on German territory must remain a matter of bilateral agreement between Germany and the United States. Faced with such intransigence, the German and American governments had no choice but to bite the bullet and work out an agreement to finance Garlstedt themselves. A figure in the range of 280 to 300 million German marks was the official estimate of the cost of the new installation by April, 1976, when the two governments began to bargain in earnest over the matter of cost distribution. A bargain was finally struck by late July when Schmidt and Ford met in Washington. In lieu of a new offset payment the German government would contribute 171.2 million marks, approximately one-half the cost of the construction of Garlstedt, leaving a similar sum to be paid by the American government. A protocol embodying the cost distribution and other details of the stationing arrangement was signed by Ford and Schmidt on July 22, 1976.[50]

In late October the Lower Saxony Landtag finally disposed of the numerous legislative petitions which had been filed and approved the arrangements, with certain stipulations to the effect that the approved area could not be enlarged and the local population would have access to the southwestern section of the area whenever training exercises were not being held. On May 3, 1977, the cornerstone of the new installation was laid by Defense Minister Georg Leber in an elaborate ceremony with many high ranking NATO commanders, American officers, and German political leaders in attendance. "I lay this cornerstone as a symbol of our alliance," intoned Leber.[51] A number of editorials used the occasion to emphasize the military and political significance of the American move to northern Germany. Said *Die Welt*:

> The stationing of the American brigade in the vicinity of Bremerhaven is, quite apart from its military meaning, an important political signal. What it shows is that America casts its fate with NATO ever more strongly as a community of common fate. The responsible political leaders in Washington have recognized that even the superpower on the North American continent could not preserve its security if Europe fell into the sphere of influence of the red opponent."[52]

The *Frankfurter Allgemeine* continued:

> A potential enemy in the entire area of the central European defense system must now reckon with the Americans. This means that no matter at which point a violent attempt is made to destroy our system, a European war would immediately become a confrontation of the superpowers. The Soviet Union would not be able to provoke a regional conflict; rather it would begin a world war. When that is the alternative to the present condition of the absence of war, then the American brigade strengthens deterrence with a deciding element.[53]

New Initiatives at Garlstedt

The movement of Americans to northern Germany created a new set of social problems for the Germans which ought not be overlooked by American observers. In southern Germany the population at large, both in cities and many small towns, had grown used to the American presence over the years with all the attendant social and cultural problems. The north Germans, in turn, were used to smaller numbers of British, Dutch, and Belgian soldiers in their midst, but had always been thankful that the more awesome American presence remained in the south. The construction of Garlstedt naturally raised fears that the intercultural problems created by huge concentrations of Americans, so endemic to the south, would now be transferred to the north. Hence, there was an effort to do things differently this time. All during the negotiations between the Land government of Lower Saxony and the federal government in Bonn and during other phases of the planning process involving local political leaders and American military leaders, there was an effort to avoid a phenomenon which was felt to be a primary culprit in causing intercultural struggle, namely, the phenomenon of the American ghetto. General George Blanchard, who succeeded General Davison as Commanding General of the U.S. Army, Europe, in 1975, had clearly articulated views on the subject. He believed that many of the worst social problems could be eliminated to the extent that American families living off base could be dispersed from ghettos surrounding bases into the wider German community. All during his tenure as Commanding General he advocated the idea of genuine German-American integration as a solution to problems of cultural misunderstanding. Most German political leaders tended to agree. Consequently, the goal of integration was pursued vigorously by the government of Lower Saxony and local authorities in Bremen and Osterholz-Scharmbeck after the army announced that the rotation principle had been abandoned in favor of the permanent stationing of the unit at Garlstedt with families. With subsidies from the federal government the Lower Saxony state government agreed to build 1,027 apartments for American families, which would be leased by the U.S. Army. In the process of planning the location of the apartments and securing the building permits, in Germany a complex and lengthy ordeal, the local authorities attempted, with the blessing of the army, to disperse the American families as widely as possible throughout the town of Osterholz-Scharmbeck.

According to many observers, the attempt succeeded as well as or perhaps even better than had been hoped. Certainly it must be said that the German authorities and the German people went much more than the proverbial extra mile to accommodate their new American guests. Operation New Neighbor, sponsored initially by Frau Dielewicz, wife of the city manager of Osterholz-Scharmbeck, eventually gained the active support of a substantial majority of the town's population. Using a computer to match German and American families with similar characteristics and interests, a German sponsor family was found for virtually every American family which desired the arrangement. Operation New Neighbor also helped to dispel the notion that racism was a serious problem for the German hosts. The answers to the questionnaries in which Germans requested participation in the program revealed that among the first four hundred registrants, only four indicated a preference for sponsorship of white families.[54] Flowers and gifts were given to new American arrivals, neighborhood welcoming parties were held, and trips to shopping facilities and points of interest were organized. Many Americans, officers and noncom's alike, were not only pleasantly surprised, but taken aback by the red carpet treatment they received from the people of Osterholz-Scharmbeck.

Despite the sweetness and light, inevitably the americanization of Osterholz-Scharmbeck brought stresses and strains. "This used to be a one-horse town," said Wilfried Iffert, the mayor's liason with the U.S. Army. "But now it's all changing. In a few months every second man on the street will be an American."[55] He was not far from wrong. Even the army's own estimates indicated that by 1979 the U.S. population in the Garlstedt area would surpass 9,000. With a German population of 24,000, Americans would constitute over one quarter of the area's population. In the end, the army was less willing to carry through on the dispersal-integration idea than the Germans. Six locations in Osterholz-Scharmbeck, including the borough of Garlstedt, were selected by the county government as the location of the new apartment complexes, though the Germans attempted unsuccessfully to persuade the Americans to accept additional locations further from the base. According to Herr Iffert, "the city council wanted to spread the U.S. housing among several communities, but the army refused."[56] Hence, an opportunity to test the integration idea to an even fuller extent was lost. Over time, perhaps inevitably, the accoutrements of military life arrived in Osterholz-Scharmbeck. Former German gaststätte near the base became military hangouts, new bars opened primarily for soldiers, and prostitutes moved into town. Given the previous efforts by the local population to truly integrate the Americans to the fullest possible extent, however, the situation remained more normal and more German than in many communities in south Germany. Even today, Osterholz-

Scharmbeck and its picturesque borough of Garlstedt remain a fairly positive example of how a large American military installation managed to settle into a largely rural setting abroad without intolerable disruption.

The actual construction of the Garlstedt base was accomplished with greater dispatch than expected by U.S. military authorities. In less than a year and a half after the laying of the cornerstone a giant complex of attractive, modern buildings was ready for occupancy in the Garlstedt Heath. The official dedication ceremony was held October 17, 1978, attended by Secretary of Defense Harold Brown, Supreme Allied Commander Alexander Haig, German Minister of Defense Hans Apel, and other officials of the German federal government, the Land Lower Saxony, local mayors, and others. The installation's name paid tribute to that great American general who so ably laid the foundation for German-American reconciliation after World War II. Appropriately, the Garlstedt base was christened the Lucius D. Clay Kaserne. The meaning of the ceremony was aptly affirmed by Herr Apel:

> We welcome our American friends.....To speak of
> defense is a very important thing. But here and now
> we have occasion to reaffirm how important to all of
> us the element of friendship is in the NATO family
> of nations. This element cements the peace which
> we are determined to preserve.[57]

A system of administrative arrangements was worked out for Clay Kaserne quite different from those applicable to American bases in southern Germany. On September 22, 1978, the German and American governments signed a protocol which provided that the grounds, buildings, furnishings, and facilities at Garlstedt would be maintained according to the prescriptions of German administrative law. In return, the army would be reimbursed for the overhead costs of maintaining the facilities by the German federal government. In addition, the German government would be responsible for security, fire protection, refuse removal, building and street cleaning, and general maintenance.[58] The new arrangements provided another demonstration that, with the move to northern Germany, the American army was making its best effort to construct arrangements which would remedy some of the longstanding problems besetting military bases in southern Germany.

Force Moves in South Germany:
Wiesbaden and Ramstein

Though our discussion has concentrated exculsively until now on the movement of Brigade '75 to Garlstedt, due to the far-reaching significance of introducing an American military presence to northern Germany, it should not be forgotten that the exchange of support for combat units required by the Nunn Amendment resulted in a Pentagon plan to bring not one, but two new brigades to Germany. In late July, 1975, army headquarters in Heidelberg (USAREUR) announced, following lengthy consultations with German federal and state authorities, that the Wiesbaden Air Base would become the new home of one of the brigades which would be transferred to Germany. The brigade would start arriving early in 1976. In the meantime, in order to make room for the army units, the air force, which had long occupied the air base and other installations in and around Wiesbaden, would begin moving its personnel west of the Rhine into the Kaiserslautern area. Similarly, army personnel in the Kaiserslautern area would have to make way for the heavier air force concentration by moving to installations east of the Rhine. In essence, the movements meant that in southern Germany army units would be moving eastward as part of the overall restructuring plans, while air force units, moving westward, would progressively become concentrated in the corridor stretching from Mainz to Trier-Saarbruecken, most especially in the Kaiserslautern-Ramstein-Sembach area. Corresponding to the movements, an air force officer would become the senior commanding officer in the Kaiserslautern area, while, for the first time, an army officer would become the senior commanding officer in Wiesbaden.

The announcement occasioned a public outcry of a magnitude hardly expected by either German or American authorities. The residents of Wiesbaden had long been used to the presence of the air force. Though constant complaints had been registered through the years about aircraft noise and other nuisances, the Germans in Wiesbaden apparently had a much more positive image of the American air force than the army. The air force was of course a much smaller and less obtrusive presence than the army. In addition the flood of publicity surrounding the army's discipline and morale problems of the recent past had not been forgotten. It was not that the air force would move out of Wiesbaden which troubled the Germans. In this case the primary concern would be over jobs lost to German nationals. What worried the people of Wiesbaden was that the air force units would be replaced by army units, planes would give way to jeeps and tanks, and pilots would be replaced by hard drinking infantrymen. Image conscious Wiesbadeners had long taken great pride in the city's reputation as one of the finest health resorts in Germany. They feared that a large army presence might diminish the city's reputation for charm and beauty and harm the tourist and health spa industries. Hence, protest movements and citizens' initiative groups were organized, though they were smaller and less obstructive than those in Garlstedt.

The arrangements for Brigade '76 caused fewer problems than those for Garlstedt for obvious reasons. The Americans had been in southern Germany since World War II, so there was no question of a new foreign presence. Installations and facilities were already in existence, so that it was merely a question of moving various force components around rather than building a large new base in an area where none had existed before. There was no need for complex negotiations between the Germans, the Americans, and NATO on financing, land usage, and environmental protection. Hence, the protests were smaller and less successful in delaying the plans than was the case in northern Germany.

Brigade '76 arrived in Germany with great pomp and ceremony on March 24, 1976. (The brigade names reflected simply the year they arrived in Germany.) Whereas Brigade '75, as noted previously, was the Third Brigade of the Second Tank Division from Fort Hood, Texas, Brigade '76, by contrast, came from Fort Carson, Colorado, and was the Fourth Brigade of the Fourth Infantry Division. The air force had largely completed the move of its equipment and personnel to the Ramstein area when Brigade '76 arrived. Hence, the Germans in Wiesbaden found themselves hosts to the second of the two new combat brigades, somewhat unwillingly, before the protest movements had had time to get fully organized. The movement of Brigade '76 to Wiesbaden took place without major incident and with all the elaborate ceremony usually afforded by the Germans. At the welcoming ceremony the mayor of Wiesbaden assured the new commanding general that, "We understand each other as partners, and I am certain that our American friends will feel at home as citizens of Wiesbaden."[59]

Nuclear Weapons and Armaments

Closely tied to the decisions to alter the "tooth to tail" ratio of U.S. forces in Germany by substituting combat troops for support troops were decisions relating to tactical nuclear weapons in Germany. In 1974 a lively debate arose in the Department of Defense and in Congress on the need for and the number of nuclear weapons stationed in Europe. At the time, the United States had about 7,000 nuclear warheads positioned in Western Europe. (The number began to decrease following the NATO dual decision in 1979. By 1986 there were only approximately 4,500 nuclear warheads.) In 1974, by official definition, all were "tactical" nuclear weapons, although many of them were far more powerful than the atomic bomb which destroyed Hiroshima. They included artillery shells, warheads for short-range missiles, bombs carried by fighter bombers to targets in eastern Europe and western Russia, warheads for anti-aircraft missiles, and demolition mines. A staff report for the Senate Foreign Relations Committee in 1974 noted that the weapons were stored at more than one hundred sites in Europe, with two-thirds of the sites containing weapons to be used jointly by NATO forces, though technically all the weapons remained under American control. In a symbolic sense the warheads assumed over the years an importance somewhat analogous to the American troops stationed in Europe. Just as American and European officials had come to regard any decrease in the troop strength as signalling a reduced American commitment to NATO, so Europeans had come to view any reduction in the nuclear stockpile below the 7,000 figure as a weakening of the American nuclear deterrent in Europe. To certain officials in the Defense Department, however, a crucial military difference had developed between the need for troops and the warheads. Together with a group of Congressmen, they argued that the troops were needed, at least for the time being, to maintain a conventional military balance with the Warsaw Pact forces, but that the 7,000 warheads were not needed to maintain a credible nuclear deterrent. Some senior defense officials also argued that the stockpile was so large that the United States and its European allies might be self-deterred against using the warheads.

For many years the stockpile had been governed by the strategic concept that, if necessary to save Western Europe against a Soviet invasion, virtually all the warheads would be used at the same time. Critics argued that though this strategic concept may have had validity ten years earlier when the United States still possessed a clear superiority over the Soviets in nuclear weaponry, such a concept could not be considered valid now that the Soviet Union had increased its capability to the point that a large-scale nuclear strike by the European allies almost certainly would result in the nuclear destruction of Western Europe. Defense Secretary Schlesinger had been trying for some time to shift to a strategic concept of selective use of the warheads against military targets in a limited fashion, so as to demonstrate allied determination without necessarily provoking all-out Soviet nuclear retaliation. A corollary of this selective use concept was that fewer nuclear warheads would be needed in the stockpile.

At the same time as this strategic reappraisal came a concern, more in Congress than the Pentagon, over the physical security of so many nuclear warheads scattered throughout Europe. This concern came to a head during the Cyprus crisis in 1973 when the Defense Department took precautionary steps to protect and, if necessary, to retrieve atomic warheads stationed in Greece and Turkey. Somewhat gingerly, because of concern over allied reactions, Mr. Schlesinger had been moving toward a review of the nuclear stockpile. But what finally provoked a full-fledged study was an amendment attached to the military authorization bill of 1974 by Senator Sam Nunn. The Nunn Amendment froze the nuclear stockpile at its then present level and directed the Defense Department to carry out a wide-ranging review of nuclear strategy and requirements in Western Europe. It ordered the department, among other things, to study the "overall concept for use of tactical nuclear weapons in Europe,"; how the use of such weapons related to deterrence and to a strong conventional defense; reductions in the numbers and types of nuclear warheads which might not be essential for the defense of Western Europe; and steps which might be taken "to develop a rational and coordinated nuclear posture by the North Atlantic Treaty Organization."[60]

The Defense Department undertook the required study in the fall of 1974 and by April, 1975, submitted a lengthy classified report to the Senate Armed Services Committee, chaired by Senator Nunn. The final report embodied the conclusions of the Pentagon as modified by intensive consultations with European allies in the NATO Council. Though the report acknowledged the need for adjustments as old systems were replaced by newer ones, its major thrust was that it would be unwise to reduce the number of tactical nuclear weapons in Europe to any significant degree so long as the NATO and Warsaw Pact countries remained at loggerheads on mutual and balanced reductions in European force levels in the MBFR talks. Any reductions in nuclear force levels would profoundly disturb the European members of the alliance. The report recommended therefore that reductions in the number and variety of tactical nuclear systems in Europe should be carefully weighed only in the context of the MBFR negotiations.[61]

In December, 1975, the NATO allies agreed on a proposal to be presented at the MBFR talks. Joining the issues of conventional force levels to nuclear force levels, the proposal suggested a reduction of 1,000 weapons in the U.S. nuclear stockpile in Europe as part of a first stage agreement involving mutual Soviet and American troop cuts in central Europe. The Soviets, as usual, rejected the proposal. Unable to achieve any progress in the Vienna talks, the U.S. government reaffirmed its intention to maintain the existing level of tactical nuclear weapons in Europe several times in 1976.[62]

In the fall of 1976 the Pentagon announced that the U.S. would significantly increase its fighter strength in Western Europe the following year. The net increase would be 84 aircraft and 3,000 men, an increase of approximately 14% in the number of aircraft deployed in Europe, making a total of nearly 550. Once again the United States was moving to reverse the cutbacks which had occurred nearly a decade previously during the Vietnam War. In the spring of 1968 the U.S. had returned 96 F-4 fighters from Europe to the United States, though the squadrons flew back to Europe once a year for maneuvers. "These deployments," said the Pentagon, "are in keeping with the congressional mandate to increase U.S. combat capability in Europe and are particularly important in the light of recent improvements in Warsaw Pact forces facing NATO."[63]

During 1977 the additional planes were phased into the NATO fighter forces in stages with little fanfare and scant notice in the press. The most significant additions were F-15 Eagle fighters, which were stationed at bases in Germany for the first time to insure aerial superiority on the NATO front. The F-4 fighter bombers that the F-15's replaced at Bitburg Air Base were reassigned to three other bases rather than sent back to the United States, thus increasing the number of F-4's at the bases at Hahn, Ramstein, and Spangdahlem. The F-15 was considered superior to the Soviet MIG-23 and 21 fighters, though the Warsaw Pact had considerably more planes than NATO. And though the F-15's were meant to assure air superiority, the Pentagon emphasized that they could also be used for close support of ground troops. They could also deliver atomic bombs into Eastern Europe and the western Soviet Union.[64]

To supplement the arrangements for increased air superiority, the American air force also established a presence in northern Germany for the first time, as did the army. In November, 1976, a new mobile radar station was established at Hessisch-Oldendorf consisting of 600 air force personnel with 200 families. A few months later in 1977 a new Allied Tactical Operations Center was established at Kalkar in the state of North Rhine Westphalia. Though the American contingent consisted of only 300 personnel, the air force thereby added materially to its intelligence and monitoring capabilities.[65]

The summer of 1977 saw the first stages of a debate over the possible stationing of cruise missiles in Germany following Congressional approval of $349 million for development and testing of the new weapons. The struggle in Congress over production of the B-1 bomber also figured in the German debate over weapons systems, though the implications of the bomber caused less consternation than those of the cruise missile. Much more important was the lively debate which began to take shape over the implications of neutron bombs, should they be developed and brought to Germany as part of the stockpile of tactical nuclear weapons. As certain commentators pointed out, the stability of detente was being questioned ever more seriously by the relentless march of technology and the development of new weapons systems. In addition, the lines between strategic and theater systems and between offensive and defensive weapons systems were becoming progressively more difficult to distinguish. To the Germans these developments were highly unsettling because of the heavy investment in detente which, they believed, was the policy best suited for the avoidance of a major war in Europe.[66] Weapons systems and the nuclear question are not the focus of this study. It is, however, important for our purposes to note how the debates over these weapons systems increased the tension in the Bonn-Washington relationship in the mid to late 1970s. The worst episode, of course, was the administration's attempts to persuade the Germans to accept the presence of neutron bombs and Carter's subsequent cancellation of the program. Clearly, the zigzag policy decisions of the Carter administration undermined German confidence in the steadfastness of American leadership. And the early debate over cruise missiles presaged a much more violent confrontation to come, following the NATO dual decision of 1979.

Force Readiness and Nuclear Security

In the mid 1970s public attention in both Germany and the United States was drawn to two other problems relating to force readiness in Germany, namely, the terrible condition of U.S. equipment in Europe and the inadequacy of security at nuclear weapons sites. Congress was the catalyst by which concern was elevated to the level of panic. In the spring of 1975 Senator John Pastore made public a secret report which had been submitted to the Senate Atomic Energy Committee by the Department of Defense two years earlier. According to the report, atomic bombs in Germany were stored, among other places, in the basement of an office building where security was minimal. During the year preceding the report 213 members of the security forces were relieved of duty for various infractions, 83 of them for drug abuse. Many weapons depots were insufficiently camouflaged; terrorists would have little difficulty in capturing weapons. The report cited as extremely serious the arrangements for storage of atomic mines. For various reasons many of them would not be usable in wartime.[67]

As the clamor began to mount, the Pentagon replied that during the two years since the issuance of the report in 1973, the security deficiencies had for the most part been remedied. In the interim period the number of sites where nuclear weapons were stored had been reduced by 20%, and the Department had plans to reduce the number by another 15 to 20% in the near future. Senator Pastore was not at all satisfied. Though he agreed that some improvements had in fact occurred in the storage of the weapons, he believed that they were entirely insufficient. The better solution, he said, would be to further reduce the number of storage depots and, more importantly, to cut in half the 7000 nuclear warheads stationed in Europe.[68]

The furor in Germany had not yet died down when, on May 12, Representative Les Aspin reported that an army patrol had found secret documents detailing the location of weapons facilities in an open trash container on April 16 near the town of Inneringen. Though the Pentagon immediately denied that any confidential information had been found, Aspin insisted that the documents contained information on the precise locations of the firing platforms for Pershing weapons as well as the storage depots of the actual warheads. Even worse, he said, the army had attempted to conceal the incident. Not surprisingly the story was carried in newspapers throughout Germany.[69]

Congress was in no mood to let the matter rest. Prompted by important members in both houses of Congress, the General Accounting Office released a report a few days later which revealed a veritable chamber of horrors in reference to readiness and equipment of U.S. forces in Germany. According to the report, the maintenance procedures of the army were nothing short of scandalous. It was a common occurrence that the units responsible for the three or four lowest levels of maintenance would skip the work and deliver the vehicle to the next highest step. Hence, hundreds of tanks would be delivered to depots where German maintenance workers would complete work which should have been done earlier, but at much higher wages in terms of the dollar exchange rate. In only three depots the U.S. government was spending $63 million annually for work which should have been completed earlier by American soldiers. Eight arsenals in Germany contained equipment with a value of $700 million which, according to regulations, should be ready for operation within six hours. In reality the six hour deadline amounted to sheer fantasy. Batteries were missing from thousands of jeeps and tanks because of thievery. To counter thievery the batteries were stored sometimes many miles from the vehicles. In order to ready the vehicles for operation the batteries would have to be filled with distilled water and installed, but no one knew where distilled water was located. It could not be ascertained how high the losses were from professional thievery or faulty accounting procedures, but in the inventory of one storage facility, as an example, it was discovered that $32 million worth of material was missing.[70]

The report cited many reasons for the equipment mess in Europe. In the opinion of many commanders the terrible conditions were created by the Pentagon's earlier preoccupation with the Vietnam War. In addition, many believed that the recruits for the all volunteer force were intellectually incapable of understanding the technical requirements for maintenance of complex pieces of equipment or lacked the motivation to do careful work. Underscoring all these reasons, however, according to the GAO, was the simple reality that the United States maintained in Europe such an enormous quantity of equipment and weapons that even under optimal circumstances it would be impossible to keep track of all of it or keep it in operating condition. The report produced a considerable furor in Congress. In the opinion of Senator Humphrey the matter needed more extensive investigation. Hence, as chairman of the Joint Economic Committee, he directed the General Accounting Office to undertake further study and prepare another detailed report, to be delivered a few months later.

Before the new report was issued, an ominous event occurred, which demonstrated how serious the situation really was. In mid June, 1976, a robbery took place at a U.S. weapons depot in Wildflecken near Wuerzburg. According to the army's Criminal Investigation Division, fifteen light anti-tank weapons, with a 66 millimeter caliber and a range of 300 meters were stolen. Although the robbers escaped without a trace, experts explained that the criminals must have had detailed knowledge of the exact storage location and applicable security procedures. The army was unable to explain how the weapons could have been stolen with the storage facility under twenty-four hour guard. The spectre of penetration of U.S. weapons storage facilities, possibly by terrorist groups was now a very real concern.[71]

When the second GAO report was issued a month later, still grimmer circumstances were portrayed in detail. Of the approximately 2000 tanks the U.S. maintained in Germany, a large percentage had defective radio communications. Equipment readiness reports were not only misleading but could not even distinguish between various categories of readiness. The locator system for equipment was totally inaccurate. Of the 314 vehicles and trailers examined at four sites, 115 vehicles had parts which were faulty, improperly installed, or missing. One unit had 23 quarter-ton trucks, 22 of which had something broken or missing. Thousands of vehicles had flat tires, broken windows, smashed mirrors and headlights. The situation with ammunition was a disgrace. Many units did not have correct information as to where various types of ammunition were stored. Very often the access roads to the ammunition depots were clogged or unusable. In many cases the equipment to load the ammunition was unavailable. As a grotesque example of indolence and negligence, the investigators came across one tank company which could not locate the key to the ammunition depot and expended over an hour searching for it.[72]

Senator Humphrey seized upon the opportunity immediately to chastise the army in no uncertain terms:

> Even the army of Field Marshall Idi Amin couldn't possibly be in worse shape. There was a time when the U.S. Army in terms of training and weapons stood at the apex of NATO troops. Now they probably share last place with the Danes and the Dutch.[73]
>
> The magnitude of the problem casts doubt on whether the army could carry out the mission assigned to it in existing war plans that require the use of pre-positioned equipment stored for U.S. based units. The present situation is not fair to our allies, to our own troops, or to the American taxpayer. ....The GAO report comes as disappointing news to those of us who have worried about the army's ability to manage the large sums appropriated by Congress to hold up our end of the NATO alliance.[74]

The Pentagon lost no time this time replying to what many considered simply a ploy to bolster Congress' declining political popularity by taking cheap shots at the most obvious unpopular target. Secretary of the Army Martin Hoffman pointed out that most of the material in the report was at least eighteen months old and did not reflect the improvements the army had undertaken in the meantime.[75] Other Pentagon spokesmen pointed out that during the Middle East war in the fall of 1973 a considerable amount of war material had been delivered to the Israeli army from stocks in Germany. Much of this the army had never been able to replace because Congress refused to appropriate money for replacement materials. Another spokesman stated that it seemed ironic that Senator Humphrey was the one to lambast the tank units in Germany, as he had been the most energetic advocate during the Middle East war of immediate removal of war supplies from Germany. In 1973 no fewer than 400 tanks, 900 armored vehicles and 100 howitzers had quickly been transferred to Israel from stocks in Germany. Since then the army had patiently and actively done everything humanly possible to remedy deficiencies in the readiness of tank units, despite the lack of cooperation from Congress.[76]

Without directly criticizing Senator Humphrey, spokesmen for the German government strongly supported the Pentagon's case. Werner Buchstaller, chairman of the Defense Committee in the *Bundestag*, pointed out that careful investigation by his committee did not bear out the conclusions of the GAO report. Other government spokesmen stated that there could be no doubt about either the quality or the quantity of American troops in Germany.[77] The German press, for the most part, also remained critical of Senator Humphrey's conclusions. Said the *Frankfurter Allgemeine*:

> H.H.H. continues to ride the same old horse.....But with whom does the fault lie, if one can speak of fault at all, that vehicles, and equipment rot in storage depots on European soil? Administration, organization, and upkeep of the materials for reserve divisions consume enormous sums of money. But the Senate Finance Committee, to which Humphrey belongs, wishes to save money. Whom will the Senator attack now? The White House, the Pentagon, the Seventh Army, or - - perhaps himself?[78]

Changing Strategic Concepts: The Nunn-Bartlett Initiatives

There can be little doubt that the GAO reports and Humphrey's criticism spurred the Pentagon to make greater efforts to remedy deficiencies in the administration and upkeep of equipment in Europe. Later in 1976, however, concern in Congress tended to shift in another direction when Senators Sam Nunn and Dewey Bartlett issued a report following an extended study trip to Europe. The report raised new questions about the warning time available to NATO forces in the case of a Soviet attack and advocated revised policy guidelines for U.S. troops in Germany. The major suggestions included shortening the deployment time for NATO troops, strengthening the conventional force levels, and relocating U.S. troops to new positions directly on the East German and Czech borders. Their conclusions were echoed by reports emanating from the newly founded "Committee on the Present Danger," which included in its ranks three former NATO supreme commanders, several former ambassadors, and former Secretary of State Dean Rusk.

NATO planners had long assumed that if the Russians ever regarded war with the West as inevitable, they would probably attempt to launch a surprise preemptive attack, as Israel did against the Arab armies in 1967. Indeed, this had been one main argument used by U.S. defense secretaries over the years in resisting congressional demands for American troop reductions in Europe. Only in the previous year or two, however, following substantial Soviet force improvements in Eastern Europe, did planners seriously begin to believe that the Russians might actually be capable of launching a surprise offensive. Hence, the issues of warning time and troop deployments now began to receive higher priority on the issue agenda. NATO began basically to reevaluate the time it would take the Russians to bring varying numbers of divisions to the front, and how quickly they might bring them into fighting formation. The Russians would probably need two days after mobilization day to prepare for the considerable task of transporting their divisions and their equipment to Eastern Europe. Then, by using a combination of air, road and rail, they might be able to move the divisions at the rate of two a day or perhaps three every four days. Allowing for some delay in filling out category three divisions and for bringing the units on line when they had arrived, analysts reckoned that the fighting formations would be ready thirty days after mobilization day, and most Pentagon planning was done on this assumption.

In 1976 NATO planning also assumed that during the first seven days no overt action would take place, because NATO would be trying to assess whether the Warsaw Pact troops were preparing for war or merely conducting exercise maneuvers. Then, even after NATO's own mobilization day, Western reinforcements, particularly the crucial American reinforcements, would arrive within thirty days to take up their positions in West Germany. The Nunn-Bartlett report began a wide-ranging debate in Congress about the sufficiency of NATO planning assumptions. In the Senators' opinion the capability of Warsaw Pact forces to mount a surprise attack with lightning speed at several border locations simultaneously meant that NATO's plans for deploying reinforcements from the U.S. were outdated and insufficient. The thirty day deployment schedule must be reduced substantially, and, in order to insure that a Soviet attack could not succeed in the initial stages, American forces must be moved closer to the border.[79]

Opposition to the Nunn-Bartlett ideas was led by Representative Les Aspin of Wisconsin. The opposition pointed out that movement of additional units close to the East German and Czech borders might well be viewed by Soviet military planners as extreme provocation or as a signal of aggressive intentions by NATO. Moreover, the plan to concentrate units at border locations smacked of a Maginot Line mentality which would reduce rather than expand the maneuverability of NATO forces. The Russians, Aspin believed, possessed no such capability to mount a massive lightning attack which could overwhelm NATO within forty-eight hours. The Nunn-Bartlett plan would also cost close to $50 billion, a totally unjustifiable sum. As a counter to the plan, Aspin offered his own three-point program: the establishment of joint NATO-Warsaw Pact observation teams which could observe maneuvers and war preparations on both sides, mutually agreed restrictions on the length and size of military maneuvers on both sides, and restrictions on the numbers and types of troop movements within defined regions on both sides.[80]

The Congressional debate on the possibility of surprise Soviet attack in Europe and NATO's strategic plans continued well into 1977. Although the Nunn-Bartlett proposals were not this time translated into specific legislation, they were in fact adopted in large measure by Pentagon planners. Indeed, there is much evidence to indicate that the Nunn-Bartlett ideas simply mirrored the thinking of senior military planners in both the Pentagon and NATO, especially General Alexander Haig, Supreme Allied Commander, and that the basic rationale of the plans had been adopted as a kind of master plan for U.S. forces in Europe some time before they were clearly articulated by Nunn and Bartlett in 1976. At any rate, it is clear that the Nunn-Bartlett proposals of 1976 were a logical continuation and extension of the Nunn Amendments which had been adopted by Congress in 1974 and 1975. And, as we shall see later, the plan to move U.S. forces closer to the eastern borders formed a central element of the Stoessel Plan pressed upon the Germans in 1980.

In 1977 the army continued its efforts to strengthen both its forces and equipment reserves in Europe. The unity of thought between Senator Nunn and army planners was seen in new plans announced by General Bernard Rogers, the army chief of staff, in a speech to the Association of the United States Army on October 18, 1977. The motivation for the plans was clearly the concern in the Pentagon and in Congress over the Soviet Union's apparent ability to launch a ground attack on Western Europe with only five to seven days of preparation, instead of the approximately three weeks of warning time formerly assumed by the Atlantic alliance. In his speech General Rogers said that the measures would improve the army's and NATO's ability to deal with an attack that might occur with little warning. The new emphasis, he indicated, was to increase to the highest level possible the readiness of the forces already deployed or to be deployed during the first thirty days of a war. The plan was to increase the weapons, ammunition and equipment stockpiles in Europe, and to increase the numbers of troops in the five mechanized infantry and armored divisions, plus other combat units principally in Germany. Though he did not specify how much additional equipment and weapons would be positioned in Europe, or the extent of the troop increase, he reminded Senator Humphrey and critics in Congress that improvements in Europe would not be without cost:

> The gains we will obtain through this focus on early force readiness for Europe will not be without their price. Yet the threat exists now, and we must act with dispatch......We have no alternative but to withdraw some equipment from both active and reserve component units and divert some existing production output previously allocated to CONUS (Continental United States) units. Similarly, in order to increase the personnel fill of our forward deployed units in Europe, our CONUS units will likely feel a decline in their strengths.[81]

A few months later, in early 1978, the army expressed concern over the need for additional artillery in Europe. Western intelligence sources reported that the Soviet Union enjoyed at least a two to one advantage in artillery over NATO forces. U.S. commanders also indicated that a shortage of artillery was one of their greatest worries. Massive fire by allied artillery and anti-tank weapons would be required to halt a heavy tank-led attack before it penetrated far into German territory. As a shortterm measure to increase allied firepower, pending action in Congress to provide real growth in army resources, the army announced in January, 1978, that several batallions of heavy and medium artillery, capable of firing atomic shells, would be sent to Europe in the coming months. The weapons would include 8-inch Howitzers and 155-mm guns, taken from U.S. based army units, and they would be capable of being armed with the controversial neutron warhead, if President Carter approved its production.[82] At the time Carter had not indicated his plans for neutron warheads in Europe beyond saying that they would not be deployed unless the NATO allies wanted them.

In 1978 the Pentagon continued full speed ahead in implementing the master plan, as expressed in the Nunn-

Bartlett proposals. President Carter indicated his support for the plans and emphasized the need to station as many U.S. forces as possible very near the front line in the border areas. General Haig told the Senate Armed Services Committee that the period of "greatest danger, greatest vulnerability" for defending NATO forces would be "a few days to a couple of weeks" after an attack, and that NATO's efforts were being heavily concentrated on meeting such a contingency.[83] Under a secret "consolidated guidance" document sent to the army over the signature of Defense Secretary Harold Brown, a plan would be implemented from fiscal 1981 through fiscal 1984 to ship additional weapons to Europe to arm three more divisions. In 1978 the army had 5 and 2/3 divisions, fully equipped, on the ground in Europe, 5 of which were stationed in Germany. Stored in Europe was combat equipment for two divisions based in the United States. Once the equipment for an additional three U.S. based divisions arrived in Europe, the army would have the arms for a total of 10 and 2/3 divisions there. Since the army had a total of 16 and 2/3 divisions, the bulk of its total combat equipment would be concentrated in Europe. Five U.S. based divisions would have equipment stored in Europe for immediate pick up in an emergency. Pentagon sources indicated that teams were already in Europe looking for places to store the arms for the three additional divisions.[84]

The plan was the subject of considerable controversy both in the Pentagon and in Congress throughout the rest of 1978. Senator Nunn and his supporters contended that storing tanks, guns, missiles, and helicopters in Europe prior to the outbreak of war was the best way to insure that American troops based in the United States could move into battle quickly and hence deny victory to Soviet forces in the first few days and weeks. Critics countered that the plan, by stripping U.S. based divisions of much of their weaponry, was a dangerous example of putting too many eggs in one basket at a time when war was most likely to occur outside of Europe. Robert Komer, a primary adviser to Defense Secretary Brown, admitted that the plan might be so costly that Congress would refuse to provide the money. The Pentagon estimated that it would cost slightly more than $2 billion to store the equipment for three divisions in Europe. Taking the weapons from the U.S. based divisions would leave those divisions with only 70 percent of the combat equipment they normally had for training. "If we're having trouble training our troops when the division has 100 percent of its equipment," asked one army critic of the plan, "how are we going to do the job with only 70 percent of the equipment?"[85] An even more worrisome matter, according to other critics, was that by storing so much equipment in Europe, the army would lessen its ability to respond to threats outside of Europe, where they were more likely to occur. One outspoken military critic of the plan was retired Rear Admiral George Miller, former navy director of strategic planning. According to Miller, the storage of equipment in Europe, where it could be easily spotted and targeted, plus concentrating troops on what should be the forward picket line for alerting forces to the rear, would "enable the Soviets to deal with them in their own time and in their own way."[86]

Debates on Force Readiness and Strategy

By this time, mid-1978, there was increasing doubt in many quarters that the multiple changes affecting U.S. forces in Germany were in the best interests of the United States' longterm strategic objectives. Since at least 1974 the congruence of thinking between senior planners in the Pentagon and the senior members of the Senate Armed Services Committee, led by Sam Nunn, had provided a clear path for the basic restructuring of U.S. forces in Germany. Indeed, much of the revolution advocated by Lawrence and Record in the pivotal Brookings Institution study of 1974 had now been accomplished, with congressional authorization provided by the Nunn Amendments and subsequent plans. The slogan of "hammering fat into swords" had been used effectively by defense secretaries Schlesinger, Rumsfeld, and Brown in persuading Congress to accept a larger defense budget and to endorse an increase of army divisions from thirteen to sixteen. All along there had been resistance to these far-reaching changes both within Congress and important segments of the army staff. As early as 1975 concern was expressed by the army chief of staff, General Frederick Weyland, that army divisions in Europe were in danger of losing their staying power in combat if the support troops, such as engineers, quartermaster and communications, were cut any further.[87] In the summer of 1975 General James Polk, army commander in Europe until his retirement in 1971, published an article in *Strategic Review* questioning the wisdom of the congressionally mandated changes. The article, which reflected one line of thought within the army staff, argued that the reductions required by the Nunn Amendment were reducing the self-sufficiency and flexibility of the army while adding very little to its combat power. Polk contended that through the reductions the army was being driven into a short-war strategy in which it could fight for only a few days or weeks before it faced possible defeat or recourse to tactical nuclear weapons.[88]

The structural changes can be seen in the changing ratio of combat to support troops between 1972 and 1977. In 1972 the ratio in the army was 59% combat troops to 41% support troops. In 1974, the year of the Nunn Amendment, the ratio was 61% combat to 39% support; by the end of 1975 it was 64% to 36%; in 1976, 68% to 32%; and by 1977, when the changes were largely completed, the ratio stood at 71% combat troops to 29% support troops. Clearly, the capacity of the army to counter a Soviet attack had improved in many respects. In 1978 General George Blanchard, the army's commanding general in Europe, expressed unrestrained optimism over the army's higher overall state of readiness. The Seventh Army, he pointed out, was at more than 100 percent of its authorized strength. More than 90 percent of the troops were in their chosen occupational specialty "doing what they have been trained to do." Equipment authorized for active units was nearing 100 percent and exceeding Department of the Army targets. The divisions and armored cavalry regiments had received all of the 320 Cobra helicopters armed with the TOW anti-tank missiles. The Dragon anti-tank weapon had gone to all units, the 155mm Howitzer had been improved, and the improved model M-60 tank would go to cavalry units later in the year.[89]

Still, however, the deeper implications of the structural changes were troubling to many commanders and military analysts. In the spring of 1978 Drew Middleton reviewed the situation for *The New York Times*. Wide ranging discussions with enlisted men, noncommissioned officers, company commanders and general officers led him to two major conclusions: first, the Seventh Army, despite some inadequacies in the most advanced equipment, was well prepared to meet and hold the first wave of any Soviet invasion from the East; second, and much more troubling, it was questionable whether the army could sustain the battle beyond the initial period of intense fighting during the first few days. Middleton concluded that the 5th Corps, deployed in the northern sector of the Seventh Army's area, was capable of handling a first attacking echelon of six or seven Soviet divisions during a first stage of five to seven days. Then, however, even assuming a two-day delay before the Russians renewed the attack, the corps would be reduced to 50 percent of its strength in weapons, munitions, and equipment. Sustaining the battle at that point was the big question mark. "It is easy to see a situation in which tank mechanics would have to work all out to load ammunition for artillery and tanks," a staff officer said. "Who would be left to service the tanks? That would be one result in war of reducing the support units in peace."[90]

Middleton found a consensus among officers that the army would be capable of a spasm of intense combat that would use up ammunition and weapons at an unprecedented rate. The movement of supplies and reinforcements to the battle area, the major function of support troops, would be the big problem. The structural changes brought about by the Nunn Amendment and Pentagon planners were consonant with a change in strategic doctrine from protracted war to short war. Now the army was in a much better position than previously to preclude the success of a Soviet *blitzkrieg* against Western Europe. What worried military commanders, however, is what would happen if allied defense plans worked less successfully than envisaged. What would happen if the initial stage of intense combat resulted in more or less of a draw, so that allied forces, in order to prevail, would have to engage in a much more protracted conflict? A vastly changed combat to support troop ratio (in military jargon the "tooth to tail" ratio) might lead to disastrous results. According to Middleton:

> The issue is not simply whether airborne reinforcements from the United States would arrive to participate in the second phase of a battle. Rather, it is whether the army would have the resources in manpower and ammunition to keep the front supplied.[91]

The Stoessel "Demarche"

Despite criticism and controversy Pentagon planners, with the blessing of Senator Nunn and a majority of the members of the Senate Armed Services Committee, continued to develop and refine the new plan for U.S. forces in Germany during the next two years. Since the major objectives were to provide the equipment for three additional U.S. based "Reforger" divisions on German soil and to move German based U.S. forces closer to the eastern borders, it was clear from the outset that a major financial contribution from the German government would be needed to provide the substantial sums the plan would require. In early November, 1980, Ambassador Walter Stoessel presented an eight-point plan to the German defense minister, Hans Apel. Though Apel received the plan cordially and with appropriate compliments concerning American resolve in the defense of Europe, he also stated immediately that, given the German government's new efforts to bring the budget deficit under control, coupled with an underfunded defense budget, he did not see where the money for a German contribution could possibly come from.[92]

The Americans lost no time in applying maximum pressure on the Germans. At a conference on military preparedness in Munich in late February, 1981, deputy defense secretary Frank Carlucci told the Germans in no uncertain terms that they could not expect the United States to strengthen and improve the forces stationed in Germany "if the other allies do not increase their own contribution to the common defense efforts." An American senator took the argument one step further by asserting that the Americans might decide to pull their forces out of Europe entirely if the Europeans were unwilling to strengthen their own defense potential substantially. Apel left the conference early with the remark, "It's likely to get much more interesting."[93]

The Germans felt they had very good reasons to stake out a hard bargaining position at the outset of the negotiations on the "Stoessel demarche," as it came to be known. In the first place the recession in Germany, which many believed had been unfairly exported by the United States, was deepening, unemployment was rising, and the German budget deficit, for the first time since the the founding of the republic, was reeling out of control. Secondly, leading German political leaders of all three parties were agreed that West Germany, despite severe material and financial difficulties, had fulfilled in good faith all of its obligations to NATO, while the Belgians, the Dutch, and the Danes had allowed their defense expenditures to decline, thereby placing a greater burden on Germany's defense establishment. Thirdly, the Germans were nonplussed by what they believed one of the main emphases of the improved force structure program really was, namely, an intention to orient U.S. forces earmarked for Europe toward non-European contingencies as much as toward the Soviet threat in Europe. Finally, the Germans felt that as the only European ally to have undertaken financial obligations for defense improvement programs in Greece, Turkey, and Portugal, West Germany had already gone an extra mile in underwriting the defense posture of the Atlantic alliance.[94]

The German government's reaction to the Stoessel Plan throughout the first half of 1981 was decidedly cold. Visits to Washington by defense minister Apel in March and by Chancellor Schmidt in May brought no progress. The German visitors used the visits mainly to recite a litany of German objections to the catalogue of unrealistic new American demands. In an interview with the *Washington Post* in July the inspector general of the German army, General Jürgen Brandt, candidly expressed the dim view the German defense ministry had of the plans: "I believe it would be easier to station cruise missiles on the moon than to move American troops closer to the border." In Brandt's opinion the enormous sums of money required to build new installations for American troops could be more profitably used for weapons, equipment, and other projects to increase the military strength of the allied forces.[95]

Throughout the negotiations the German government made public very little information about the demands contained in the Stoessel demarche. Quite naturally the government found it difficult to justify stringency measures and budget cutbacks and at the same time announce that substantial sums might have to be made available to the Americans for new programs involving the troops. Since American troops had been stationed in the same garrisons throughout southern Germany for over thirty-five years, the German government found it troublesome to explain why the troops would now have to be moved closer to the borders and why enormous new supply installations would be necessary for the the Reforger troops. The construction of large new garrisons in the border regions would require government land acquisition programs on a vast scale, which would be certain to arouse vigorous, perhaps violent protests from farmers, environmentalists, and other groups opposed to a general military buildup.

It is important to appreciate the multiple and conflicting pressures the German government faced in the Stoessel negotiations. The growing German budget deficit, coupled with recession and growing unemployment, dictated caution and resistance to the American demands. And, given the enormous legal and practical difficulty of acquiring government land in a densely populated country, the government had good reason to fear the hard-nosed protest movement that might be generated by the proposal to move American troops to new locations. The rationale of a revised military strategy is difficult for any government to explain to its people in the best of times. In this case, the broad catalog of demands in the Stoessel program would require a herculean effort to explain and justify the technicalities and nuances of a new military policy. There was little enthusiasm for the plan in German military circles, since German military leaders were inclined to the view that the costs of the Stoessel changes far outweighed the benefits in terms of improved defense capability. Despite German sympathy for the American morale problem caused by old, outmoded facilities, the Germans did not feel they were obligated to foot the lion's share of the bill for brand new installations. In addition, the Germans resented what they believed to be insufficient understanding and appreciation by the Americans for their substantial contributions to allied defense in recent years. As the *Frankfurter Neue Presse* put it:

Washington's plans to move American combat troops in Germany closer to the borders of the Warsaw Pact states are meeting only with a tired smile in Bonn. The main reason for this response: no one can afford to pay for such a super expensive undertaking. The costs are estimated at 15 to 20 billion marks. And besides, experts view such measures as militarily useless, since the American units are already stationed as far forward as necessary. .....On the German side higher military authorities have made it crystal clear that according to NATO agreements the Americans are fully responsible for the renovations of their barracks. .....As a further argument against the American plan it is pointed out in Bonn that (the plan) is in no way consonant with the political landscape. From it would arise unnecessary emotions, which could not be countered. .....Also, the Soviet party newspaper *Pravda* immediately reacted and let it be known that the proposed American step would 'increase tensions and the danger of war in central Europe.' .....Representatives of the **Bundeswehr** have not tried to conceal their opinion that they would rather see the money necessary for the realization of the American plans used more profitably for weapons and other military provisions, which are necessary for building the strength of the Atlantic alliance.[96]

Despite the unfavorable domestic political landscape, the German government was faced on the other hand with unrelenting American pressure. On a trip to Europe to inspect American military installations in April, 1981, Senator Strom Thurmond found conditions in the outmoded American facilities so deplorable as to demand immediate, forthright action. At a press conference in Frankfurt in July, the army chief of staff, General Edward Meyer, declared that German objections to the costs of restationing American troops were hardly justifiable, since the installations vacated by the Americans would be returned to the German government. Since the value of the real estate returned, often located in or around urban areas, would be much higher than the value of the real estate acquired in the more remote areas, the German government might well gain from the exchanges.[97]

More than anything else, however, it was the Damocles sword of threatened troop withdrawals which the American Congress held over the German government which propelled it toward reaching accommodation with the Americans over the Stoessel proposals. Congressional pressure increased considerably in late 1981 and early 1982 as a result of three convergent circumstances. First, many members of the Reagan administration were angered with what they believed was insufficient German support of American initiatives in reference to Soviet-inspired crises in Afghanistan and Poland. Consequently, for a while at least, the administration did not attempt to counter a growing inclination in Congress to question the continued stationing of American troops in Germany. Second, Congress was influenced by a growing chorus of critics of the American presence in Germany which could be heard in newspaper and television editorials and other media forms throughout the country. Third, a catalyst was present in the form of Senator Ted Stevens, the assistant majority leader in the Senate, who, after years of reflection, decided to succeed Senator Mansfield as the sponsor of long moribund proposals to withdraw American troops from Germany.

For many years successive American administrations had used the threat of troop withdrawals to gain greater respect from the Germans on all manner of American initiatives. Though both the Johnson and Nixon administrations had expended great energy in combatting the Mansfield program in Congress, the initiative nevertheless served as a convenient threat whenever the administration found it necessary to negotiate with the Germans on issues involving money or support for American-inspired NATO initiatives. With the defeat of Mansfield's proposals in 1974 and the senator's retirement in 1976, the matter appeared to have been laid to rest, and the Germans had grown more self-confident in negotiations with Washington, knowing that the threat of troop withdrawals was not a significant issue in Congress. Now, after a hiatus of seven years, the troop withdrawal issue surfaced again, placing the Germans once again in the unpleasant position of either giving in to Washington's demands or facing Congressional retaliation in the most sensitive matter of the country's security. In late 1981 relations between Bonn and Washington were at a low ebb owing to American disenchantment with the growing peace movement in West Germany and President Reagan's profound frustration over Germany's hard-nosed attitude in the gas pipeline deal with the Soviet Union. In early December Ambassador Arthur Burns warned the Germans that "they (the American troops) will not stay, if they are not welcome."[98] He repeated the warning again in mid-January, 1982, in an interview with the SPD weekly newspaper *Vorwärts.*[99] Two weeks later Senate majority leader Howard Baker declared in a newspaper interview that a proposal in Congress to withdraw American troops might produce a wave of support which could not be resisted.[100]

Some of the details of the American plan were revealed in the summer of 1981, when the negotiations apparently reached the stage of serious bargaining. The plan envisaged the movement of three combat brigades to existing installations which could be expanded at Wildflecken, Grafenwoehr and Giessen during a first stage which would take approximately five years. The restationing of an additional fourteen brigades would be effected over a period of twenty-five years, during which time entirely new barracks and facilities would be constructed in the border areas. The program would cost approximately eleven to thirteen billion German marks, according to Pentagon estimates.[161]

As might have been expected, the CDU opposition in the *Bundestag* pressed the government early on in the negotiations to reach an acceptable accommodation with the Americans. Werner Marx, chairman of the defense committee in the *Bundestag,* expressed strong approval of an idea which, in the opinion of the CDU leadership, would strengthen America's engagement in Europe, lend higher credibility to the concept of forward defense and diminish the danger of a conquest of the eastern third of the Federal Republic by Soviet forces in case of war. In comments to the press Marx admitted that the restationing of forces would create large problems, especially in the acquisition of the necessary land, but, he added, "we must accustom ourselves to the fact that the preservation of freedom is not accomplished by demonstrations and slogans against weapons, but requires concrete sacrifices." The government, he felt, had so far handled the American requests in an awkward and uncouth manner. It was time to stop making limp excuses and to face up to the real sacrifices which were now required.[102]

The Stoessel plan was debated vigorously in the press as well as in the *Bundestag* for a period of several months. As might be expected, the major newspapers in Bavaria took the lead in championing the plan, while papers in the remainder of the country expressed much more skepticism. The issue of costs was a paramount consideration. As the *Frankfurter Allgemeine* expressed it:

> The costs of this strategic reorientation would extend into the billions (of marks). There can be no doubt that the restationing of American divisions to more 'forward' positions might be necessary to reinforce the 'credibility of forward defense.' However, the reality of our federal form of government, the difficulty of land acquisition, and most especially the empty treasury all argue against this undeserving initiative of the Pentagon.[103]

Der Spiegel was even less enthused:

> The 'master restationing plan,' proposed over and over by the Americans for years, and resisted by the Germans with equal tenacity, would demand, according to experts in Bonn, at least four billion marks just in the first phase. Who is going to find the money for land acquisition, the construction of training grounds, barracks, vehicle maintenance facilities, workshops, and storage depots is as quarrelsome a matter between the Germans and the Americans as the military necessity of the action to 'Go East.' .....The Americans are less concerned about forward defense than they profess. What they are really after is to remove their soldiers from the urban conurbations in the Rhine-Main area, where they have been since the Second World War. The temptations at the end of the work day are simply too near and too great: bars, alcohol, girls, and drugs. .....The more important reasons for moving, in German opinion, relate above all to the terrible conditions of the barracks of the Fifth Corps. They are in fact slums. But, according to the NATO Troop Statute, the users of the facilities, i.e. the Americans, are responsible for the repair and maintenance of the installations. If the federal government should agree to pay for renovations and new facilities, as it did in 1972, similar demands could also be made by the British, the Dutch, the Belgians, and the Canadians. The French have already made known their wishes: to the tune of 1.3 billion marks.[104]

By the fall of 1981 the German government let it be known that it would be willing to meet at least some of the American demands. In mid-September the foreign ministry announced that some money could be made available for the expansion and the security of storage depots on the territory of the Federal Republic. The payments would be, however, strictly for the logistical support of the American reinforcement troops. The *Bundeswehr* would make available approximately one billion marks over several years for various projects. For fiscal 1982, 150 million marks would be available for projects connected with the storage of American weapons and equipment. According to the Pentagon's plans, six American divisions would be flown to Germany within a few days in case of war or extreme crisis. The German government, in turn, had now agreed to make available

2000 German troops in peacetime to guard and maintain the stored material and equipment. At the same time, the German government also let it be known that it had not changed its mind about the restationing provisions of the Stoessel proposals. An undertaking of such enormous cost could not be underwritten by the German government due to its precarious financial situation at the time. The renovation of the present barracks and the construction of new ones would have to remain the responsibility of the American government.[105]

The movement of the German government toward accommodation of at least some of the demands was met in Washington with increased Congressional pressure to bring the Germans to heel on the remaining demands in the Stoessel plan. In addition, the acts of terrorist groups in Germany served to exacerbate American public opinion on all aspects of the military relationship between Germany and the United States. In the fall of 1981 two spectacular terrorist attacks on American military installations placed additional strains on the relationship: the bombing of air force headquarters at Ramstein and the attempt to assassinate USAREUR commander General Kroesen in Heidelberg. Though General Kroesen managed to escape the assassination attempt with only minor injuries, several lives were lost and substantial property damage was done in the bomb blast at Ramstein. The terrorist onslaughts, widely reported in the American media, excited public opinion to an extent not seen in years in reference to American troops in Germany. Combined with repeated administration statements about insufficient German support of NATO defense plans and reams of negative editorial opinion concerning the growth of neutralist tendencies in Germany, the result was an outpouring of letters to Congress demanding the withdrawal of American troops from Germany.

In September Klaus Francke, a leading CDU deputy in the *Bundestag* and member of the defense committee, returned from a trip to Washington with an alarming description of the mood on Capitol Hill and in American public opinion in general. Thousands of letters were pouring into Congressional offices from throughout the country demanding action in reference to events in Germany. There was even an increasing flow of letters to Congressmen from American soldiers stationed in Germany demanding that something be done about their miserable living conditions. Francke found an ever hardening mood in Congress concerning the need for immediate action on the Stoessel proposals. "The members of Congress are not ready to be put off by the Germans any longer. They want a clear answer to the Stoessel plan," he said. Alluding to the origin of the plan, he declared further: "The Stoessel plan was not a proposal of then President Carter, but rather a demand of the members of

Congress. And they aren't going to be led around by the nose any longer."[106]

Negotiations between the two governments continued for several months in secret, with no details made public. By early February, 1982, the basic outline of an agreement had been drawn up. Final agreement was delayed, however, by an angry outcry in the German *Bundestag* over the McDade Amendment passed by Congress the previous December, which forbade the purchase of weapons for American forces from European NATO partners. Leading members of the SPD insisted that the German government refuse to sign the treaty until the offensive McDade Amendment had been repealed. After all, the SPD spokesmen argued, the intolerable pressure and interference being exercised by the Americans on the Germans were reaching proportions which no government in its right mind would tolerate.[107] CDU spokesmen answered, in reply, that there was no time to be lost in concluding the negotiations. If no treaty were forthcoming soon, there would certainly be a new initiative in the Congress to withdraw American troops from Germany in substantial numbers or altogether. If Germany wished to maintain and strengthen the American commitment to the defense of the Federal Republic, the Germans had no choice but to accept the necessary sacrifices. German intransigence would serve only to increase America's disillusionment with its German ally.[108]

The Wartime Host Nation Support Treaty

Finally, on April 15, 1982, the Wartime Host Nation Support Treaty was officially signed at a ceremony in Bonn by German foreign minister Hans-Dietrich Genscher and American ambassador Arthur Burns. The major purpose of the treaty was to enable the United States to effect a rapid reinforcement in crisis or war of its ground and air forces in Germany to more than twice their strength. The forward defense of the alliance area would thereby be enhanced by the deployment to Germany of six combat divisions from the U.S. within ten days. According to the terms of the treaty, the Federal Republic would train and equip some 93,000 *Bundeswehr* reservists to provide support to U.S. forces in the areas of transportation, supply, airfield repair, logistics and security of U.S. army facilities, in addition to those German troops who would already be on active duty. The German military reserve manpower would be made available from the general reserve manpower pool, and would not diminish the current or proposed reserve military structure, nor would it in any way diminish the combat effectiveness of the *Bundeswehr*. Germany undertook also to make available additional civilian

support in the form of transportation, material handling,
facilities and other services. The agreement was viewed by both
sides as a significant step in reducing the strategic airlift
requirements on the United States for support forces, thereby
making it possible for the U.S. to provide a higher percentage of
combat troops in an emergency. For this reason, and because of
the intensified use of in-country assets, the agreement was
expected to result in increased cost effectiveness for the alliance.
The investment costs of the treaty would be approximately 570
million dollars. These, plus all operating expenses, would be
shared equitably by the United States and the Federal Republic.

The treaty was greeted in Germany with a mixture of
approval and skepticism. The *Sonntagsblatt* in Hamburg
observed:

> The defense ministry seems to be able to do what
> the common man thought was impossible: to grab a
> naked man by the pocket. Despite the existing and
> ever deepening financial difficulties, a whole series
> of new projects is being planned and carried out.
> .....Burden-sharing is the watchword here. The
> more the USA groans under the burdens of the
> Reagan armament plans, the stronger the demands
> get in Congress that the Europeans must shell out
> more money for defense.[109]

Other commentators protested the signing of a new treaty as long
as the Congress refused to repeal the offensive McDade
Amendment.[110] From the German point of view, the Federal
Republic had come much more than halfway in meeting the
American demands by undertaking expensive new commitments.
In the view of American critics, however, the Germans had not
done nearly enough. Congressional critics could not fail to notice
that only one or two of the proposals in the original Stoessel plan
had been addressed by the new treaty. As far as other demands
were concerned, especially the plan to restation American forces
nearer the border areas, the German government was still
refusing to budge. Any agreement is, of course, a compromise
package which leaves both sides partially satisfied and partially
dissatisfied. In the case of the Wartime Host Nation Support
Treaty, apart from hard-line Congressional critics, leading
political figures on both sides of the Atlantic were pleased that a
series of complex negotiations had been amicably concluded and
had resulted in a substantial and meaningful new German
contribution to an enhanced strategy of forward defense. Not
only had long-standing NATO plans been activated on a treaty
basis, but the German-American political relationship had been
revitalized by concessions and sacrifices on both sides.

Recent Developments in Strategy and Tactics:
The Airland Battle Doctrine

In 1982 and 1983 the debate continued in Germany and the United States on military doctrine, strategy, weapons, and the structure and positioning of U.S. forces in Germany. In September, 1982, General Rogers forcefully advocated, as he had done before, that a continued buildup of the conventional forces of NATO members must be undertaken, if Western Europe were to be defended against Soviet attack without the early use of nuclear weapons. The alternative to a Western effort to bolster conventional defenses, he said, would be "a steady widening of the gap between the military strength of the Soviets and the Warsaw Pact and NATO." Raising conventional force levels would involve an annual increase of four percent in real terms in West European military outlays. He believed, however, that the balance in conventional forces in Europe was not as unfavorable to the West as was often portrayed, though there were other factors which increased the Soviet margin, such as mechanized divisions, divisions available after mobilization, main battle tanks, artillery tubes, medium bombers, fighter planes and interceptor aircraft. General Rogers was convinced, in contrast to other observers, that he had the means to oppose a second echelon of Soviet forces if the West were invaded.[11]

The most recent changes in strategy and tactics in Europe have again demonstrated a convergence of thinking between Senator Nunn and his allies on the Senate Armed Services Committee, Supreme Allied Commander General Bernard Rogers, army Chief of Staff General Edward C. Meyer, and central planning staffs in the Pentagon. In the fall of 1982 the army developed a new field manual based upon a new doctrine known as Airland Battle. Designed to move the army away from the traditional emphasis on defense along the front line, the new doctrine emphasizes a more mobile, maneuverable, "counterstroke" style of fighting that would make it easier to strike behind enemy lines in case of hostilities. Another purpose of the doctrine is to increase conventional fighting capabilities to the point that an early first use of nuclear weapons would not be necessary. Traditionally, NATO doctrine relied heavily upon the threat of nuclear response as a deterrent to Soviet aggression in Europe. The longterm Soviet strategic buildup of the 1960s and 1970s, however, undermined the credibility of the American nuclear umbrella. Beginning in 1977, when General Donn A. Starry became the head of the Training and Doctrine Command, the new ideas began to ripen and to be developed on an experimental basis. The changes were given impetus by General Edward C. Meyer, when he became army chief of staff in 1979 and by the emergence of the military reform movement in Congress in the early 1980s, a caucus of Republicans and Democrats from both houses seeking to alter military priorities by increasing fighting effectiveness with fewer expensive, high technology weapons.

The older doctrine stressed that defensive firepower should be concentrated wherever the enemy's attack occurred, while the new doctrine's goal is to "disrupt the enemy timetable, complicate command and control, and frustrate his plans, thus weakening his grasp on the initiative." According to the guidelines of the doctrine:

> Opposing forces on the next battlefield will rarely fight along orderly, distinct lines. Faced by an enemy who expects to sustain rapid movement during the offensive.....the United States Army must be prepared to fight campaigns of considerable movement, complemented by intense volumes of fire. The fluid environment of modern war will place a premium on leadership, unit cohesion, and effective, independent operations.[112]

In essence the new doctrine calls for a counteroffensive in case of attack to carry the battle 75 to 100 miles behind the line of enemy advance. Traditionally, the army concentrated on the forward defense line, rather than behind it. But a new counteroffensive, the new doctrine holds, does not put defenders at risk; rather, it is the only way to throw the attacker off guard and seize the initiative. Stressing the link between military operations and political bargaining, the doctrine emphasizes that:

> ....Once political authorities commit military forces in pursuit of political aims, military forces must win something - else there will be no basis from which political authorities can bargain to win politically. Therefore, the purpose of military operations cannot be simply to avert defeat - but rather it must be to win.[113]

The Airland Battle doctrine comprises two principal ideas. The first is that of a counterattack deep behind enemy lines carried out by the corps commander, who is also coordinating the main battle in the forward area. The second idea involves maneuver, concealment and surprise, elements that must influence leadership and fighting at all levels, down to the platoon. Major computerized war games the army has played using the new doctrine and using the weapons it plans to have in hand by 1986 seem to demonstrate, according to army planners, that the defenders could hold the invaders without the use of nuclear or chemical weapons, a development which might alter NATO's assumption that it would have to use tactical nucear weapons to defeat a Warsaw Pact invasion. Robert W. Komer, who was under secretary of defense for policy in the Carter administration, states that the doctrine "is the most encouraging thing going on in any of the armed services today. The army has traditionally been the stodgiest of the armed services and has also traditionally been the low man on the totem pole. What I think has happened is that the army, being third, has decided to try harder."[114]

By 1983 there was good evidence that the doctrine had already influenced the army's research and development program. Four areas were given priority: advanced surveillance and targeting systems; improved battlefield command, control and intelligence; munitions that can change as their targets move; and advances in biotechnology which, it is hoped, will make it possible to vaccinate soldiers against possible encounters with chemical weapons.

In the early 1980s the doctrine seemed to enjoy a kind of honeymoon of consensus in Pentagon planning staffs and Congress. With time, however, as with any other new program, a lively controversy has developed. Some Congressional critics charge that the army sees the new doctrine mainly as a good way to enlarge its traditionally small slice of the military budget. Others worry that the army may construe the doctrine merely as an excuse to purchase glamorous new weapons systems. Though some members of the military reform movement in Congress approve of the basic outline of the plan, others reject it, calling for new tactics and better training which could give the army better fighting power for the same money or less. What is not entirely clear is the relationship between the new fighting doctrine and the army's "master restationing plan" to move combat units closer to the eastern borders in Europe. There is, as some critics point out, an inherent contradiction between the restationing plan, which seems to emphasize "holding the line" at point of attack, and the Airland Battle doctrine which stresses counterattack and maneuver. The controversy is likely to continue for some time to come. According to former defense secretary Harold Brown:

> The army is changing, but when you ask them exactly what they're doing, they're not clear about it. At least until recently, the army hasn't had a clear idea of what direction it's going in. The

change may not be very deep, but it's deeper than
the critics say it is.[115]

Support for the new doctrine and for the modernization plans
based on it also seemed to wax and wane on the part of the
Reagan administration. According to Milton Benjamin in the
Washington Post:

> The army's modernization program won support
> early in the Reagan Administration as strategists
> sought ways to reduce NATO's reliance on nuclear
> weapons to deter or stem a Soviet attack with non-
> nuclear forces in Europe. Modernizing U.S.
> conventional forces would reduce NATO's
> dependence on atomic weapons, it was argued.
> ....However, the Administration's commitment to
> the army program has appeared to wane as the
> White House concentrates its attention on nuclear
> strategic weapons, such as the MX missile system
> and the theater nuclear missiles planned for
> installation in Germany next year. In a recent
> speech, presidential assistant Thomas C. Reed
> ranked conventional military modernization fifth
> on a list of military priorities.[116]

Clearly, the debates over strengthening conventional forces in
Germany and over weapons and strategies of the forces are likely
to continue for several years in the late 1980s and 1990s.

The NATO Dual Decision

One important NATO decision of the late 1970s has been
treated only in passing in this study. This is the so-called NATO
"dual decision" of December, 1979, to strengthen nuclear forces in
Europe. The dual decision approved the deployment of 572
Pershing-II and cruise missiles in five European countries
beginning in late 1983 if agreement could not be reached with the
Soviet Union in the meantime on reducing or eliminating Soviet
missile forces targeted on Western Europe. A rich literature
exists elsewhere on this issue, and since the focus of this study is
conventional forces in Germany, we have avoided a lengthy
treatment of nuclear issues and nuclear strategies. It is
important, however, to consider briefly the relationship of the
dual decision to the major developments traced in this chapter
and other issues raised in this study.

Of primary interest here is the relationship of the dual decision to other decisions concerning the size and composition of U.S. conventional forces in West Germany. It is important to realize that the dual decision to strengthen the nuclear deterrent came *after* major decisions had been taken to beef up and restructure U.S. conventional forces in Germany. Two additional brigades had been brought to Germany and a major change in the ratio of combat to support troops had been effected well before the dual decision of 1979. The timing itself shows that even in the 1970s the U.S. and German governments, as well as the other NATO allies, attempted to avoid a situation of placing too much reliance upon nuclear weapons for the defense of Europe.

The primary German concern has long been and remains today the level of the U.S. commitment to the defense of Germany and Western Europe. The German government seeks constant reassurance in every possible form that the United States remains absolutely committed to the defense of West Germany in case of any form of Soviet aggression. Few analysts, of course, expect the Soviet Union to mount either a conventional or a nuclear attack in the near future. Defense, however, always deals with the contingency of the "what if." Moreover, what negates any Soviet plans or ideas to take over Western Europe militarily is the credibility of the NATO deterrent and the certain knowledge that an attempted military conquest of Europe would mean all out war with the United States.

In the German view there are two definite legs of the American deterrent, the conventional and the nuclear. Too great an imbalance on either side of the defense equation might either tempt the Soviets to undertake an aggression or to exercise undue political pressure or blackmail. Inadequate conventional forces, or a conventional force structure not insuring full American participation in a possible war, might tempt the Soviets at some time to mount a preemptive conventional attack on Western Europe, which would surely begin in Germany. On the other hand, an inadequate nuclear deterrent undermines the credibility of the conventional forces, especially in the case of a sustained war. The nuclear deterrent, i.e. the tactical nuclear weapons stationed on German soil, has a dual purpose. First, it insures that the Soviets cannot use nuclear blackmail against the German government or threaten a preemptive strike without having to reckon with an American nuclear response. Secondly, it insures the credibility of the conventional forces by guaranteeing that they will not lose a major battle in Western Europe without resort to nuclear weapons at some point.

The balance between concern with the nuclear and the conventional sides of the NATO deterrent has shifted back and forth from time to time with changes in strategic thinking and technological developments. Throughout the decade of the 1970s the record would seem to show that primary NATO and American concern lay with strengthening the conventional side of the Western deterrent. This was in response to two developments: the deterioration in the quantity and quality of American forces in Germany as a result of the Vietnam War, and the continued Soviet conventional military buildup in Eastern Europe throughout the 1970s. The concern with the nuclear side of the deterrent came later in the decade, largely as a result of the Soviet move, begun in the mid-1970s, to deploy a new generation of SS-20 missiles targeted on Western Europe. It is important to realize, however, that NATO planners and German political leaders have never believed that an attrition of conventional forces would be a viable alternative by placing greater reliance on nuclear forces. Concern for the viability of the conventional forces has always been paramount, with the nuclear deterrent seen as a necessary backdrop to the conventional deterrent. Only when the conventional deterrent seemed to lag too far behind and to lose its credibility as a counterweight to an ever larger number of Soviet SS-20 missiles did concern shift in a major way to the nuclear deterrent. Even then, concern with the conventional forces was maintained intact with the programs for modernization, increased force levels, and changes in strategic doctrine.

It is also important to realize that the impetus for beefing up the American nuclear forces in West Germany came from the NATO allies, primarily the Germans. Discussion of the issue began in 1977, and a decision was reached only after protracted rounds of discussion among the NATO allies which lasted over two years. The Americans, reluctant at first, were persuaded by the cogent arguments presented primarily by Chancellor Schmidt and defense minister Apel. The decision was a "dual" decision in the sense that Pershing II's and cruise missiles would be brought to Europe only if the Soviets would not agree to reduce or eliminate the SS-20 missiles targeted on Western Europe. It was meant both as a bargaining mechanism with the Soviets at missile negotiations in Geneva and as a genuine military program to correct the imbalance of nuclear forces in Europe should the political effort in Geneva fail.

Given the enormous fear of nuclear war in Europe and the presence of a powerful anti-nuclear movement in West Germany, both the German and American governments realized that the emplacement of new nuclear missiles in Europe would be politically very difficult. It is probably true, however, that the strength and organization of the opposition movement came as an unpleasant surprise. What is not true, as portrayed in some analyses and press reports, is that the concern with strengthening conventional forces in Europe came about as a reaction to the German anti-nuclear movement. The record, as traced in this chapter, clearly shows that concern with the viability of conventional forces in Europe predates the dual decision and probably would have activated the programs to reform and strengthen the forces even had the Soviets not begun the deployment of SS-20 missiles. Though strongly linked at the level of overall grand strategy, the subjects of U.S. conventional forces and U.S. nuclear forces in Germany have always been treated somewhat separately, with strong attention being given at all times to the deterrent value and fighting capability of the conventional forces, with tactical nuclear weapons seen as the backdrop. And, as we have seen, even the more recent modernization program and change in military doctrine in the 1980s is an effort to maintain the viability of the conventional deterrent, so that overreliance on the nuclear deterrent can be avoided.

Notes

[1] Frankfurter Allgemeine, February 12, 1973.

[2] TIME Magazine, April 16, 1973.

[3] The Christian Science Monitor, April 30, 1973.

[4] Neue Ruhrzeitung, July 16, 1973; Frankfurter Rundschau, July 4, 1973 Bremer Nachrichten, July 20, 1973.

[5] Rheinische Post, September 20, 1973.

[6] The Financial Times (London), September 21, 1973.

[7] The Daily Telegraph, November 7, 1973.

[8] General Anzeiger (Bonn), November 27, 1973.

[9] Schwarzwälder Bote (Oberndorf), November 29, 1973.

[10] Die Welt, December 29, 1973.

[11] International Herald Tribune, February 6, 1974.

[12] Westdeutsche Allgemeine (Essen), March 26, 1974; Der Spiegel, March 25, 1974; Neue Zürcher Zeitung, April 27, 1974.

[13] Neue Zürcher Zeitung, April 27, 1974.

[14] International Herald Tribune, March 22, 1974.

[15] Financial Times (London), March 22, 1974.

[16] Süddeutsche Zeitung, July 11, 1975; General Anzeiger (Bonn), June 28, 1975; New York Herald Tribune (European Edition, Paris), September 11, 1975.

[17] Die Welt, May 29, 1975.

[18] The Times (London), September 29, 1975.

[19] Kölner Stadt-Anzeiger, September 30, 1975; Münchener Merkur, September 30, 1975.

[20] See for example Frankfurter Neue Presse, July 16, 1976; Stuttgarter Nachrichten, July 17, 1976; Südwest Presse (Ulm), July 20, 1976.

[21] International Herald Tribune, July 26, 1976.

[22] See, for example, Stuttgarter Zeitung, November 9, 1976; Westfälische Rundschau (Dortmund), December 20, 1976.

[23] TIME Magazine, March 19, 1973.

[24] James Goldsborough, "The Case for Reducing U.S. Forces in Europe," International Herald Tribune, April 12, 1973; Alain C. Enthoven, "U.S. Forces in Europe? How Many? Doing What?" Foreign Affairs, Vol. 53, No. 3 (April, 1973), pp. 513-532; Eliot L. Richardson and Mike Mansfield, "American Forces in Europe - The Pros and the Cons," Atlantic Community Quarterly, Vol. 8, No. 1 (Spring, 1970), pp. 5-16; John Yochelson, "The American Presence in Europe: Current Debate in the United States," Orbis, Vol. 15, No. 3 (Fall, 1971), pp. 784-807.

[25] Stuttgarter Zeitung, April 27, 1973; Bayern Kurier, May 5, 1973; Neue Zürcher Zeitung, May 19, 1973; Süddeutsche Zeitung, July 12, 1973; Frankfurter Allgemeine, July 27, 1973, and August 4, 1973; Bayern Kurier, August 4, 1973; International Herald Tribune, April 19, 1973, and September 1, 1973; Leslie H. Gelb and Morton H. Halperin, "Why West Europe Needs 300,000 GI's," Atlantic Community Quarterly, Vol. 9, No. 1 (1971), pp. 56-60; Elliot L. Richardson and Mike Mansfield, "American Forces in Europe - The Pros and the Cons," Atlantic Community Quarterly, Vol. 8, No. 1 (Spring 1970), pp. 5-16; John Yochelson, "The American Military Presence in Europe: Current Debate in the United States," Orbis, Vol. 15, No. 3 (Fall, 1971), pp. 784-807.

[26] Stuttgarter Zeitung, July 27, 1973.

[27] Bayern Kurier, August 4, 1973.

[28] Süddeutsche Zeitung, May 18, 1974.

[29] International Herald Tribune, June 7, 1974.

[30] Richard D. Lawrence and Jeffrey Record, U.S. Force Structure in Nato: An Alternative (Washington, D.C.: The Brookings Institution, 1974).

[31] Ibid.

[32] Deutsche Tagespost (Würzburg), November 5, 1974; The Daily Telegraph (London), November 6, 1974; Süddeutsche Zeitung, November 6, 1974; Die Welt, December 24, 1974.

[33] International Herald Tribune, December 14, 1974.

[34] Süddeutsche Zeitung, November 6, 1974.

[35] Deutsche Zeitung - Christ und Welt (Stuttgart), November 8, 1974.

[36] International Herald Tribune, July 1, 1975.

[37] Frankfurter Rundschau, August 8, 1974.

[38] The Daily Telegraph (London), August 9, 1975.

[39] Frankfurter Allgemeine, August 22, 1975.

[40] Bremer Nachrichten, October 1, 1975.

[41] Augsburger Allgemeine, October 16, 1975.

[42] Weser Kurier (Bremen), October 18, 1975.

[43] Vorwärts (Bonn), January 8, 1976.

[44] In German, die Vereinigten Burgerinitiativen zum Schutze der Garlstedter Heide.

[45] In German, die Burgeraction Garlstedter Heide.

[46] Hannoversche Allgemeine, April 24, 1976.

[47] Bremer Nachrichten, May 14, 1976.

[48] Weser Kurier (Bremen), May 15, 1976.

[49] Hannoversche Allgemeine, April 17, 1976.

[50] Rheinische Post (Düsseldorf), July 23, 1976; Süddeutsche Zeitung, July 23, 1976.

[51] Suddeutsche Zeitung, May 4, 1977.

[52] Die Welt, May 4, 1977.

[53] Frankfurter Allgemeine, May 4, 1977.

[54] Frankfurter Allgemeine, October 18, 1978; Weser Kurier (Bremen), October 28, 1978.

[55] International Herald Tribune, April 15, 1978.

[56] Ibid.

[57] Osnabrücker Zeitung, October 18, 1978.

[58] Weser Kurier, October 18, 1978.

[59] Wiesbadener Kurier, June 16, 1976.

[60] The Times (London), September 23, 1974.

[61] Financial Times (London), April 21, 1975.

[62] The Guardian (Manchester), November 2, 1976.

[63] International Herald Tribune, October 28, 1976.

[64] The Christian Science Monitor, October 28, 1976.

[65] Rheinische Post (Düsseldorf), September 3, 1976; Neue Westfälische (Bielefeld), December 14, 1976.

[66] Frankfurter Allgemeine, June 23, 1977; Die Welt, June 25, June 29, and July 18, 1977.

[67] Frankfurter Rundschau, May 2, 1975.

[68] Ibid.

[69] See, for instance, Münchener Merkur, May 13, 1975; Frankfurter Rundschau, May 13, 1975, and many others.

[70] Stuttgarter Nachrichten, May 14, 1975.

[71] Die Welt, June 16, 1976.

[72] Stuttgarter Zeitung, July 10, 1976.

[73] Deutsche Tagespost, July 16, 1976.

[74] The Sunday Times (London), August 8, 1976.

[75] Die Welt, July 12, 1976.

[76] Stuttgarter Zeitung, July 10, 1976.

[77] Die Welt, July 10, 1976.

[78] Frankfurter Allgemeine, July 30, 1976.

[79] Die Welt, November 20, 1976.

[80] Die Welt, November 20, 1976; Frankfurter Allgemeine, March 15, 1977

[81] International Herald Tribune, October 20, 1977.

[82] International Herald Tribune, January 13, 1978.

[83] International Herald Tribune, June 29, 1978.

[84] Ibid.

[85] International Herald Tribune, June 29, 1978.

[86] Ibid.

[87] International Herald Tribune, September 15, 1975.

[88] General James H. Polk, "The New Short War Strategy," Strategic Review, 3, No. 3 (Summer, 1975), pp. 52-56.

[89] International Herald Tribune, May 19, 1978.

[90] Ibid.

[91] Ibid.

[92] Stuttgarter Nachrichten, March 19, 1981.

[93] Ibid.

[94] Südwest Presse (Ulm), October 29, 1980.

[95] General-Anzeiger (Bonn), July 11, 1981.

[96] Frankfurter Neue Presse, July 14, 1981.

[97] Stuttgarter Zeitung, July 11, 1981.

[98] Stuttgarter Nachrichten, December 3, 1981; Münchener Merkur, December 3, 1981.

[99] Neue Rhein Ruhr Zeitung (Essen / Köln), January 19, 1982; Die Welt, January 20, 1982.

[100] Bayern Kurier, January 30, 1982.

[101] Die Welt, July 13, 1981; General Anzeiger (Bonn), July 11, 1981; Süddeutsche Zeitung (München), July 24, 1981.

[102] Frankfurter Allgemeine, July 17, 1981; Die Welt, July 17, 1981.

[103] Frankfurter Allgemeine, July 20, 1981.

[104] Der Spiegel (Hamburg), July 20, 1981

[105] Süddeutsche Zeitung, September 14, 1981; Die Welt, September 14, 1981.

[106] Hamburger Abendblatt, September 17, 1981; Berliner Morgenpost, September 18, 1981.

[107] Frankfurter Allgemeine, February 12, 1982.

[108] Die Welt, February 2, 1982; Frankfurter Allgemeine, February 12, 1982.

[109] Sonntagsblatt (Hamburg), March 14, 1982.

[110] Neue Zürcher Zeitung, February 27, 1982.

[111] International Herald Tribune, September 20, 1982.

[112] Quoted in Deborah Shapley, "The Army's New Fighting Doctrine," New York Times Magazine, November 28, 1982, p. 37.

[113] Ibid.

[114] Ibid.

[115] Ibid.

[116] Washington Post, November 20, 1982, p.1.

6

CONCLUSION: THE CARE AND MAINTENANCE
OF A POLITICO-MILITARY RELATIONSHIP

Until a major reordering of East-West relations takes place, either in terms of a broad settlement of the Soviet-American confrontation or a stunning breakthrough in nuclear and MBFR negotiations, the United States will continue to station a large contingent of military forces in West Germany. American forces have been in Germany now for over forty years. It is not unlikely that they will remain for many years to come. If history provides indispensable insight needed to interpret present reality, what have we learned from our near half-century of experience in stationing American forces in Germany?

The reader must of course formulate his own conclusions as to which aspects of the past impact most profoundly in specific ways upon present reality. Nevertheless, a few suggestions can be offered as to some of the lessons which might have been learned. As with any historical exercise, the lessons range from the grandiose variety to the mundane, macro and micro to use other terms, and there are perhaps quite different lessons to be garnered from each of the five broad historical periods, since each period had its own special characteristics in terms of the environmental factors affecting American forces.

The period of the military occupation from 1945 to 1949 established an overall tone and texture which served as a powerful influence on the development of relations between the United States and West Germany for the next many years. The occupation period turned out to be much shorter than most people, either Germans or Americans, expected. Though some major errors were obviously made by the American occupiers, by and large the occupation period was gentler and less oppressive than most Germans had expected. The American conquerors were, by and large, not avengers. Viewing themselves primarily as liberators of a people trampled upon by a brutal totalitarian regime, they seemed to the Germans to have mosly good intentions in regard to the future. Brutality was seldom witnessed. It occurred in isolated instances, but these were largely overshadowed by acts of kindness or by measures which showed a basic respect for the dignity of any person who had not actively coopted for a leadership position in the Nazi regime. Within four short years the German-American relationship was profoundly transformed by the larger events shaping the postwar period. Indeed, the most important legacy of the military occupation was the active and intentional creation of preconditions which later could serve as the viable foundation stones of an alliance relationship.

If the occupation period was shorter than initially expected, so too was the period of semi-sovereignty. The allied tutelage, like the occupation, was not seen by the Germans as particularly oppressive, since the Federal Republic's new-found freedom, within well defined limits, could be quite freely exercised. The occupation gave way to a carefully constructed partnership between the Federal Republic and the United States in the sphere of security. The West German government's search for a viable security policy, one which would be acceptable to the German people as well as the western allies, was, following the failure of the grandiose attempt at European military integration, eminently successful. The Truman administration's troops to Europe decision had momentous implications not only for the future security of the Federal Republic but for all of Western Europe. By providing a security grarantee which was real, constantly visible, and completely credible, it also set the stage for firmly integrating the West German state and West German military forces into the NATO alliance. By 1955 the Federal Republic and the United States had established a relationship of mutual respect based largely upon the status of defense protectorate for West Germany under the security umbrella of the United States. Throughout the period the relationships between American military personnel and the German population seemed to blossom and mature. By 1955 a kind of basic friendship had been established between Germans and Americans which lasts, in altered form, even today.

The period of consolidation and normalcy from 1955 to 1967 could be called, without much exaggeration, the "golden age" of the security relationship between the U.S. and West Germany. A vast range of friendships between American military personnel and Germans was elaborated, cemented, and allowed to mature. Both the Germans and the Americans became over time adjusted to and reasonably comfortable with the situation of Germany's security dependence upon the United States. As in any marriage, however, stresses and strains developed which could have led to two different outcomes: resolution or divorce. What is significant about the normalcy period in German-American security relations is that the partners learned to cope with the stresses and strains in a successful manner. Both the MLF plan and the offset payments issue, if not settled amicably within a reasonable period of time, could have created tensions that might have resulted in irreparable fissures in the security relationship. Instead, however, the alliance partners learned to use processes of conflict management through negotiation and compromise which led, in case after case, to an amicable resolution of conflict. In this way an even more solid foundation was laid for weathering the severe crises yet to come.

The lessons which might be learned from the period of deterioration, 1967-1973, derive mainly from the spinoff effects of the Vietnam War in West Germany. What became painfully evident to security policy makers as well as to the American public at large in the late 1960s and early 1970s was that, seen in global terms, the ratio of responsibilities to actual capabilities of American forces was entirely out of balance. The results of such an imbalance were disastrous. Not only were U.S. forces unable to "win" the Vietnam War in any meaningful way, but the complications which the war brought to U.S. forces stationed in Germany produced highly unfortunate consequences. As the forces themselves became less manageable, so too did the entire phenomenon of the American military presence in Germany. The rise in racial strife, combined with increased problems of druge usage, crime, and violence, led to successive crises in military morale which seemed almost beyond control. Though the military leaders managed to muddle through the crises and eventually reestablished a semblance of order, the price paid for this protracted period of difficulty was exorbitantly high. A not insubstantial measure of German respect for the quality of American forces was lost, never to be regained. As German confidence in the viability of the American security guarantee declined, so also did tolerance for the large scale American military presence, bringing a certain estrangement into the German-American security relationship for the first time since the war. Many Germans, in policy relevant and lay positions alike, began to take seriously the search for alternative security policies to fill the void left by the lack of confidence in the American guarantee.

Though the damage to the German-American politico-military relationship during this period was not irreparable, it was nevertheless severe. American forces never again enjoyed the enormous prestige they had had previous to the mid 1960s. The problems of this period, even after they were brought under control in a later period, complicated the management of the alliance relationship in every possible way. Disputes tended to be expressed and argued in shriller tones on both sides of the Atlantic. Reaching a settlement of serious disputes tended to be a more painful process, with less harmonious overtones at the conclusion. The end of the period saw the Germans in general less satisfied with the security dependency arrangement than they had been previously. Impetus was thereby given to the rise of a new kind of neutralist sentiment in West Germany which found its primary expression in the large "peace movements" of the 1970s and 1980s which sought to interrupt altogether the security arrangements between Germany and the United States.

The final period in our analysis, 1973 to the mid-1980s, was a period of rehabilitation and renewal, both of American forces in Germany and of the security relationship built upon them. Though things never returned to the way they had been prior to the period of deterioration, it was still possible, painfully and step by step, to rebuild and regain much of the vitality of the alliance relationship. The recurrent struggles over offset payments ended finally in 1976 when both sides decided, in effect, to liquidate a program which was more quarrelsome than beneficial. In the remaining years of the 1970s a number of structural changes were undertaken in the forces in Germany, some arising from changes in strategic doctrine and others arising from the general effort to regenerate the forces and reestablish their credibility. As part of the restructuring process the decision was made to establish a major American military presence in North Germany for the first time. The initiatives undertaken in reference to the new base at Garlstedt included efforts to integrate American military personnel into German communities and German society in new ways. The modest success of these programs provided a powerful example of the positive results which could be reaped from innovative investments in community relations programs.

The decade of the 1980s has been a decade of continuing debate on many aspects of strategy and force readiness. One important part of this debate concerns the longterm effects of the changes in the combat-to-support troops ratio mandated by the Nunn-Bartlett initiatives of previous years. This debate, as well as related debates on other aspects of force strategy and readiness, continues today and will most likely continue on into the 1990s. In 1980 a whole new catalogue of demands was presented to the German government by Washington in the form of the "Stoessel Demarche." The most noteworty result of the protracted Stoessel negotiations was the Wartime Host Nation Support Treaty signed in 1982 which establishes a higher level of German-American cooperation and support, hence a higher capability level, in case hostilities with the Soviet Union should occur. Other issues related to the Stoessel demands remain unsettled. It is unlikely that major progress on these issues can be achieved until fundamental decisions are made by the two governments in reference to proposals for major reforms in the NATO alliance.

In reviewing the history of the American military presence in West Germany as the continuous story of a developing security relationship from 1945 until the mid-1980s, one is struck by several striking features. Perhaps the most compelling aspect about the American military presence in West Germany is its durability. American forces arrived in Germany as conquerors in 1945. They remain nearly a half century later as the concrete expression of an American security guarantee of West Germany. Second, this history is, by and large, a long success story in many ways. The Federal Republic of Germany and the United States have worked together successfully for over forty years in the operation of a security arrangement which served the vital interests of both countries and the western alliance as a whole. American forces were perceived as friends by the German civilian population as early as the late 1940s. They are accepted by most Germans as friends yet today.

In terms of the historical time periods delineated for this study, two broad conclusions seem to emerge clearly and logically. First, the three periods from 1945 to 1967 - occupation, semi-sovereignty, and normalcy - all contributed to the building of a solid foundation for the German-American politico-military relationship. Even a relationship involving the potentially troublesome element of security dependency by one partner upon the other could be managed upon this firm foundation. Second, the period of deterioration from 1967 to 1973 exacted a heavy toll upon the bilateral politico-military relationship. The toll was not fatal, but it was indeed severe. If the initial foundation of the relationship had not been consolidated and secured to the extent it was by 1967, the difficulties of the 1967-1973 period might well have weakened the relationship beyond the point of no return. As it was, the relationship weathered the difficulties well, though it was never quite the same again. The loss of respect for American forces by the German population and the inclination or willingness to search seriously for alternative security arrangements has altered the basic parameters of the relationship and diminished, to a certain extent, its resiliency.

The policy implications which emerge from this historical analysis, though hardly revolutionary, are nevertheless vital to an understanding of the future dynamics of U.S.-West German relations, and they need to be repeated over and over again with clarity and certitude. They apply both to the executive and legislative branches of the U.S. government, though in somewhat different ways. First, the failure to maintain close consultations on vital bilateral security issues with the most strategic member of the Atlantic Alliance, West Germany, always has deleterious results. As Americans, we seem to understand this in an abstract sense, but we fail over and over again to translate the need for consultation with close allies into integral procedures of the policy making process. A recent case in point is the presentation of the "Stoessel Demarche" to the German government without adequate prior consultation on the practical implications of these rather sweeping proposals. The results were predictable. The Stoessel proposals met with an initial resolute rejection by the Germans. Apart from the Wartime Host Nation Support Treaty signed in 1982, they have borne little fruit, and created needless tension. Similarly, when Congress mandates major changes in military strategy or the structure of American forces without close consultation with members of the German government and *Bundestag*, it inevitably produces bitterness and resentment at all levels of the German government. The Nunn-Bartlett amendments of the mid-1970s were resented by the Germans at the time quite strongly; some of the resentment carries over to this day.

Second, constant reprimands, constant pressure, constant nagging - whatever one wishes to call it - demeans and diminishes the vitality of the relationship. This is especially true when one party feels strongly that its side of the issue is not being properly grasped, either intellectually (in terms of the facts) or emotionally (in terms of political or psychological needs) by the other partner. This leads back to, perhaps even derives from, the failure of consultation noted above. In this sense, a diplomatic or military relationship really is a bit like a marriage. Too much biting or nagging by one partner will finally cause the other to become disillusioned with the relationship, perhaps abandon it altogether. Examples from this historical account are abundant. The offset negotiations from start to finish clearly showed the American tendency to browbeat the Germans into submitting to American demands, regardless of whether the American demands were empirically well founded or not.

In recent years both members of Congress and high ranking executive officials have tended to exert undue pressure on the German government in reference to the issue of burden sharing within the NATO alliance. What American officials fail to see is the depth of conviction Germans of all political persuasions have on this issue. Not only do the Germans believe very strongly that they carry more than their fair share of the defense burden of NATO, but that, even worse, much of the German contribution is not even understood or properly credited in Washington. A fair reading of all the empirical evidence, no matter how one interprets the statistics, tends to support the conclusion that the Germans have a very strong case. Hence, constant carping and constant criticism of the German contribution by officials in Washington serve only to cause resentment on the part of the Germans and to create unnecessary strains in the alliance relationship.

Finally, the actions of the Congress in recent years have worked powerfully to undermine the viability of the German-American relationship. For many years, Congress has used the threat of withdrawing American troops from Germany as a means of coercing the Germans into submission to Congressional demands on a variety of security issues. It should by this time be abundantly clear that these threats are not only time worn and patently stale, but that they are very likely to backfire with the German government and the German people in the long run, perhaps even in the short run. Attempts to browbeat the Germans into submission by threatening to withdraw American troops will from now on be a self-defeating tactic. As German officials patiently point out, either the American military presence in Germany serves the vital defense needs of the United States, or it does not. If not, the troops should be withdrawn forthwith. If so, then Congress should make and stick to a commitment which can be viewed as reliable. Congress cannot have it both ways. In Senator Mansfield's era it was still possible to coerce the Germans to submit to American demands by the threat of troop withdrawals. With rising German impatience with this tactic, however, it is patently unwise to persist in these threats. American troops are not stationed in Germany as a favor to the Germans or even primarily to safeguard the security of the Federal Republic. They are there, in the final analysis, as the forward defense line of the United States itself. If members of Congress or the administration persist in using the threat of troop withdrawals to force the Germans to accede to American demands in the future, the threat may well become a self-fulfilling prophecy. Hence, the better part of wisdom would be to make a firm commitment and to stick by it resolutely in the best traditions of true partnership.

Books

Anderson, Martin. *The Military Draft*. Stanford: Hoover Institution Press, 1982.

Anderson, Martin, ed. *Registration and the Draft*: *Proceedings of the Hoover-Rochester Conference on the All-Volunteer Force*. Stanford: Hoover Institution Press, 1982.

Arkin, William M. *Research Guide to Current Military and Strategic Affairs*. Washington, D.C.: Institute for Policy Studies, 1981.

Bachman, Jerald G., et al. *The All-Volunteer Force*: *A Study of Ideology in the Military*. Ann Arbor: University of Michigan Press, 1972.

Baker, Kendall L., et al. *Germany Transformed*: *Political Culture and the New Politics*. Cambridge: Harvard University Press, 1981.

Baldwin, Hanson W. *Strategy For Tomorrow*. New York: Harper and Row, 1970.

Bell, Coral. *Negotiation From Strength*. New York: Alfred A. Knopf, 1963.

Beres, Louis Rene. *Myths and Realities*: *U.S. Nuclear Strategy*. Muscatine, Iowa: The Stanley Foundation, 1982.

Bergsten, C. Fred. *The Dilemmas of the Dollar: The Economics and Politics of United States International Monetary Policy*. New York: New York University Press, 1975.

Binkin, Martin. *America's Volunteer Military: Progress and Prospects*. Washington, D.C.: The Brookings Institution, 1984.

Binkin, Martin, et al. *Blacks and the Military*. Washington, D.C.: The Brookings Institution, 1982.

Binkin, Martin. *The Military Pay Muddle*. Washington, D.C.: The Brookings Institution, 1975.

Binkin, Martin, and Shirley J. Bach. *Women and the Military*. Washington, D.C.: The Brookings Institution, 1977.

Binkin, Martin, and Irene Kyriakopoulos. *Youth or Experience?: Manning the Modern Military*. Washington, D.C.: The Brookings Institution, 1979.

Blechman, Barry M., et al. *The Soviet Military Buildup and U.S. Defense Spending*. Washington, D.C.: The Brookings Institution, 1977.

Boston Study Group. *The Price of Defense: A New Strategy for Military Spending*. New York: Times Books, 1979.

Bowman, William, Roger Little, and G. Thomas Sicilia, eds. *The All-Volunteer Force After A Decade: Retrospect and Prospect*. Elmsford, N.Y.: Pergamon-Brassey's International Defense Publishers, 1986.

Brown, James, et al., eds. *Changing Military Manpower Realities*. Boulder: Westview Press, 1982.

Buck, James H., and Lawrence J. Korb, eds. *Military Leadership*. Beverly Hills: Sage Publications, 1981.

Calleo, David P. *The Atlantic Fantasy: The U.S., NATO, and Europe*. Baltimore: Johns Hopkins University Press, 1970.

Carlton, David, and Carlo Schaerf. *Arms Control and Technological Innovation*. New York: Halsted Press, 1977.

Chambers, John Whiteclay, ed. *Draftees or Volunteers: A Documentary History of the Debate Over Military Conscription in the United States, 1787-1973*. New York: Garland Publishing, Inc., 1975.

Chapkis, Wendy. *Loaded Questions: Women in the Military*. Amsterdam: Transnational Institution, 1981.

Cleveland, Harlan. *NATO: The Transatlantic Bargain*. New York: Harper and Row, 1970.

Coffey, Kenneth J. *Manpower for Military Mobilization*. Washington, D.C.: American Enterprise Institute for Public Policy Research, 1978.

Coffey, Kenneth J. *Strategic Implications of the All-Volunteer Force*. Chapel Hill: University of North Carolina Press,1979.

Collins, John M. *American and Soviet Military Trends Since the Cuban Missile Crisis*. Washington, D.C.: Center for Strategic and International Studies, Georgetown University, 1978.

Committee for the Study of National Service. *Youth and the Needs of the Nation*. Washington, D.C.: The Potomac Institute, 1979.

Cortright, David, and Strom Thurmond. *Unions in the Military?* Washington, D.C.: American Enterprise Institute for Public Policy Research, 1977.

Council on Foreign Relations. *Nuclear Weapons and World Politics*. New York: McGraw-Hill, 1977.

Craig, Gordon A. *The Germans*. New York: G.P. Putnam's Sons, 1982.

Cromwell, William C., et al. *Political Problems of Atlantic Partnership*. Brugge: College of Europe, 1966.

Czempiel, Ernst Otto, and A. Dankwart Rustow, eds. *The Euro-American-System: Economic and Political Relations Between North America and Western Europe*. Boulder: Westview Press, 1976.

Davis, Franklin M. Jr. *Come as a Conqueror: The United States Army's Occupation of Germany, 1945-1949*. New York: MacMillan Publishing Co., 1967.

Dietchmann, Seymour J. *New Technology and Military Forces for the 1980's and Beyond*. Boulder: Westview Press, 1979.

Doenhoff, Marion. *Foe into Friend*. (Translated by Gabriele Annan) London: George Weidenfeld and Nicolson, 1982.

Eden, Anthony. *The Memoirs of Anthony Eden: Full Circle*. Boston: Houghton Mifflin, 1960.

Endicott, John E. and Roy W. Stafford, eds. *American Defense Policy*. Baltimore: Johns Hopkins University Press, 1977.

Gabriel, Richard A., and Paul L. Savage. *Crisis in Command: Mismanagement in the Army*. New York: Hill and Wang, 1978.

Gallois, Pierre. *The Balance of Terror: Strategy for the Nuclear Age*. Boston: Houghton Mifflin, 1961.

Gatzke, Hans W. *Germany and the United States*. Cambridge: Harvard University Press, 1977.

Gerhardt, James M. *The Draft and Public Policy: Issues in MIlitary Manpower Procurement, 1945-1970*. Columbus: Ohio State University Press, 1971.

Germany: Keystone to European Security. A Symposium. AEI, Foreign Policy and Defense Review, Vol. 4, Nos. 3 and 4, Washington, D.C.: American Enterprise Institute for Public Policy Research, 1983.

Gimbel, John. *A German Community Under Occupation: Marburg, 1945-1952*. Stanford: Stanford University Press, 1961.

Gimbel, John. *The American Occupation of Germany: Politics and the Military, 1945-1949*. Stanford: Stanford University Press, 1968.

Golay, John Ford. *The Founding of the Federal Republic of Germany*. Chicago: University of Chicago Press, 1958.

Goldman, Nancy L., and David R. Segal, eds. *The Social Psychology of Military Service*. Beverly Hills: Sage Publications, 1976.

Goodpaster, Andrew J. et al. *Toward a Consensus on Military Service: Report of the Atlantic Council's Working Group on Military Service*. Elmsford, N.Y.: Pergamon Press, 1982.

Gottlieb, David. *Babes in Arms*. Beverly Hills: Sage Publications, 1980.

Goulden, Joseph C. *The Best Years: 1945-1950*. New York: Atheneum, 1976.

Gray, Colin S. *The Soviet-American Arms Race*. Lexington, Mass.: Lexington Books, 1976.

Hartmann, Frederick H. *Germany Between East and West: The Reunification Problem*. Englewood Cliffs, N.J.: Prentice-Hall Inc., 1965.

Hartmann, Frederick H. *The Relations of Nations*. Sixth Edition. New York: Macmillan Publishing Co., Inc., 1983.

Hauser, William L. *America's Army in Crisis*. Baltimore: Johns Hopkins University Press, 1978.

Hillenbrand, Martin J. *The Future of Berlin*. Montclair, N.J.: Allanheld, Osmun Publishers, 1980.

Hitch, Charles J., and Roland N. Mckean, eds. *The Economics of Defense in the Nuclear Age*. Cambridge: Harvard University Press, 1960.

Hoeber, Francis P., et al. *Arms, Men and Military Budgets: Issues for Fiscal 1981*. New Brunswick, N.J.: Transaction Books, 1980.

Hoeber, Francis P. *Slow to Take Offense: Bombers, Cruise Missiles, and Prudent Deterrence*. Washington, D.C.: Georgetown University Center for Strategic and International Studies, 1977.

Hope, Richard. *Racial Strife in the U.S. Military: Toward the Elimination of Discrimination*. New York: Praeger Publishers, 1979.

Huntington, Samuel P. *The Soldier and the State: The Theory and Polities of Civilian Military Relations*. Cambridge: The Belknap Press of Harvard University Press, 1957.

Jensen, Lloyd. *Return From the Nuclear Brink*. Lexington, Mass.: Lexington Books, 1974.

Kaiser, Karl. *Europe and the United States: The Future Relationship*. Washington, D.C.: Columbia Books, 1973.

Keely, John B. ed. *The All-Volunteer Force and American Society*. Charlottesville: University Press of Virginia, 1978.

Kelleher, Catherine. *Germany and the Politics of Nuclear Weapons*. New York: Columbia University Press, 1975.

Kennan, George F. *Memoirs 1925-1950*. Boston: Little, Brown and Company, 1967.

Kennan, George F. *Memoirs 1950-1963*. Boston: Little, Brown and Company, 1972.

Kim, Choongsoo, et al. *The All-Volunteer Force: An Analysis of Youth Participation, Attrition, and Reenlistment*. Columbus: Ohio State University Center for Human Resource Research, 1980.

Krendel, Ezra S., and Bernard Samoff. *Unionizing the Armed Forces*. Philadelphia: University of Pennsylvania Press, 1977.

Laird, Melvin R. *People, Not Hardware: The Highest Defense Budget Priority*. Washington, D.C.: American Enterprise Institute for Public Policy Research, Public Policy Project on National Defense, 1980.

Lawrence, Richard D., and Jeffrey Record. *U.S. Force Structure in NATO: An Alternative*. Washington, D.C.: The Brookings Institution, 1974.

Long, Franklin A., and George W. Rathjens, eds. *Arms, Defense Policy and Arms Control*. New York: W.W. Norton, 1976.

Luttwak, Edward N. *Strategic Power: Military Capabilities and Political Utility.* Beverly Hills: Sage Publications, 1976.

Mako, William P. *U.S. Ground Forces and the Defense of Central Europe.* Washington, D.C.: The Brookings Institution, 1983.

Mandelbaum, Michael. *The Nuclear Question: The United States and Nuclear Weapons, 1946-1976.* New York: Cambridge University Press, 1979.

Margiotta, Franklin D., ed. *The Changing World of the American Military.* Boulder: Westview Press, 1978.

Marmion, Harry A. *The Case Against a Volunteer Army.* Chicago: Quadrangle Books, 1971.

McGeehan, Robert. *The German Rearmament Question.* Chicago: University of Illinois Press, 1971.

Mendershausen, Horst. *Troop Stationing in Germany: Value and Cost.* (Memorandum RM-5881-PR) Santa Monica: Rand Corporation, 1968.

Merritt, Anna J. and Richard L. Merritt, eds. *Public Opinion in Occupied Germany: the OMGUS Surveys.* Chicago: University of Illinois Press, 1970.

Merritt, Anna J. and Richard L. Merritt. *Public Opinion in Semisovereign Germany.* Chicago: University of Illinois Press, 1980.

Millett, Allan R., and Anne F. Trupp, eds. *Manning American Armed Forces.* Columbus: Mershon Center of Ohio State University, 1981.

Moodie, Michael. *Sovereignty, Security and Arms.* Beverly Hills: Sage Publications, 1979.

Morgan, Roger. *The United States and West Germany, 1945-1973.* London: Oxford University Press, 1974.

Nelson, Daniel J. *Wartime Origins of the Berlin Dilemma.* University, Ala.: University of Alabama Press, 1978.

Newhouse, John. *U.S. Troops in Europe: Issues, Costs, and Choices*. Washington, D.C.: The Brookings Institution, 1971.

Noelle-Neumann, Elisabeth, ed. *The Germans: Public Opinion Polls, 1967-1980*. Westport, Conn.: Greenwood Press, 1981.

O'Sullivan, John, and Alan M. Meckler, eds. *The Draft and Its Enemies: A Documentary History*. Chicago: University of Illinois Press, 1974.

Osgood, Robert E. *NATO: The Entangling Alliance*. Chicago: University of Chicago Press, 1962.

Paul, Roland A. *American Military Commitments Abroad*. New Brunswick: Rutgers University Press, 1973.

Peterson, Edward N. *The American Occupation of Germany: Retreat to Victory*. Detroit: Wayne State University Press, 1977.

Petrov, Vladimir. *U.S.-Soviet Detente: Past and Future*. Washington, D.C.: American Enterprise Institute for Public Policy Research, 1975.

Pierre, Andrew J., ed. *Nuclear Weapons in Europe*. New York: Council on Foreign Relations, Inc., 1984.

Plischke, Elmer. *Contemporary Government of Germany*. Boston: Houghton Mifflin Company, 1961.

Potomac Institute. *National Youth Service: What's at Stake?* Washington, D.C.: Potomac Institute, 1980.

Pranger, Robert J., and Roger P. Labrie, eds. *Nuclear Strategy and National Security: Points of View*. Washington, D.C.: American Enterprise Institute for Public Policy Research, 1977.

Record, Jeffrey. *Revising U.S. Military Strategy: Tailoring Means to Ends*. Elmsford, N.Y.: Pergamon-Brassey's International Defense Publishers, 1984.

Record, Jeffrey. *U.S. Nuclear Weapons in Europe: Issues and Alternatives*. Washington, D.C.: The Brookings Institution, 1974.

Ruhm von Oppen, Beate. *Documents on Germany Under Occupation, 1945-1954*. London: Oxford University Press, 1955.

Sabrosky, Alan Ned. *Defense Manpower Policy: A Critical Reappraisal*. Philadelphia: Foreign Policy Research Institute, 1978.

Sarkesian, Sam C., ed. *Combat Effectiveness, Cohesian, Stress, and the Volunteer Military*. Beverly Hills: Sage Publications, 1980.

Sarkesian, Sam C., ed. *Defense Policy and the Presidency: Carter's First Year*. Boulder: Westview Press, 1979.

Schlissel, Lillian, ed. *Conscience in America: A Documentary History of Conscientious Objection in America, 1757-1967*. New York: E.P. Dutton and Co., 1963.

Scowcroft, Lt. Gen. Brent C., ed. *Military Service in the United States*. Englewood Cliffs: Prentice-Hall, Inc., for the American Assembly, 1982.

Sherraden, Michael W., and Donald J. Eberle, eds. *National Service: Social, Economic, and Military Impacts*. Elmsford, N. Y.: Pergamon Press, 1982.

Shmitt, Hans A., ed. *United States Occupation in Europe After World War II*. Lawrence: The Regents Press of Kansas, 1978.

Spanier, John. *American Foreign Policy Since World War II*. 4th Revised Edition. New York: Praeger Publishers, 1971.

Stein, Harold, Ed. *American Civil-Military Decisions: A Book of Case Studies*. University, Ala.: University of Alabama Press, 1963.

Stockholm International Peace Research Institute. *World Armaments and Disarmament, SIPRI Yearbook*. London: Taylor and Francis, Ltd., 1980.

Sweet, William. *The Nuclear Age: Power, Proliferation, and the Arms Race*. Washington, D.C.: Congressional Quarterly, Inc., 1984.

Taylor, William J. Jr., et al. *Defense Manpower Planning: Issues for the 1980's.* Elmsford, N. Y.: Pergamon Press, 1981.

Tax, Sol, ed. *The Draft.* Chicago: University of Chicago Press, 1967.

Thies, Wallace J. *The Atlantic Alliance, Nuclear Weapons and European Attitudes: Reexamining the Conventional Wisdom.* Policy Papers in International Affairs, No. 19. Berkeley: Institute of International Studies, University of California, 1983.

Thompson, W. Scott, ed. *National Security in the 1980's: From Weakness to Strength.* San Francisco: Institute for Contemporary Studies, 1980.

Treverton, Gregory F. *The Dollar Drain and American Forces in Germany.* Athens, Ohio: Ohio University Press, 1978.

Trezise, Philip H. *The Atlantic Connection: Prospects, Problems, and Policies.* Washington, D.C.: The Brookings Institution, 1975.

U.S. Army War College. *Army Command and Management: Theory and Practice.* Carlisle Barracks: Army War College, 1977.

U.S. Defense Policy: Weapons, Strategy, and Commitments. Second Edition. Washington, D.C.: Congressional Quarterly, Inc., 1980.

U.S. Defense Policy. Third Edition. Washington, D.C.: Congressional Quarterly, Inc., 1983.

Weigley, Russel F. *History of the United States Army.* New York: Macmillan Publishing Co., 1967.

Zink, Harold. *The United States in Germany 1944-1955.* Princeton: D. Van Nostrand Company, Inc., 1957.

Book Chapters

Faris, John. "Leadership and Enlisted Attitudes." *Military Leadership.* Eds. James H. Buck and Lawrence J. Korb. Beverly Hills: Sage Publications, 1981.

Faris, John H. "The Military Occupational Environment and the All-Volunteer Force." *Manning the American Armed Forces*. Eds. Allan R. Millett and Anne F. Trupp. Columbus: Mershon Center of Ohio State University, 1981.

Joffe, Josef. "Germany and the Atlantic Alliance: The Politics of Dependence, 1961-68." Ed. W.C. Cromwell, et al. *Political Problems of Alliance Partnership*. Bruges: College of Europe, 1969.

Kaufmann, William W. "U.S. Defense Needs in the 1980's." *Military Service in the United States*. Ed. Lt. Gen. Brent C. Scowcroft. Englewood Cliffs: Prentice-Hall, Inc., for the American Assembly, 1982.

Martin, Laurence W. "The American Decision to Rearm Germany." *American Civil-Military Decisions*. Ed. Harold Stein. University, Ala.: University of Alabama Press, 1963.

Nixon, Richard M. "The All-Volunteer Force." *The Military Draft*. Martin Anderson, ed. Stanford, Calif.: Hoover Institution Press, 1982.

Peters, B. Guy, and James Clotfelter. "The Military Profession and its Task Environment." *The Changing World of the American Military*. Ed. Franklin D. Margiotta. Boulder: Westview Press, 1978.

"The Post War Atlantic System and its Future." *The Euro-American System: Economic and Political Relations Between North America and Western Europe*. Eds. Otto Czempiel, and A. Dankwart Rustow. Boulder: Westview Press, 1976.

Sarkesian, Sam C. "An Empirical Reassessment of Military Professionalism." *The Changing World of the American Military*. Ed. Franklin D. Margiotta. Boulder: Westview Press, 1978.

Segal, David R., et al. "Institutional and Occupational Values in the U.S. Military." *Changing Military Manpower Realities*. Eds. James Brown, et al. Boulder: Westview Press, 1982.

Sorley, Lewis. "Prevailing Criteria: A Critique." *Combat Effectiveness, Cohesian, Stress, and the Volunteer*

Military. Ed. Sam Sarkesian. Beverly Hills: Sage Publications, 1980.

Journal Articles–Authored

Altman, Stuart. "Earnings, Unemployment, and the Supply of Enlisted Volunteers." *Journal of Human Resources*, 4, Winter 1969, pp. 38-59.

Anderson, Frederic M. "Weapons Procurement Collaboration: A New Era for NATO?" *Orbis*, Winter 1977, pp. 965-990.

Andrews, Michael A. "Women in Combat?" *Military Review*, June 1979, pp. 28-34.

Bare, Gordon C. "Burden Sharing in NATO: The Economics of Alliance." *Orbis*, 21, No. 2, Summer 1976, pp. 417-436.

Barlow, Jeffrey G. "Western Europe and the NATO Alliance." *Journal of Social and Political Studies*, Spring 1979, pp. 3-15.

Betit, Eugene D. "Soviet Tactical Doctrine and Capabilities and NATO's Strategic Defense." *Strategic Review*, Fall 1976, pp. 95-107.

Bloemer, Klaus. "Freedom for Europe, East and West." *Foreign Policy*, No. 50, Spring 1983, pp. 22-38.

Boutwell, Jeffrey. "Politics and the Peace Movement in West Germany." *International Security*, Spring 1983, pp. 72-139.

Brooks, William W., et al. "A Current Perspective on Military Unionization: Can It Happen Here?" *Journal of Collective Negotiations in the Public Sector*, No. 2, 1979, pp. 97-104.

Brzezinski, Zbigniew. "America and Europe." *Foreign Affairs*, 49, No. 1, October 1970, pp. 11-30.

Callaghan, Thomas A. "Can Europe Be Defended?" *Policy Review*, 24, Spring 1983, pp. 75-86.

Cameron, Juan. "It's Time to Bite the Bullet on the Draft: Both in Number and Quality, Volunteer Forces are Inadequate to

Meet a Real Emergency." *Fortune*, 7 April, 1980, pp. 52-54.

Clarke, John L. "NATO, Neutrals and National Defense." *Survival*, 24, No. 6, Nov./Dec. 1982, pp. 260-265.

Cortwright, David. "Our Volunteer Army: Can a Democracy Stand It?" *The Nation*, 16 October, 1976, pp. 357-362.

Deporte, A. W. "NATO of the Future: Less is More." *The Fletcher Forum*, 7, No. 1, Winter 1983, pp. 1-16.

Doherty, Thomas. "Don't Sell the Army Short." *Newsweek*, 1 February, 1982, p. 13.

Douglas, Dr. Joseph D., Jr. "What Happens if Deterrence Fails?" *Air University Review*, 34, No. 1, Nov./Dec. 1982, pp. 2-17.

Doyle, James. "Retreat in the Senate." *The Progressive*, 35, No. 7, July 1971, pp. 26-29.

Enthoven, Alain C. "U.S. Forces in Europe? How Many? Doing What?" *Foreign Affairs*, 53, No. 3, April 1973, pp. 513-532.

Feld, M. D. "Arms and the Woman: Some General Considerations." *Armed Forces and Society*, 4, No. 4, Summer 1978, pp. 557-568.

Fisher, Anthony C. "The Cost of the Draft and the Cost of Ending the Draft." *American Economic Review*, 59, June 1969, pp. 239-254.

Fouquet, David. "The Atlantic Arms Race." *European Community*, Aug./Sept. 1976, pp. 26-29.

Frye, Alton. "Strategic Restraint, Mutual and Assured." *Foreign Policy*, Summer 1977, pp. 3-24.

Gabriel, Richard A., and Paul L. Savage. "Cohesian and Dissintegration in the American Army." *Armed Forces and Society*, 2, No. 3, Spring 1976, pp. 340-376.

Garnett, John. "BAOR and NATO." *International Affairs*, 46, No. 4, 1970, pp. 670-681.

Gelb, Leslie H. and Morton H. Halperin. "Why West Europe Needs 300,000 GI's." *Atlantic Community Quarterly*, 9, No. 1, 1971, pp. 56-60.

Gray, Colin S. "NATO Strategy and the Neutron Bomb." *Policy Review*, Winter 1979, pp. 7-26.

Gray, Colin S., and Keith Payne. "Victory is Possible." *Foreign Policy*, Summer 1980, pp. 14-27.

Hanrieder, Wolfram F. "West German Foreign Policy: Background to Current Issues." *Orbis*, 113, No. 4, Winter 1970.

Haseler, Stephan. "The Euromissile Crisis." *Commentary*, 75, No. 5, May 1983, pp. 28-32.

Hassner, Pierre. "The Shifting Foundation." *Foreign Policy*, No. 48, Fall 1982, pp. 3-36.

Heiberg, Anne, ed. "Women as New 'Manpower'." *Armed Forces and Society*, 4, No. 4, Summer 1978, pp. 555-556.

Hoag, Malcolm W. "Economic Problems of Alliance." *Journal of Political Economy*, 65, No. 1, December 1957, pp. 522-534.

Holmes, John W. "The Dumbbell Won't Do." *Foreign Policy*, No. 50, Spring 1983, pp. 3-22.

Ingraham, Larry H., and Frederick J. Manning. "Personnel Attrition in the U.S. Army in Europe." *Armed Forces and Society*, 7, No. 2, Winter 1981, pp. 256-270.

Jacob, James B. "Legal Change Within the United States Armed Forces Since World War II." *Armed Forces and Society*, 4, No. 3, Spring 1978, pp. 391-422.

Janowitz, Morris. "The Citizen Soldier and National Service." *Air University Review*, 31, No. 1, Nov./Dec. 1979, pp. 2-16.

Janowitz, Morris, and Charles C. Moscos Jr. "Five Years of the All-Volunteer Force: 1973-1978." *Armed Forces and Society*, 5, No. 2, Winter 1979, pp. 171-218.

Jenson, John W. "Nuclear Strategy: Differences in Soviet and American Thinking." *Air University Review*, March/April 1979, pp. 2-17.

Jervis, Robert. "Why Nuclear Superiority Doesn't Matter." *Political Science Quarterly*, Winter 1979/1980, pp. 617-633.

Joffe, Josef. "Europe and America: The Politics of Resentment." *Foreign Affairs*, 61, No. 3, Winter 1983, pp. 569-590.

Jones, Christopher D. "Equality and Equal Security in Europe." *Orbis*, 26, No. 3, Fall 1982, pp. 637-664.

Klotz, Benjamin. "The Cost of Ending the Draft: Comment." *American Economic Review*, 60, December 1970, pp. 970-979.

Koenig, Ernest F. "Force Reduction and Balance of Power in Europe: A Neutral's View." *Military Review*, February 1977, pp. 37-47.

Kohl, Wilfrid L., and William Taubman. "American Policy Toward Europe: The Next Phase." *Orbis*, 17, No. 1, 1973. pp. 51-74.

Komer, Robert W. "Ten Suggestions for Rationalizing NATO." *Survival*, 19, No. 2, Mar./Apr. 1977, pp. 67-72.

Kravis, Irving B., and Michael W. S. Davenport. "The Political Arithmetic of International Burden-Sharing." *The Journal of Political Economy*, 71, No. 4, August 1963, pp. 309-330.

Kressler, Diane A. "Germany, NATO, and Europe." *Orbis*, 10, No. 1, 1966, pp. 223-239.

Luns, Joseph M. A. H. "A Turbulence of Wind off NATO." *The Atlantic Community Quarterly*, 20, No. 4, Winter 1982/1983, pp. 295-300.

Mansfield, Mike. "Policies Respecting Germany." *Vital Speeches of the Day*, 25, No. 11, March 15, 1959, pp. 335-339.

Moskos, Charles C. Jr. "Compensation and the Military Institution." *Air Force Magazine*, April 1978, p. 35.

Moskos, Charles C. "Making the All-Volunteer Force Work: A National Service Approach." *Foreign Affairs*, 60, 1981, pp. 17-34.

Nitze, Paul H. "Assuring Strategic Stability in an Era of Detente." *Foreign Affairs*, January 1976, pp. 207-232.

Novak, Michael. "Moral Clarity in the Nuclear Age." *National Review*, April 1983, pp. 354-392.

Nunn, Sam. "Those Who Do Not Serve in the All-Volunteer Armed Forces." *Journal of the Institute of Socioeconomic Studies*, Autumn 1979, pp. 10-21.

Pfalzgraff, Robert L., Jr. "NATO and European Security: Prospects for the 1970's." *Orbis*, 15, No. 1, 1971, pp. 154-177.

Pfalzgraff, Robert L., Jr. "The United States and Europe: Partners in a Multipolar World." *Orbis*, 17, No. 1, 1973-1974, p. 31ff.

Polk, Gen. James H. "The New Short War Strategy." *Strategic Review*, 3, No. 3, Summer 1975, pp. 52-56.

Richardson, Elliot L., and Mike Mansfield. "American Forces in Europe: The Pros and Cons." *Atlantic Community Quarterly*, 8, No. 1, 1970, pp. 5-17.

Rogers, Bernard W. "Improving Public Understanding of NATO Objectives." *The Atlantic Community Quarterly*, 20, No. 4, Winter 1982/1983, pp. 301-306.

Schreffler, R. G. "The Neutron Bomb for NATO Defense: An Alternative." *Orbis*, Winter 1978, pp. 959-973.

Schwenk, Edmund H. "Liability of the Stationing Forces for 'Scope Claims' and 'Ex Gratia Claims' in the Federal Republic of Germany." *Military Law Review*, 65, Summer 1974, pp. 57-84.

Seignious, George, James Callaghan, and Raoul Girardet (Symposium). Theme: "The Present and Future of the Atlantic Alliance: How to Improve Public Understanding of its Objectives." *The Atlantic Community Quarterly*, 20, No. 4, Winter 1982/1983, pp. 307-326.

Seybold, Calvin C. "Mutual Destruction: A Deterrent to Nuclear War?" *Military Review*, September 1979, pp. 22-28.

Slobodenko, A. "The 'Bases Strategy'-A Strategy of Expansion and Diktat." *International Affairs*, No. 7, 1981, pp. 75-84.

Stray, Svenn. "Challenges to NATO Cooperation." *The Atlantic Community Quarterly*, 20, No. 4, Winter 1982/1983. pp. 291-294.

Strobridge, Truman R. "USEUCOM." *Armed Forces*, April, 1982, pp. 98-107.

Taylor, Maxwell D. "Changing Military Priorities." *American Enterprise Institute Foreign Policy and Defense Review*, No. 3, 1979, pp. 2-13.

Ullman, Richard H. "The Euromissile Mire." *Foreign Policy*, No. 50, Spring 1983, pp. 39-52.

Vermaat, J. A. Emerson. "Moscow Fronts and the European Peace Movement." *Problems of Communism*, Nov./Dec. 1982, pp. 43-58.

Vershbow, Alexander R. "The Cruise Missile: The End of Arms Control?" *Foreign Affairs*, October 1976, pp. 133-146.

Wallace, William. "Atlantic Relations: Policy Co-ordination and Conflict. Issue Linkage Among Atlantic Governments." *International Affairs*, No. 2, April 1976, pp. 163-179.

Webb, James. "The Draft: Why the Army Needs It." *The Atlantic Monthly*, April 1980, pp. 34-44.

Wesbrook, Stephen D., et al. "Combat Readiness for a Deterrent Strategy." *Armed Forces and Society*, 6, No. 2, Winter 1980, pp. 169-312.

Wesbrook, Stephen D. "Sociopolitical Alienation and Military Efficiency." *Armed Forces and Society*, 6, No. 2, Winter 1980, pp. 170-189.

Wiegele, Thomas C. "The Origins of the MLF Concept, 1957-1960." *Orbis*, 12, No. 2, Summer 1968, pp. 465-489.

Williams, Phil, and Scott D. Sagan. "Congressional Demands for American Troop Withdrawals From Western Europe: The Past as Prologue." *Journal of the Royal United Service Institute for Defense Studies*, 121, No. 3, 1976, pp. 52-56.

Williams, Phil. "Whatever Happened to the Mansfield Amendment?" *Survival*, 18, No. 4, July/Aug. 1976, pp. 146-153.

Wood, Frank R. "Air Force Junior Officers: Changing Prestige and Civilization." *Armed Forces and Society*, 6, No. 3, Spring 1980, pp. 483-506.

Yochelson, John. "The American Military Presence in Europe: Current Debate in the United States." *Orbis*, 15, No. 3, Fall 1971, pp. 784-807.

Yochelson, John. "MBFR: The Search for an American Approach." *Orbis*, 17, No. 1, 1973, pp. 155-175.

Yost, David S., and Thomas C. Glad. "West German Party Politics and Theater Nuclear Modernization Since 1977." *Armed Forces and Society*, Summer 1982, pp. 525-560.

Ypersele de Strihou, Jacques van. "Sharing the Defense Burden Among Western Allies." *Review of Economics and Statistics*, 49, No. 4, November 1967, pp. 527-536.

Journal Articles-No Author

"Controversy Over Proposed Draft Registration: Pro and Con." *Congressional Digest*, April 1980, pp. 99-128.

"Today's American Army." *The Economist*, 25 April, 1981, pp. 23-25.

Government Documents

"Final Report on NATO Offset: Message Transmitted from President Ford to the Congress." *Department of State Bulletin*, 72, No. 1878, 23 June, 1975, p. 877.

Goldich, Robert L. "Recruiting, Retention, and Quality in the All-Volunteer Force." *CRS Report No. 81-106F*, Washington, D.C.: Congressional Research Service, 1981.

Goldich, Robert L. "Women in the Armed Forces: Proceedings of a CRS Seminar Held on 2 November, 1979." *CRS Report No. 80-27F*, Washington, D.C.: Congressional Research Service, 1980.

Jones, Gen. David C., USAF, Chairman, Joint Chiefs of Staff. *United States Military Posture for Fiscal Year 1981*. Washington, D.C., Department of Defense, January 1980.

Military Manpower Task Force: A Report to the President on the Status and Prospects of the All Volunteer Force. Department of Defense, October, 1982.

Nunn, Sam, and Dewey F. Bartlett. *NATO and the Soviet Threat: Report to the Committee on Armed Services*, U.S. Senate. 95th Cong., 1st Sess., 24 January, 1977. Washington, D.C.: GPO, 1977.

The President's Commission on an All-Volunteer Armed Force. *The Report of the President's Commission on an All-Volunteer Armed Force* Washington, D.C.: GPO, 1970.

The President's Commission on Military Compensation. *Report*. Washington, D.C.: GPO, 1978.

President's Reorganization Project. *Selective Service System Reorganization Study-Final Report*. Washington, D.C.: Office of Management and Budget, 1978.

President's Commission on an All-Volunteer Armed Force. *Studies Prepared for the President's Commission on an All-Volunteer Armed Force*, 2 Vols. Washington, D.C.: Government Printing Office, 1970.

Public Papers of the Presidents of the United States, Harry S. Truman, 1950. Washington, D.C.: GPO, 1965.

Smith, Gen. W. Y. "Reinforcing NATO Rapidly." *Defense 80*, Washington, D.C.: Government Printing Office, 1980.

"U.S. and Germany Conclude Talks on U.S.-Troop Costs." *Department of State Bulletin*, 59, No. 1514, 1 July, 1968, pp. 14-15.

U.S. Central Intelligence Agency. *Soviet and U.S. Defense Activities, 1970-1979: A Dollar Cost Comparison*. Washington, D.C., 1980.

U.S. Congress. Congressional Budget Office. *Costs of Manning the Active Duty Military*, 31 May, 1980. Washington, D.C.: Government Printing Office, 1980.

U.S. Congress. Congressional Budget Office. *The Effect of Foreign Military Sales on the U.S. Economy*, Washington, D.C.: Government Printing Office, 1976.

U.S. Congress. Congressional Budget Office. *Improving Military Educational Benefits: Effects on Costs, Recruiting, and Retention*, Washington, D.C.: Congressional Budget Office, 1982.

U.S. Congress. Congressional Budget Office. *The Selective Service System: Mobilization Capabilities and Options for Improvement*. Washington, D.C.: Government Printing Office, 1978.

U.S. Congress. House. Ad hoc Subcommittee of the Committee on Armed Services. *Hearings: U.S. Military Commitments to Europe*, 93rd Con., 2nd Sess., 15 Feb.-Mar. 1974. Washington, D.C.: GPO, 1974.

U.S. Congress. House. Committee on Armed Services. *Hearings: Full Committee Briefing on German Offset Agreement*, 93rd Cong., 2nd Sess., 7 May, 1974. Washington D.C.: GPO, 1974.

U.S. Congress. House. Military Compensation Subcommittee of the Committee on Armed Services. *Report: Junior Enlisted Personnel Stationed Overseas*, 95th Cong., 2nd Sess., 19 December, 1978. Washington, D.C.: GPO, 1979.

U.S. Congress. House. Special Subcommittee on the North Atlantic Treaty Organization Commitments of the Committee on Armed Services. *Report: The American Commitment to NATO*, 92nd Cong., 2nd Sess., 17 August 1972. Washington, D.C.: GPO, 1972.

U.S. Congress. House. Subcommittee on Investigations of the Committee on Armed Services. *Report: National Defense Funding Levels for Fiscal Year 1981*, 96th Cong., 2nd Sess., 21 July, 1980. Washington, D.C.: GPO, 1980.

U.S. Congress. Senate. Combined Subcommittee of Foreign Relations and Armed Services Committees. *Report to the Committee on Foreign Relations and Committee on Armed Services: United States Troops in Europe*, 90th Cong., 2nd Sess., 15 October, 1968. Washington, D.C.: GPO, 1968.

U.S. Congress. Senate. Combined Subcommittee of Foreign Relations and Armed Services Committees. *Hearings: United States Troops in Europe*, 90th Cong., 1st Sess., S. Res. 49 and S. Res. 83, 26 April, 3 May, 1967. Washington, D.C., GPO, 1967.

U.S. Congress. Senate. Committee on Armed Services. *NATO and the New Soviet Threat*, 95th Cong., 1st Sess., 24 January, 1977. Washington, D.C.: GPO, 1977.

U.S. Congress. Senate. Committee on Foreign Relations. *United States Foreign Policy Objectives and Overseas Military Installations*. 96th Cong., 1st Sess., April 1979. Washington, D.C.: GPO, 1979.

U.S. Congress. Senate. Committee on Foreign Relations. Subcommittee on United States Security Agreements and Commitments Abroad. *Hearings: United States Security Agreements and Commitments Abroad: United States Forces in Europe*. 91st Cong., 2nd Sess., April, 1970. Washington, D.C.: GPO, 1970.

U.S. Congress. Senate. Subcommittee on Arms Control, International Law, and Organization of the Committee on Foreign Relations. *Hearings: U.S. Forces in Europe*, 93rd Cong., 1st Sess., 25 and 27 July, 1973. Washington, D.C.: GPO, 1973.

U.S. Congress. Senate. Subcommittee on Manpower and Personnel of the Committee on Armed Services. *Hearings: Military Recruiting Practices*, 95th Cong., 2nd Sess., 10 and 12 October 1978. Washington, D.C.: GPO, 1979.

U.S. Congress. Senate. Subcommittee on United States Security Agreements and Commitments Abroad of the Committee on Foreign Relations. *Hearings: United States Forces in Europe*, 91st Cong.,2nd Sess., 25 May-15 July, 1970. Washington, D.C.: GPO, 1970.

U.S. Congress. Subcommittee on Economy in Government of the Joint Economic Committee. *Hearings: The Military Budget and National Economic Priorities*, 91st Cong., 1st Sess., 1-9 June, 1969. Washington, D.C.: GPO, 1969.

U.S. Defense Manpower Commission. *Defense Manpower: The Keystone of National Security*, Washington, D.C.: Government Printing Office, 1976.

U.S. Department of Defense. *Annual Reports, Fiscal Years 1981-1984*, Washington, D.C., 1981-1984.

U.S. Department of Defense. *Defense Report on President Nixon's Strategy for Peace*. Statement of Secretary of Defense Melvin R. Laird before the House Armed Services Committee on Fiscal Years 1972-1976 Defense Program and 1972 Defense Budget, March 9, 1971.

U.S. Department of Defense. Directorate for Management Information Operations and Control. *Selected Manpower Statistics*, Washington, D.C., 1980.

U.S. Department of Defense. Military Manpower Task Force. *A Report to the President on the Status and Prospects of the All-Volunteer Force*, Washington, D.C.: October, 1982.

U.S. Department of Defense. Office of the Assistant Secretary of Defense for Manpower, Reserve Affairs, and Logistics. *America's Volunteers: A Report on the All-Volunteer Armed Forces*, Washington, D.C., 1978.

U.S. Department of Defense, Office of the Assistant Secretary of Defense for Manpower, Reserve Affairs and Logistics. *Manpower Requirements Report for Fiscal Year 1980*, Washington, D.C., 1979.

U.S. Department of Defense. Office of the Assistant Secretary of Defense for Manpower, Reserve Affairs and Logistics. *Use of Women in the Military*, 2nd ed., Washington, D.C., 1978.

U.S. Department of Defense. The Organization of the Joint Chiefs of Staff. *United States Military Posture for Fiscal Year 1984*, Washington, D.C., 1983.

U.S. General Accounting Office. Comptroller General. *Report to the Congress: The Congress Should Act to Establish Military Compensation Principles*, 9 May, 1979. Washington, D.C., 1979.

U.S. General Accounting Office. Comptroller General. *Report to the Congress: Observations on the United States Balance-of-Payments Position*, Washington, D.C., 1967.

U.S. General Accounting Office. Comptroller General. *Report to the Congress: Status of Efforts to Offset Balance-of-Payments Deficit for Fiscal Year 1974, Attributable to Maintaining U.S. Forces in Europe*, 7 February, 1975. Washington, D.C., 1975.

U.S. General Accounting Office. *Report: Improvements Needed in Army's Determination of Manpower Requirements for Support and Administrative Functions*, 21 May, 1979. Washington, D.C., 1979.

"U.S., G.B., and Germany Conclude Trilateral Talks." *Department of State Bulletin*, 56, No. 1456, 22 May, 1967, p. 788.

Miscellaneous Publications

Cooper, Richard V. L. "Military Manpower and the All-Volunteer Force." *Rand Report R-1450-ARPA*. Washington, D.C.: Rand Corporation, 1977.

Federal Republic of Germany. Federal Minister of Defense. *White Paper 1979: The Security of the Federal Republic of Germany and the Development of Federal Armed Forces*. Bonn: Federal Ministry of Defense, 1979.

Federal Republic of Germany. Federal Minister of Defense. *White Paper 1983: The Security of the Federal Republic of Germany*. Bonn: Federal Ministry of Defense, 1983.

"Focus On U.S. Troops in Germany." *Focus On...* Series, No. 3, July 1983. New York: German Information Center, 1983.

Harris, Lewis. "Support for Reinstatement of the Draft Growing." *ABC News-Harris Survey*, 2, No. 102, 18 August, 1980.

NATO: Facts About the North Atlantic Treaty Organization. Paris: NATO-Information Service, 1965.

NATO Handbook. Brussels: NATO Information Service, 1980.

Truitt, Wesley Byron. *The Troops to Europe Decision: The Process, Politics, and Diplomacy of a Strategic Commitment.* Doctoral Dissertation, Faculty of Political Science, Columbia University, 1968.

REFERENCES
GERMAN LANGUAGE

Books and Monographs

Dettke, Dieter. *Allianz im Wandel*. Schriftenreihe des Forschungsinstituts der Deutschen Gesellschaft für Auswärtige Politik, Bonn. Rüstungsbeschränkung und Sicherheit, Bd. 12. Frankfurt: A. Metzner, 1976.

Haftendorn, Helga. *Abrüstungs-und Entspannungspolitik zwischen Sicherheitsbefriedigung und Friedenssicherung: Aussenpolitik der BRD 1955-1973*. Düsseldorf, Verlagsgruppe Bertelsmann Gambit, 1974.

Joffe, Josef. *Europapräsenz und Europapolitik der Vereinigten Staaten. Eine Untersuchung über Motivation, Funktion und Evolution der Amerikanischen Stationierungspolitik in Europa*. Ebenhausen: Stiftung Wissenschaft und Politik, November 1968.

Löwenthal, Richard, und Hans Peter Schwarz. Hrsg. *Die zweite Republik. 25 Jahre Bundesrepublik Deutschland-eine Bilanz*. Stuttgart: Seewald Verlag, 1974.

Rehbinder, Manfred. *Die Rechtsnatur der Arbeitsverhältnisse deutscher Arbeitnehmer bei den ausländischen Streitkräften unter besonderer Berücksichtigung der Verhältnisse in West-Berlin*. Berlin: Dunker und Humbolt, 1969.

Thiel, Elke. *Dollar Dominanz, Lastenteilung und Amerikanische Truppenpräsenz in Europa*.

Internationale Politik und Sicherheit, Band 6. Baden-Baden: Nomos Verlagsgesellschaft, 1979.

Witzsch, Günter. *Deutsche Strafgerichtsbarkeit über die Mitglieder der U. S.-Streitkräfte und deren begleitende Zivilpersonen.* Karlsruhe: C. F. Müller Verlag, 1970.

Chapters from Edited Works

Czempiel, Ernst Otto. "Die Bundesrepublic und Amerika. Von der Okkupation zur Kooperation." *Die Zweite Republic. 25 Jahre Bundesrepublik Deutschland-eine Bilanz* Hrsg. Richard Löwenthal, und Hans Peter Schwarz. Stuttgart: Seewald Verlag, 1974, pp. 554-579.

Journal Articles-Authored

Arndt, Claus. "Zu einem Problem der deutsch-alliierten Truppenverträge." *Aussenpolitik*, 10, No. 1, 1959, pp. 29-31.

Arnolds, Josef. "Die Abgeltung von Truppenschäden nach dem NATO-Truppenstatut." *Deutsche Richterzeitung*, 41, No. 8, 1963, pp. 249-255.

Arnolds, Josef. "Die Geltendmachung von Entschädigungsansprüchen nach dem Stationierungsschadensrecht. Eine Kritik an der Rechtssprechung des BGH." *Neue Juristische Wochenschrift*, 15, No. 28, 1962, pp. 1234-1235.

Ball, George W. "Atlantische Partnerschaft im Werden." *Europa-Archiv*, 17, No. 8, 1962, pp. 251-262.

Baumann, Gerhard. "Devisenausgleichsabkommen als rechtlich-wirtschaftliches und strategishes Problem." *Wehrkunde*, 15, No. 12, Dezember 1966, p. 628.

Baumann, Gerhard. "Devisenausgleich und Sicherheit." *Wehrkunde*, 17, No. 5, Mai 1968, pp. 245-251.

Baur, Gieselher. "Beitrag zur Problematik des Truppenschmuggels." *Zeitschrift fur Zölle und Verbrauchssteuern*, 33, No. 13-14, 1957, pp. 199-201.

Birrenbach, Kurt. "Der europäisch-amerikanische Dialog." *Europa-Archiv*, 28, No. 10, 1973, pp. 699-710.

Bleckmann, Albert. "Deutsche Zuständigkeit zur Scheidung amerikanischer Soldatenehen." *Neue Juristische Wochenschrift*, 15, No. 50, 1962, pp. 2283-2286.

Boeck, Klaus, and Henry Krägenau. "Truppenstationierung. Devisenausgleich und Burden-Sharing." *Wirtschaftsdienst*, 51, No. 2, 1971, pp. 91-94.

Boeck, Klaus. "Zahlungsbilanzeffekte und Kosten des Devisenausgleichs." *Wehr und Wirtschaft*, 15, No. 12, pp. 587-589.

Borner, Silvio. "Die Dollarkrise in amerikanischer Sicht." *Aussenwirtschaft*, 26, No. 4, Dezember 1971, pp. 368-391.

Brunn, Jochen. "Dollars für Divisionen: Devisen-und Lastenausgleich in der NATO." *Loyal, das kritische Wehrmagazin*, No. 11, 1970, pp. 7-8.

Czempiel, Ernst Otto. "Entwicklungslinien der amerikanisch-europäischen Beziehungen." *Europa-Archiv*, 28, No. 22, 1973, pp. 781-790.

Diebold, William, Jr. "Europa und die Vereinigten Staaten. Perspektiven der Wirtschaftlichen Beziehungen." *Europa-Archiv*, 25, No. 15-16, 1970, pp. 597-608.

Duckwitz, Georg Ferdinand. "Truppenstationierung und Devisenausgleich." *Aussenhandelspolitik*, 18, No. 8, August 1967, p. 473.

Ehlers, Kurt. "Übergang vom Ersatz-zum Entschädigungsanspruch (bzw. umgekehrt) im ardentlichen Verfahren bei NATO-Truppen-Schäden." *Neue Juristische Wochenschrift*, 17, No. 32, 1964, pp. 1461-1462.

Erbenbach, H. "Strafverfolgung im Rahmen des NATO-Truppenstatuts und der Zusatzvereinbarung." *Kriminalistik*, 18, No. 3, 1964, pp. 130-132.

Friedel, Alois. "Amerikanische Truppenpräsenz in Europa und ihr Preis." *Wehrkunde*, 19, No. 12, Dezember 1970, pp. 620-624.

Geissler, Markus. "Die Geltendmachung und Betreibung von Ansprüchen aus Truppenschäden nach dem NATO-Truppenstatut." *Neue Juristische Wochenschrift*, 33, No. 48, 1980, pp. 2615-2620.

Grafe, Horst. "Die Abgeltung der Truppenschäden nach dem NATO-Truppenstatut in der Bundesrepublik Deutschland." *Neue Juristische Wochenschrift*, 14, 41, 1961, pp. 1841-1846.

Grossmann, Otto. "Allierte Truppen in der Bundesrepublik Deutschland und ihre Bewaffnung." *Europäische Wehrkunde*, 30, No. 11, 1981, pp. 500-501.

Grossmann, Otto. "Zur Problematik des Aufenthaltes ausländischer Streitkräfte in Deutschland." *Wehrkunde* 17, No. 8, 1968, pp. 399-401.

Joffe, Josef. "Amerikanische Truppenpräsenz und europäische Stabilität." *Europa-Archiv*, 25, No. 6, 1970, pp. 191-204.

Kalckreuth, Jurg von. "Zu Problemen der U. S.-amerikanischen Landstreitkräfte in der Bundesrepublik Deutschland." *Europäische Wehrkunde*, 31, No. 2, 1982, pp. 61-63.

Maier, Bernhard. "Zur Frage der Verjährung in den Fällen des Art. VII Abs. 3 des NATO Truppenstatus." *Neue Juristische Wochenschrift*, 27, No. 43, 1974, pp. 1935-1936.

Marenbach, Ernst. "Aktuelle Probleme des NATO Truppenstatuts." *Neue Juristische Wochenschrift*, 27, No. 10, 1974, pp. 394-396, und 27, No. 24, 1974, pp. 1070-1073.

Neubauer, J. "Die Rechtsstellung ausländischer NATO-Streitkräfte in der Bundesrepublik Deutschland." *Archiv des Völkerrechts*, 12, No. 1, 1964, pp. 34-65.

Nordheim, Manfred von. "Der amerikanische Kongress und die Stationierung von U. S.-Truppen in Westeuropa." *Wehrkunde*, 24, No. 12, pp. 618-621.

Nothlichs, Matthias. "Zivile NATO-Bedienstete." *Arbeitsschutz*, 4, 1975, pp. 121-124.

Otto, Franz. "Neuregelung für Schäden durch ausländische NATO-Truppen ab 1. Juli 1963." *Staats-und Kommunalverwaltung*, No. 1, 1964, pp. 17-18.

Pursch, Ernst-Richard. "Die Rechtsstellung der Stationierungsstreitkräfte. Auswirkung für Polizei und Verwaltung." *Die Polizei*, 54, 11, 1963, pp. 335-339.

Pursch, Ernst-Richard. "Die Regelung von Truppenschäden. Stand nach dem Beitritt der Bundesrepublik zum NATO-Truppenstatut." *Der Städtetag*, 15, No. 4, 1962, pp. 190-193.

Reichel, Hans. "Die Arbeitsrechtlichen Bestimmungen des NATO-Truppenstatuts und seiner Zusatzvereinbarung." *Bundesarbeitsblatt*, 12, No. 20, pp. 711-721.

Rieger, Walter. "Klagen der Arbeitnehmer bei den ausländischen Streitkräften von den Sozialgerichten." *Die Sozialgerichtsbarkeit*, 5, No. 9, 1958, pp. 275-276.

Rumpf, Helmut. "Zum Problem der Übungsplätze für die NATO-Streitkräfte." *Bulletin*, No. 70, 1973, pp. 690-692.

Schauer, Hartmut. "Die Kampf- und Kampfunterstützungstruppen der Vereinigten Staaten in der Bundesrepublik Deutschland." *Kampftruppen*, 24, No. 1, 1982, pp. 31-33.

Schneider, Fritz. "Scheinbare Unzulänglichkeiten: Wann kann die deutsche Justiz gegen Mitglieder der NATO-Streitkräfte Strafverfahren durchführen?" *Staatszeitung*, 15, No. 39, 1964, pp. 7-8.

Schroer, Friedrich. "Zur Anwendung deutscher ordnungs-und sicherheitsrechtlicher Vorschriften auf Truppen der Stationierungsstreitkräfte." *Deutsches Verwaltungsblatt*, 87, No. 13, 1972, pp. 484-489.

Schweizer, Jochen. "NATO-Partner zweiter Klasse?" *Der Volkswirt*, 22, No. 41, 1968, p. 9.

Schwenk, Edmund H. "Die strafprozessäulen Bestimmung des NATO-Truppenstatuts, des Zusatzabkommens und des Unterzeichnungsprotokolls zum Zusatzabkommen." *Neue Juristische Wochenschrift*, 16, No. 32, 1963, pp. 1425-1430.

Schwenk, Edmund H. "Strafprozessäule Probleme des NATO-Truppenstatuts." *Juristenzeitung*, 31, No. 19, 1976, pp. 581-583.

Schwenk, Edmund H. "Die zivilprozessäulen Bestimmungen des NATO-Truppenstatuts und der Zusatzvereinbarung." *Neue Juristische Wochenschrift*, 29, No. 35, 1976, pp. 1562-1566.

Schwenk, Edmund H. "Zustellung und Vollstreckung in nichtstrafrechtlichen Verfahren nach dem NATO-Truppenstatut." *Neue Juristische Wochenschrift*, 17, No. 22, 1964, pp. 1000-1004.

Thiel, Elke. "Der Preis für währungspolitische Selbstständigkeit." *Wirtschaftswoche*, 25, No. 33, 1971, pp. 19-22.

Thiel, Elke. "Devisenausgleich und Lastenteilung im Atlantischen Bündnis." *Europa-Archiv*, 26, No. 10, 1971, pp. 353-362.

Thiel, Elke. "Dollarkrise und Bündnispolitik." *Europa-Archiv*, 28, No. 11, 1973, pp. 373-381.

Thiel, Elke. "Truppenstationierung und Devisensausgleich. Vorverhandlung für ein neues amerikanisches Offset-Abkommen." *Europa-Archiv*, 24, No. 7, 1969, pp. 221-228.

Thiel, Elke. "Truppenstationierung und Wirtschaft: Betrachtung zum Devisenausgleich." *Wehrkunde*, 17, No. 9, 1968, pp. 470-474.

Tolmein, Horst Günter. "Stationierungstruppen. Unsere schussbereiten Gäste." *Dialog*, 4, No. 2, 1973, pp. 32-36.

Tschinsky, Nikolaus. "Devisionen und Devisen." *Loyal*, 5, 1974, pp. 3-4.

Volger, Gernot. "Devisenausgleich als militäre und zahlungsbilanzpolitisches Instrument." *Konjunktur-politik*, 20, No. 5-6, 1974, pp. 346-381.

Wenski, Carl, Lt. Colonel (U. S. Army). U. S. Army Europe. Kräftestruktur sowie taktische Führungs-und Einsatzgrundsätze, mit denen die 'erste Schlacht' gewonnen werden soll." *Truppenpraxis*, 21, No. 9, 1977, pp. 670-678.

Wieck, Hans-Georg. "Politische und militärische Probleme ausgewogener Truppenreduzierungen in Europa." *Europa-Archiv*, 25, No. 22, 1970, pp. 807-814.

Journal Articles-No Author

"Amerikaner in Berlin. Was GI's in der geteilten Stadt erleben." *Information für die Truppe*, 6, No. 80, 1980, pp. 3-10.

"Amerikaner in Deutschland." *Loyal, das kritische Wehrmagazin*, 6, No. 11, pp. 3-6.

"Der höchste Devisenausgleich, den es je gab..." *Wehr und Wirtschaft*, 16, No. 1, 1972, p. 15.

"Devisenausgleich: Schmidts Kontertaktik." *Wirtschaftswoche*, 25, No. 50, 1971, pp. 22-25.

"Devisenausgleich und U. S. Truppenreduzierungen." *Wehr und Wirtschaft*, 14, No. 10, 1970, p. 535.

"Rechtsstellung der Stationierungsstreitkräfte im Bundesgebiet und Aufgabenbereich der Polizei." *Ministerialblatt für das Land Nordrhein-Westfalen*, Ausgabe A, 25, No. 66, 1972, pp. 1115-1119.

"Truppenstationierung-ein Anachronismus?" Editorial. *Wehr und Wirtschaft*, 14, No. 9, 1970, pp. 457-458.

"Zur nächsten Devisenausgleichsrunde." *Wehr und Wirtschaft*, 15, No. 9, 1971, p. 409.

Government Documents

Abkommen über das Ausserkrafttreten des Truppenvertrages des Finanzvertrages und des Steuerabkommens. Verträge der Bundesrepublik Deutschland, Serie A Bd. 20, No. 229, 1965, pp. 468-473.

Abkommen zur Änderung des Zusatzabkommens vom 3 August 1959 zu dem Abkommen zwischen den Parteien des Nordatlantik Vertrages über die Rechtsstellung ihrer Truppen hinsichtlich der in der Bundesrepublik Deutschland stationierten ausländischen Truppen. BGBP, 1973, 2, No. 41, 8 August, 1973.

238 References German Language

Bundesrepublik Deutschland. Presse- und Informationsamt der Bundesregierung. *Jahresbericht der Bundesregierung. (Jahre 1970 durchgehend bis 1981).* Bonn: 1970-1981.

Bundesrepublik Deutschland. Presse- und Informationsamt der Bundesregierung. Referat III A2. *Die Alliierten Stationierungs-streitkräfte in der Bundesrepublik Deutschland.* Bonn: 1981.

Bundesrepublik Deutschland. Presse- und Informationsamt der Bundesregierung. *Die Alliierten Streitkräfte in der Bundesrepublik Deutschland.* (Aktuelles Basismaterial Chroniken, Nrs. 4 und 5, 1982.) Bonn: 1982.

Gesetz zu der Vereinbarung zwischen der Regierung der Bundesrepublik Deutschland und der Regierung des Vereinigten Königreichs von Grossbrittanien und Nordirland über eine Devisenhilfe an Grossbrittanien gemäss Art. 3 des Nordatlantik Vertrages vom 19. Mai 1959. BGBP, 1959, 2, No. 22, 30 Mai, 1959.

Gesetz zu den Vereinbarungen zwischen der Regierung der Bundesrepublik Deutschland und den Regierungen der Vereinigten Staaten von Amerika, des Vereinigten Königreichs von Grossbrittanien und Nordirland, der Republik Frankreich, des Königreichs Dänemark, des Königreichs Belgien, und des Königreichs der Niederlande über gegenseitige Hilfe gemäss Art. 3 des Nordatlantik Vertrages vom 11.3.1959. Bundesgesetzblatt (BGBP) 1959, 2, No. 17, 21.4.1959.

Zusatzabkommen zu dem Abkommen zwischen den Parteien des Nordatlantik Vertrages über die Rechtsstellung ihrer Truppen. Verträge der Bundesrepublik Deutschland, Serie A, Bd. 20, No. 228, 1965, pp. 142-467.

Miscellaneous Publications

Die deutschen Devisenausgleichs-Abkommen mit den U. S. A. dpa Hintergrund-Archiv-und Informationsmaterial. Hamburg: deutsche presse Agentur, 1971.

Kaufmann, Bernhard. "Amerikanische Soldaten und ihre Angehörigen als Opfer strafbarer Handlungen in Deutschland." Diss. Johannes Gutenburg Universität, Mainz, 1963.

Rumpf, Helmut. *Das Recht der Truppenstationierung in der Bundesrepublik.* Vortrag gehalten vor der Juristischen Studiengesellschaft, Karlsruhe. 23. Januar 1969. Karlsruhe: C. F. Müller Verlag, 1969.

Schneider, Gerhard. "Die Extraterritorialität der Truppen in strafrechtlicher Hinsicht, unter besonderer Berücksichtigung der das deutsche Territorium betreffenden Truppenverträge." Diss. Albert Ludwig Universität, Freiburg im Breisgau, 1964.

"About Face," (newspaper), 110
ACC. See Allied Control Council
Acheson, Dean, 41, 42, 50, 51
Adenauer, Konrad, 38, 46, 66
Adenauer government, 74, 77
AFN. See American Forces
    Network
Airland Battle doctrine, 189-190
Alliances, 1, 2, 7-8
Allied Control Council (ACC), 12,
    22, 30
Allied High Commission, 30,
    37-38, 53
Allied Kommandatura, 12
Allied Tactical Operations Center,
    166
All-Volunteer Force (AVF), 8, 91,
    169
    development, 92-96
    German views, 119-120
    transition to, 87, 89, 120-121
    See also German-American
        relations; Poverty; Race
        relations; Troops; Troop
        strength
Ambassadors, 38
America. See United States
American Forces Network (AFN),
    26
American-German relations. See
    German-American relations
America Houses, 35
Americanization, 3-4, 6
American Military Government.

See Office of Military
    Government of the United
    States for Germany
Americans. See German-
    American relations; United
    States
American Zone (AMZON), 54-55
AMZON. See American Zone
Anderson, Robert, 76, 77
Anti-nuclear movement, 67
Apel, Hans, 178
Aspin, Les, 168, 173
Augsburg, 33
AVF. See All-Volunteer Force

Baader-Meinhof gang, 115
Balance of payments, 76-77, 98,
    100-101, 102-103, 138. See
    also Offset payments
Bamberg, 122-123
Bartlett, Dewey, 171
Basic Law. See Basic Law of the
    Federal Republic of Germany
Basic Law of the Federal Republic
    of Germany, 29-30, 37
Bavaria, 12
Belgium. See Benelux countries
Benelux countries, 29, 39, 49
Bergen-Hohne, 153
Berlin, 12, 62-63. See also East
    Berlin; West Berlin
Berlin Airlift, 62
Berlin blockade, 29, 62
Berlin Wall, 64